Patriarchy in Practice

Patriarchy in Practice

Ethnographies of Everyday Masculinities

Edited by
Nikki van der Gaag, Amir Massoumian and
Dan Nightingale

BLOOMSBURY ACADEMIC
LONDON • NEW YORK • OXFORD • NEW DELHI • SYDNEY

BLOOMSBURY ACADEMIC
Bloomsbury Publishing Plc
50 Bedford Square, London, WC1B 3DP, UK
1385 Broadway, New York, NY 10018, USA
29 Earlsfort Terrace, Dublin 2, Ireland

BLOOMSBURY, BLOOMSBURY ACADEMIC and the Diana logo are
trademarks of Bloomsbury Publishing Plc

First published in Great Britain 2023
This paperback edition published in 2024

Copyright © Nikki van der Gaag, Amir Massoumian and Dan Nightingale, 2023

Nikki van der Gaag, Amir Massoumian and Dan Nightingale have asserted their right under
the Copyright, Designs and Patents Act, 1988, to be identified as Editors of this work.

For legal purposes the Acknowledgements on p. xiv constitute an
extension of this copyright page.

Series design by Adriana Brioso
Cover image © egor/Adobe Stock

A catalogue record for this book is available from the British Library.

A catalog record for this book is available from the Library of Congress.

ISBN: PB: 978-0-7556-4008-9
         ePDF: 978-0-7556-4006-5
        eBook: 978-0-7556-4005-8

Typeset by Integra Software Services Pvt. Ltd.

To find out more about our authors and books visit www.bloomsbury.com
and sign up for our newsletters.

Contents

Figure

List of contributors

Editors

Dan Nightingale is a PhD candidate in anthropology at the University College London. Whilst his doctoral thesis focuses on the informational politics of vaccination in Ireland, he maintains a long-standing interest in feminism, masculinities, gender justice and participatory research. His other work has involved investigating the relationship between ethics and rationality in the London Effective Altruist community and ethnographic work on the ethics of algorithms in local government.

Amir Massoumian is a PhD candidate at the SOAS University, researching the far-right in London. Following on from his previous thesis '*We Want Our Country Back*': *Attitudes towards Immigration in London Pubs,* his recent work focuses on aspects of masculinity, humour and identity.

Nikki van der Gaag is an independent gender consultant and a Senior Fellow at Equimundo (formerly Instituto Promundo), a leading global organization on engaging men and boys in promoting gender equality and preventing violence. From 2016 to 2019 she was Director of Gender Justice and Women's Rights at Oxfam GB. She has worked with a wide range of organizations; from UN Women to the corporate sector, small local NGOs, donor organizations and the media. Books and reports include *Feminism and Men* (Zed 2014), the *No-nonsense Guide to Feminism* (New Internationalist 2017), six *State of the World's Girls* reports and four *State of the World's Fathers* reports.

Contributors

Alvi A. H. is an Indonesian writer. He currently works as a freelance journalist and contributor to Solider.id, a social inclusion and people with disability rights website. He obtained an undergraduate degree in law with the specialization in criminal law. His latest personal essay is published in the collection of queer personal essays, Queer etc. (EA Books, 2021). He is interested in exploring the intersection of gender, sexuality and disability issues in his future writings and activism.

Debarati Chakraborty is presently serving as an Assistant Professor in the Department of Sociology at Jhargram Raj College (Girls' Wing), West Bengal, India. She has completed MPhil from the Department of Sociology at Jadavpur University and presently pursuing her doctoral studies from the same university. Her area of interest is gender and sexuality, disability studies, sociology of science and technology, sociology of childhood and youth.

Lucy Clarke is an accomplished anthropologist with an interest in self-forming practices and subjectivity. Her research with Alcoholics Anonymous (AA) groups explores the experiences of members in the AA programme. As a result of AA engagement, members start to experience themselves and others differently. They find themselves thinking and feeling differently. These new ways of being, she argues, interrupt and transfigure modern individualistic concepts of self. Bringing this research into conversation with post-structural feminist theory, she investigates the ways in which our experiences of self impact upon gender identity. When the experiencing self transforms, so too does masculinity.

Ed Forniels (*1983, UK) is an artist working in London. His most recent project Cel uses immersive role play to investigate the effects of hierarchical structures and how the psychology of extremist views feed off each other and negatively impact the world in which we live. Fornieles' work focuses on exploring alternative tools and patterns of behaviour through role play. He has exhibited at The Serpentine Gallery, Chisenhale Gallery, Martin Gropius Bau, amongst various other institutions and galleries. Fornieles ran The Wallis Gallery with Vanessa Carlos between 2006 and 2009 in which time he hosted Making Mistakes a performance evening in which artists were invited to experiment with new works in a relatively safe space. Since then Fornieles has run events out of his space, often addressing the themes in his work through discussions, reading groups and open mic therapy.

Chris Haywood is a Reader in Critical Masculinity Studies in the Department of Media, Culture and Heritage at the Newcastle University, UK. He is interested in exploring how different conceptual deployments of masculinity shape what we know and are able to know about gender and sexuality. His current research explores the hidden world of sex clubs. His book, *Sex Club: Recreational Sex, Fantasies and Cultures of Desire* (2022, Palgrave), explores sex club cultures through themes such as power and erotic hierarchies, hypersexualized black bodies, 'sexually insatiable women', queer heterosexualities, trans desires and spaces of non-consent in dangerous, high-risk spaces.

Annie Kelly is a journalist and researcher specialising in antifeminist and far-right digital cultures. She is the UK Correspondent for the QAnon Anonymous podcast, and a postdoctoral researcher on the AHRC-funded 'Everything is Connected: Conspiracy Theories in the Age of the Internet' project at the University of Manchester and King's College London.

Cristina Oddone is currently a lecturer in Sociology at the Faculty of Social Sciences and an associated member of LINCS – Lab for Interdisciplinary Cultural Studies, at the University of Strasbourg in France. She has previously worked for the GREVIO Secretariat contributing to the monitoring procedure on the implementation of the Istanbul Convention by state parties. As an expert on violence against women, she has conducted research for the Italian National Research Council and for the Gender Equality Division of the Council of Europe. Sha has authored the book *Uomini normali. Maschilità e violenza nell'intimità*, Rosenberg&Sellier, Torino (2020).

Ceri Oeppen is a Senior Lecturer in Human Geography at the University of Sussex, and Co-Director of the Sussex Centre for Migration Research. Her primary specialism is the geography of forced migration but she is also building on her research about community, transnationalism and inclusion/exclusion of minority groups, in order to reflect on the current conjuncture in cultural politics – particularly associated with the rise of the so-called alt-right in Western liberal democracies.

Elisa Padilla works at the University of Sussex teaching Film Studies. She wrote a thesis on bodies, taste and pleasures in the cinema of John Waters and is currently working on a book on the topic. Her research interests are drag performances, nostalgia, humour and star studies.

Shannon Philip is a Postdoctoral Research Associate at the University of Cambridge. His research looks at gender, masculinities, sexualities, development and violence in India and South Africa. His first academic monograph entitled

Becoming Young Men in a New India: Masculinities, Gender Relations and Violence in the Postcolony is forthcoming with Cambridge University Press in 2022.

Lauren Redfern is currently based at the London School of Hygiene and Tropical Medicine where she is working towards obtaining her PhD in Medical Anthropology. Ethnographically exploring the sociocultural dimensions of testosterone, Lauren is interested in the ways in which the medical and biological are imbued with social meaning. Lauren graduated from the University of Exeter with a BA in Sociology and Anthropology (Hons), after which she decided to pursue her interest in public health further and obtained an MSC in Reproductive and Sexual Health Research from the London School of Hygiene and Tropical Medicine (LSHTM). She conducts interdisciplinary research with a focus on the intersectional relationship between gender, sexuality and medicine. Prior research has included in depth content analysis of young people's depictions of sexual intimacy and the implications of gendered identities during these encounters.

Hendri Yulius Wijaya is the author of 'Intimate Assemblages: The Politics of Queer Identities and Sexualities in Indonesia' (Palgrave Macmillan 2020). His most recent academic publications have been published in *Laws* and *Indonesia and the Malay World* Journal. He obtained a research Master's in Gender and Cultural Studies from Sydney University and a Master's in Public Policy from Lee Kuan Yew School of Public Policy – National University of Singapore.

Foreword

Andrea Cornwall

Patriarchy, bell hooks observed, 'is the single most life-threatening social disease assaulting the male body and spirit in our nation' (2004:17). In a world threatened by the hypermasculinity inherent in war mongering and as country after country experiences the toxic effects of the resurgence of patriarchal values, it's never felt so urgent to tackle the questions with which this book is concerned. Violence against women continues unabated. The gains feminism claimed in the last thirty years are being unpicked with the rise of neo-populism and its associated masculinisms. It is a time to regroup, to rethink and to reconstitute forms of progressive politics that can suture the fissures that have appeared across and within movements inspired by the ideals of feminism and gender justice.

This volume brings together papers initially assembled to address the possibility of post-patriarchal masculinities. But, as the editors observe, to talk of *post*-patriarchy at a time when the resurgence of noxious, repressive patriarchal views, practices and behaviour is so evident, may imply – wrongly – that we're beyond the worst of it. Like a virus, patriarchy replicates, mutates, infects and spreads faster than attempts to despatch it or repair its effects. To talk of post-patriarchy is to conceive of a world that is difficult to imagine in the current conjuncture to be just on the horizon; such a possibility appears to be fast receding the world over. Instead, the editors refocused on identifying and documenting a panoply of practices that, together, might give succour or inspire hope in a time of backlash. They and the authors gathered here explore how the documenting the enactment of masculinities in all its particularity in different instances and locales can provide an entry point for thinking in a more complex and nuanced way about the relationship between masculinity and patriarchy, and where and how that relationship can be redressed and reimagined.

The collection of cases in this volume offers a dynamic constellation of contexts and relational possibilities for closer inspection, seeking in bringing them together to identify alternative ways of being a man and performing masculinities that can aid the possibility of imagining a post-patriarchal social order. They take a common methodological approach: the use of ethnography, a methodology well suited to examining at close range and in quotidian detail the practices of everyday life. Ethnographic research produces fine-grained, contextually rich descriptions of life as lived. Ethnographies can offer powerful challenges to preconceptions and normativities for this reason, as they take the reader into worlds that they may never have encountered or imagined, enabling them to 'see' and 'hear' perspectives and experiences that might otherwise lie out of reach.

Through these ethnographies, in all their diversity, we are transported into the lives of a diversity of subjects and gain some fascinating insights into the very different worlds that are evoked through these studies. Annie Kelly's 'Alpha and Nerd Masculinities' looks at performative masculinities in anti-feminist digital cultures. 'Phantom masculinities' is another variant of contemporary masculinities introduced by Amir Massoumian, in his account of men in pubs in London's borough of Walthamstow, in reveries that are nostalgic and xenophobic by turns as they reflect on immigration in a time of Brexit. Alvi A. H. and Hendri Yulius Wijaya write of the 'tenuous masculinities' of Indonesian transmen, who feel that it is only through constant re-enactment they can mitigate the risk of rejection and denial.

Others write of masculinities gained and lost, emerging and embodied. Shannon Phillip's 'new male heroes' of 'new thinking' 'new men' in New Delhi, which offers us another trope, one familiar from the cultural contexts in which the global elite circulate, and one that, as they show, can serve to entrench male privilege and misogyny. And Chris Haywood's chapter on dark rooms in sex clubs in the UK speaks of the 'loss of masculinity' as those who frequent them relate how they lose themselves in the pursuit of pleasure in these liminal, dark spaces. Chapters by Christina Oddone, Ceri Oeppen, Elisa Padilla, Lucy Clarke and Debarati Chakraborty tackle a diversity of manifestations of masculinities – attitudes towards women in accounts of French perpetrators of sexual violence, the performative identities of drag icons, the 'moral-existential reconfiguration of masculinity' in Alcoholics Anonymous meetings, participation in sports, gaming and role-play, the disabling ways in which patriarchal masculinities intersect with the bodies of the physically disabled, and the reflections of testosterone users.

Bringing together such an interesting, unusual and varied constellation of masculinities, this collection complicates any straightforward association between men, masculinities and power. Together, these studies offer a rich contribution to the wider anthropological and sociological literature on masculinities. In their focus on the practice of patriarchy in such very disparate settings, they open windows into lesser-studied worlds and attest to the value of ethnography in surfacing voices and perspectives that are rarely heard.

Acknowledgements

First and foremost, we would like to express our gratitude to the many feminist scholars across all disciplines who have made our work possible. For allowing us to create and host the conference (towards) Post-Patriarchal Masculinities from which this volume has arisen, we would like to extend our gratitude to the Department of Anthropology at the University College London (UCL) for their generous support in funding the event, as well to the School of Oriental and African Studies (SOAS) for allowing us to host the conference in the university space. We would like to show our extreme gratitude to the invaluable support of Emma Crewe, who beyond helping us in the creation of the conference was a source of continual guidance and encouragement throughout the various stages in developing this volume.

We are also grateful for the assistance of Jeff Hearn, whose experience in the field, along with many conversations and active involvement in the editing process, greatly aided the formation of this volume. We also wish to thank Bloomsbury for their support in preparing the volume for publication, in particular Nayiri Kendir and Tomasz Hoskins, who have been as patient as they were supportive in the process. We also wish to thank Andrea Cornwall for writing the foreword for the volume.

The editors of the volume also wish to thank the contributors for their patience and perseverance in working with us through multiple iterations of their chapters during the uncertainties and challenges of the pandemic. It has been a genuine pleasure and privilege to have worked with you all on the production of such a diverse collection of chapters.

We also wish to collectively thank the participants whose data is presented in this volume and whose generosity makes ethnographic inquiry possible.

Finally we would like to thank the family and friends who have been anchors of support through the difficulties of recent times.

Introduction: Patriarchies in practice

Dan Nightingale, Nikki van der Gaag and Amir Massoumian

The study of masculinities, and how patriarchy plays out in practice, is a matter of urgency for anyone engaged in the struggle for gender equality. It has been thrown into stark relief by the fact that as we finalize this book in 2022, Vladimir Putin has invaded Ukraine in the largest military conflict in continental Europe since the Second World War. Putin is one in a line of new 'strong-men' (Ben-Ghiat 2020), whose autocratic style has a distinctly hypermasculine foundation.[1] The unaccountability allows amplifies its affects and projects it onto the world stage with catastrophic consequences (Wood 2016). A close examination of masculinities, patriarchy and their role in current events is critical to understanding the volatile shifts taking place in the world today. Indeed, it was the twin events of Trump and Brexit in 2016 that drove us to organize a conference at the School of African and Oriental Studies (SOAS) in London in 2019 to explore the nature of masculinities in this context from an ethnographic perspective. The events in the world are not just confined to the corridors of state power, but cascade into wider social contexts. From continued and increasing violence by men against women around the world (Fried 2003; Htun and Jensenius 2020), to men's attempts to control women's bodies, to the current surge in far-right politics and its evident associations with hyper-masculinity and misogyny (Kutner 2020), we are reminded time and time again that patriarchy is far from dead.

This volume consists of the chapters that were presented at the event, which was originally titled '(towards) post-patriarchal masculinities'. Our intent was to interrogate the relationship between personhood, patriarchies and masculinities from an anthropological and ethnographic perspective. Yet as we prepared the

---

[1] The now near-mythic photograph of his riding a bear shirtless comes to mind. Indeed, the excess of his hypermasculinity has rendered him a grim yet tongue-in-cheek gay icon in LGBT+ Russian activism (Baker, Clancy and Benjamin 2019). The interplay between (hegemonic) masculine icons and queer culture is complex (e.g. Demetriou 2001).

manuscript for this volume, it became clear that we risked implying that we were already done with patriarchy. While envisioning post-patriarchal forms of masculinity is an ultimate aspiration, it can be achieved through patient examination of different, situated examples. To the extent that masculinities might be considered patriarchies in practice, close attention to the various local, social contexts is an avenue to understanding and opening possible avenues for liberation, transformation and healing. Yet it is dangerous – perhaps now more than even in 2016 – to only dream of a Utopian future when faced with a dire present. The current wave of autocratic populism and backlash against feminism and women's rights is not the first and will not be the last. As US feminist Susan Faludi pointed out thirty years ago:

> The last decade has seen a powerful counterassault on women's rights, a backlash, an attempt to retract the handful of small and hard-won victories that the feminist movement did manage to win for women. … And in every case, the timing coincided with signs that women were believed to be on the verge of breakthrough. In other words, the antifeminist backlash has been set off not by women's achievement of full equality but by the increased possibility that they might win it.
>
> (Faludi 1992:13)

Today's 'backlash', as with others in the past, points towards the success of feminist and women's rights organizations as much as it now risks such work being undone. These are familiar tropes of masculinity's 'crisis tendencies' (Connell 2005) coupled with a renaissance of far-right, misogynist politics (Vieten 2018). Cas Mudde, a Dutch political scientist who focuses on political extremism and populism in Europe and the United States, notes: 'it is clear that gender, and specifically masculinity … plays a role in terms of the propaganda and appeal of radical right parties and politicians' (Mudde 2019). Right-wing movements – old and new, online and offline – have spilled over from the margins to the mainstream (e.g. Asahina 2015; Main 2018; Miller-Idriss 2017; Wendling 2018). While the current situation in many countries cannot be reduced to a conflict based only on gender, it remains a powerful axis of mobilization with enormous potential consequences; from the significant increase in online abuse towards women (see Chapter 1 of this volume) to far-right terror attacks founded on the notion that masculinity in the West is in decline (Conway, Scrivens and Macnair 2019).

These backlashes can be seen at least in part as a reaction to the continuing resistance of feminist organizations, individuals and their allies against patriarchal practices (Zetkin, Taber and Riddell 2017). The struggle for reproductive justice – especially access to safe and legal abortion – is a particularly notable case in point. While many countries have liberalized abortion laws,[2] huge numbers of women around the world (and disproportionately in the Global South) still lack access to safe reproductive healthcare (Singh et al. 2018). Women's bodies have always been a key locus of male control; and this is also true today. In December 2021 a case challenging Roe versus Wade was brought before the US Supreme Court, where the balance of power has shifted in favour of conservative, anti-abortion justices which in June 2022 resulted in the overturning of the federal right to abortion (Liptak 2021). In Poland, after a series of legal challenges since 2011 (Hussein et al. 2018) the government passed a controversial law amounting to a near-total ban on abortion in October 2020, which was met by widespread protests. The consequences became real all too quickly: in 2021 a mother died of septic shock in Pszczyna hospital after doctors refused to remove a non-viable foetus for fear of the new legislation (Dyer 2021). Yet victories still occur; in Colombia, abortion was decriminalized in February 2022, marking an historic achievement for women's rights (Oppenheim 2022). It may generally have been possible to speak of a 'slow and steady' improvement in access to abortion since the 1960s (ibid.); we should be wary of assuming that such trends will necessarily continue with a hard fight. No situation is immutable, in any direction; freedoms that are hard-won can be lost, just as seemingly insurmountable barriers can be overcome.

Thus, while the gains made over the past decades in terms of women's rights are a cause for celebration, each advancement has galvanized various forms of right-wing resistance. Movements organized around the achievement of justice in gender, race and sexuality represent an almost existential threat – not just to individual men, but to the wider patriarchal systems and structures that they valorize and seek to defend. Indeed, as chapters by Oddone and Massoumian in this book explore, there is a sense of disenfranchisement and alienation amongst many men, some even going so far as to believe that patriarchy has been supplanted and replaced by a 'matriarchy' that is actively hostile to their interests as men.

A narrative in many of these groups is that there is a perceived 'war on masculinity', a particular flashpoint being the American Psychological Association's (APA) identification of 'toxic masculinity' as a threat to men's

---

[2]   Singh et al. report that twenty-eight have liberalized laws from 2000 to 2017 (2018).

mental health. Podcaster Joe Rogan has made the claim that 'woke culture' will 'silence straight men' (Moschella and Wong 2021), while other counter-cultural 'public intellectuals' continue sustained attacks on so-called cultural Marxism and critical race theory that they see infiltrating public life (Barg 2022). Yet the surge in anti-feminist rhetoric and 'strongman' politics also presents a unique opportunity to interrogate masculinity's relationship with patriarchy as well as how it may be extricated from it. It is this particular moment of crisis for masculinity and its relationship with patriarchy that sets the frame for this book. To what extent is patriarchy expressed in and linked to masculinities, or the various shapes that these take? In what ways and contexts can specific enactments of masculinity make visible, undermine, challenge or reconfigure patriarchal power structures? And perhaps most importantly, what might masculinity look like if it were not linked to patriarchy, but rather grounded in feminist principles of gender justice?

We believe that one – though by no means the only – reason for the continued backlash is an absence of meaningful alternatives to patriarchal masculinities. In many ways, this is the core preoccupation of this book; insofar as masculinity is inextricably bound to patriarchy, the diminution of its power and privilege is indeed an existential threat to men, for there is no other way to live or find meaning. Gender is not by any means the whole of an identity, but it is certainly a potent part. We are inspired by bell hooks in her statement that: 'if men are to reclaim the essential goodness of male being, if they are to regain the space of openheartedness and emotional expressiveness that is the foundation of well-being, we must envision alternatives to patriarchal masculinity. We must all change' (hooks 2004).

At its simplest, the current crisis of masculinity opens a vista onto the relationship between masculinities, patriarchies and the various individuals or groups that enact, sustain, challenge or subvert them. The collection of ethnographic chapters in this book is from a range of countries and contexts, intended to explore the spaces where masculinity and patriarchy are at work. In particular, we are interested in the question of the extent to which masculinities may be thought of as patriarchy in practice. In doing so, we hope to open space for exploring the alternatives that hooks speaks of. It is a long and winding path, considering patriarchy's resilience – yet we hope that the chapters assembled here might give some thought (and some hope) as to how it might be accomplished. In the remainder of the introduction we move to set out the key terms of patriarchy, masculinity and ethnography before providing and overview of the sections and chapters of the volume.

Patriarchy in practice

In order to understand the nature of the backlash, we need to consider what is meant by patriarchy and how its practices are embodied in everyday life. Many of the contributors to this book explain this in their particular contexts – for example, as Amir Massoumian explores in British pubs in Walthamstow, Debarati Chakraborty for disabled men in Kolkata and Shannon Philip for 'New men' in entrepreneurial, forward-looking New Delhi.

Patriarchy, from the Greek *patros* 'father' and 'authority' *archos*, is the concentration of power in the hands of the figurative and literal father (or patriarch). While this may have once literally meant the head of powerful families, it also points to gender inequalities in wider social, economic and political terms. The concept was used in social-scientific analysis in the nineteenth century, but its more recent history can be traced back to the 1960s and 1970s where it became a cornerstone of feminist theory and praxis. One of the earliest ventures was proffered by Kate Millet (1970) in her work *Sexual Politics,* who states that 'sexual dominion ... [is] perhaps the most pervasive ideology of our culture and provides its most fundamental concept of power. This is so because our society, like all other historical civilisations, is a patriarchy' (25).[3] Patriarchy was explored by other feminist scholars in detail, one summation being offered by Veronica Beechey at the height of feminist theorizing of patriarchy in 1979:

> Politically, feminists of a variety of different persuasions have seized upon the concept of patriarchy in the search for an explanation of feelings of oppression and subordination and in the desire to transform feelings of rebellion into a political practice and theory. And theoretically the concept of patriarchy has been used to address the question of the real basis of the subordination of women and to analyse the particular forms which it assumes. Thus the theory of patriarchy attempts to penetrate beneath the particular experiences and manifestations of women's oppression and to formulate some coherent theory of the basis of subordination which underlies them.
>
> (1979:66)

While patriarchy fell out of vogue as a primary theoretical pursuit particularly following the emergence of non-binary and queer theorizations of gender in the late 1980s (e.g. Butler 1990), it was not abandoned; rather it became a part of the

---

[3] Millet's writing made the case that patriarchy and gender-based oppression were more pervasive and primary than racial or class-based oppressions. This aspect of her writing was a fault-line in early theorizations of patriarchy.

theoretical furniture. Both patriarchy and hegemonic masculinity (see section below) remain central to lively and critical debates around gender, power and justice. Despite the movement towards deconstructing gender, patriarchy is often something an axiom of feminist analysis even though it is not a primary focus of contemporary theorizing. For example, in her work *Down Girl*, Kate Manne identifies misogyny as a practical manifestation of patriarchal power through the use of violence against women (2019). Even in the absence of fully-fledged patriarchal systems, misogyny still connects with 'expectations and norms' of a patriarchal nature (67). As such, while individual acts of misogyny are significant in and of themselves, patriarchy remains 'a ubiquitous and arguably causally necessary aspect' of misogynist violence and behaviour (ibid.:101). Our intention is not to focus solely on masculinities, but the patriarchal systems that masculinities are entangled with and to understand and explore their potential separability.

The concept of patriarchy has also been criticized by feminist scholars for a lack of breadth. Mohanty (1988) famously challenged the way 'Western' feminism universalized the experiences of a small group of (mostly white) women, letting the concerns of a minority be the organizing priorities for a totality of women. Even as a movement for emancipation along gendered lines, Western hegemony manifests across the intersection of race, culture and class, generating new forms of disparity. Mohanty stated that the 'process of discursive homogenization and systematization of the oppression of women in the "third world" needs to be unpicked and the nuances of that power named' (p.62). The existence of localized patriarchal orders and gendered oppressions requires a more fine-tuned analysis with a range of differing voices. More recently, African-American studies professor Imani Perry, in an interview with *The Nation*, states that:

> Patriarchy is a project that coincided with the transatlantic slave trade and the age of conquest. It's not just attitudes. It's legal relations between human beings, which lead to very different encounters with violence and suffering. The book begins with where patriarchy comes from, and then morphs into the current landscape, in which conditions are different but where that foundational structure is still present. Feminism is ultimately a way of reading the world with an eye towards reducing or eliminating unjust forms of domination, violence, and exploitation.
>
> (Arjini 2019)

As Kimberlé Crenshaw notes in discussions of her conceptualization of intersectionality (Crenshaw 1991), gender cannot be parsed as a universal concept, just as positivist approaches to particular gender identities cannot be ignorant of wider social factors. Nothing stands alone – and it is precisely the unmarked character of privileged categories that often grant themselves the power to be heard while at the same time drowning out other voices. Our focus on patriarchy follows that the conditions of women's oppression are a near-universal constant (with varying forms in respect to class, race and age), but that analyses at the level of specific actors require additional theoretical tools.

The meanings of masculinity

We follow Rees in the statement that 'there is no single or simple origin to masculinity, and it cannot be isolated as beginning in a single place or at a single point … [there is] no single creator … [or] originary form' (2010:18). As Melanie Lee also states (2020), there has been a profound shift from 'a fixed, singular definition shaped by patriarchal constructions to evolving, expansive definitions that recognize multiple masculinities defined by context-dependent, culturally conditioned behaviours' (69). Within this, the task of providing a neat definition of masculinity is remarkably challenging, not least because the experiences of masculinity or masculinities in different social contexts are deeply embedded in the personal lives of those that study it, as well as being almost inseparable from definitions of patriarchy. Outlining the difficulties of providing a neat definition, masculinities scholar Raewyn Connell (2005) sets out and critiques four broad, overlapping approaches used in social science and humanities to date:

1. Essentialist: 'pick a feature that defines **the core of the masculine**, and hang an account of men's lives on that'. We may recognize this as referring to a set of behaviours or attributes that define manhood – by implication, anybody that wants to be a man should reflect these things. They may be ordained by religion, God, science or otherwise – deviation from them is heavily censured and challenge to them is a challenge to the wider social (and gender) order.
2. Positivist: A classic social-scientific approach that looks at 'what men actually are' by examining and documenting their behaviours, inferring that this is the substantive content of masculinity. Social science can use statistical analysis to find those patterns of behaviour amongst differing groups. Connell makes the argument that these forms of masculinity rely on underpinning assumptions about a male-female gender binary – that

'positivist procedure thus rests on the very typifications that are supposedly under investigation' (69). Yet, the internal differentiation between men and women or the transgression of those boundaries – men who are feminine, women who are masculine (let alone non-binary and queer identities) – challenges the validity of the approach.

3. Normative: Positions masculinity as 'what men ought to be', in relation to social, cultural and behavioural expectations. The challenge is the gap between ideas of masculinity and how actual men relate to them. If masculinity is associated with abstracted characteristics, icons or ideals they are only ever partially instantiated. While this might adequately describe certain ideological masculinity, the divergence from specific or individual men renders the approach far too narrow for a sustained social analysis.

4. Semiotic: Perhaps the most challenging to get a handle on, 'abandon the level of personality and define masculinity through **a system of symbolic difference** … in effect … not-femininity'. For Connell, these approaches are particularly effective at the level of generalized cultural analysis, drawing on (post)structuralist theories, psychology and linguistics. Masculinity is encountered in systems of meanings, although unmoored it neglects those very same specificities that are left behind.

What is generalized by Connell is what she refers to as a 'principle of connection' – that is, we should not move to treat masculinity or gender as 'an object' (that is, 'a natural character type, a behaviour or a norm') but as rather embedded in particular fields of social and gendered relations. The definition that she ultimately offers is that masculinity is 'a place in gender relations, the practices through which men and women engage that place in gender and the effects of these practices in bodily experience, personality and culture'. The systems of meaning that are analysed in cultural or semiotic approaches are brought 'back down' and grounded in empirical situations. Any analysis of masculinity needs to take into account situated, specific instantiations of gendered relations and the power dynamics involved in them.

As an additional note, much has been produced in the way of new types or categories of masculine identity. Lee (2020), in her overview of the discipline of masculinity studies, provides an outline of a dozen such examples explored within contemporary scholarship.[4] Such typological contributions are of great utility

---

[4] The typology includes adolescent, competitive, ecomasculinity, female, gay, hegemonic, hypermasculine/machosexual, hypomasculinity/metrosexuality, inclusive, mythopoetic, patritheologist, retrosexual/neosexual. Lee gives some further emphasis to five 'widespread, influential types' in 'adolescent, female, hegemonic, inclusive and patritheologist' (2020:77–9).

in distilling decades of research. Although Lee acknowledges clearly that the different types are fluid, overlapping and 'only a partial sampling of masculinity's possible variations' (79), a taxonomic way of thinking is counter-productive to what we want to achieve here. It is easy to slip into a mindset that considering masculinity need result in the production of 'types' or a contribution to the extension of a taxonomy. Typifications may well emerge from the ethnographic chapters in this book, but it is not our primary intent. The benefit of Connell's concept of hegemonic masculinity (explained below shortly) is that it presents a model of how particular types of masculinity functions within a patriarchal context. The types are part of a systematic analysis, having explanatory value. Our question is how masculinities – such as they are, wherever they are – interact with those systems of oppression. Put simply, we do not wish to lose sight of the patriarchal wood for the different (although fascinating) varieties of masculine trees.

To summarize, we should not assume that masculinity is what men should (or can) be, what men are, what men do or what women are not. Within this kaleidoscope of approaches to defining masculinity, another key observation is that masculinities are multiple and (all-too-often) hierarchical, embedded in the inequalities of power that define patriarchy in practice.

Patriarchy and the link to hegemonic masculinity

A core part of Connell's theorization of masculinity was the concept of hegemonic masculinity – something in response to the 'problem of legitimation of patriarchy' (e.g. Connell 1987; Connell and Messerschmidt 2018). The rhetorical question she was responding to is straightforward 'If gender relations are as dire and unequal as feminist analyses claim, why do people go along with such a status quo?' The analysis drew from Antonio Gramsci's concept of hegemony that became popular in the 1970s. If the working class were so utterly oppressed, why had the revolution not yet happened? Under a strict Marxist or dialectical-materialist view of history a proletarian uprising was all-but-inevitable in the correct conditions alongside revolutionary organization. The mitigating factor was the concept of hegemony, which Bates summarizes as 'political leadership based on the consent of the led, a consent which is secured by the diffusion and popularisation of the world view of the ruling class' (1975:352).

As regards gender, Connell states that brute force 'at the point of a gun, or by the threat of unemployment, is not hegemony' yet subtle coercion of 'religious doctrine and practice, mass media content, wage structures ... and so forth, is' (1987:184). And yet 'the public face of hegemonic masculinity is not necessarily what powerful men are, but what sustains their power and what large members of men are motivated to support' (ibid.:185). The linkage of ideology to specific groups is not a direct or obvious correspondence. As such, different types of masculinity or femininity and different groups of men or women intersect in radically different ways. Put simply, an 'average' Euro-American man of a particular age possessed of 'complicit' masculinity may idolize Arnold Schwarzenegger's physical strength without equalling it, but still criticize what they perceive as 'effeminate' men in what Connell describes as 'subordinate' or 'marginalized' masculinities. In tandem with this, she argues that forms of femininity under a patriarchal regime may be 'emphasized' without having hegemonic power themselves (although hegemonic femininity may well be a theoretical possibility), given her argument that femininity's general structural subordination to masculinity in existing systems or gender orders.[5]

What we wish to question is not just the type of masculinity, but the specific spaces in between and around masculinity, patriarchy and the actors that sustain, are sustained by or otherwise influenced by it. By looking at how masculinities are subverted (see Section 2 on normativity and diversity), reinforced (see Section 1 on backlash), combined and otherwise interact in a variety of richly described situations, we hope to answer questions from the 'bottom-up' by providing a collection of contemporary ethnographic material that explores these questions. The material in question is purposefully diverse and provocative, organized thematically yet ill-suited to providing new theorizations of masculinity or its putative 'types'. Indeed, this may be considered an anti-ontological exercise; that some parts of masculinity are better encountered in live traces than through finely crafted, abstracted instruments.

Masculinities and patriarchies are plural not purely in order to, as Cuboniks (2018) puts it 'generate plural but static constellation' (43) in which gender continues to bear the weight of signifying something beyond itself, but in order to acknowledge the fact that the discussions surrounding 'post-patriarchal' are,

---

[5] It should be noted that Connell and Messerschmidt acknowledge the critique that a general structural subordination of femininity to masculinity undermines women's agency and needs to be reformulated with different scales in mind (2005). Quite ironically, the 'categorical models of patriarchy' that Connell were the foil for Connell's theorizing were criticized for their over-simplistic view of men. Both concepts are flawed, but powerful and eminently applicable. A more in-depth critique of both concepts (let alone their disciplinary ties) is beyond the scope of this introduction, but we recommend Messerschmidt (2018) for an overview of the ongoing conversations around hegemonic masculinity and Beasley (2012, 2015) for a critique.

in fact, the initial steps required in the refusal to 'accept *any* gender as a basis of stable signification' (Hester 2018:31). While an ultimate, near-utopian aim might be the imagination of such concepts, it does little to speak towards their operationalization. Our intent here is not to comment on the undesirability of a scenario in which oppression (gendered or otherwise) of any form does not exist. Rather, it is to say that we cannot claim to be 'post-patriarchal' in any sense of the word yet – to be caught exploring that imaginary makes light of pressing challenges. Without meaningful alternatives, moving 'beyond' masculinity leaves those that are still attached to it behind. In the face of patriarchy's profound resilience, multiplicity and adaptability, the researchers in this conference presented ethnographic data which detailed how patriarchy and masculinity are situated in their respective field sites. Our collective focus was thus shifted to the examination of 'patriarchies in practice' through the ethnographic method.

Ethnography: Examining how patriarchy is 'done'

The studies of masculinities in this volume take an ethnographic perspective. Ethnography typically entails close, empirical examination of particular people and groups in specific situations over a long period of time. The telling of a story that looks at what people do in the day-to-day, making sense of the messiness of highly complex concepts in everyday life. It is less about what patriarchy 'is' in a static sense, but rather how it is 'done'. This doing of patriarchy reflects the study of masculinities in their specific empirical situations, how they manifest and are embodied in their particular contexts; an in-depth study of 'gendered places in production and consumption, places in institution and in natural environments, places in social and military struggles' as noted by Connell (2005:71).

Thus, if patriarchal ideology is seen to be embedded within every facet of our social world, ethnographic enquiry can assist in bringing to the fore how such ideology manifests, what aspects of it are reproduced and how it is resisted. A unique aspect of such a methodology is how the conditions under which these social worlds are being observed and studied are outside the control of the ethnographer (Atkinson and Hammersley 2007:3). The fact that ethnographic research does not involve the adherence of controlled, fixed and rigid research designs means that the performative aspect of gender identities is not conjured by a space created by the researchers involved. Therefore, data pertaining to gender expressions (in this case, masculinities) that are outlined in this volume, follow the lived experiences of the interlocuters over an extended period in particular settings outside the 'control' of the researcher. The advantages of such a research methodology are in its ability to capture how it is (in the context of this volume) that men relate to one another, themselves, women, their social group, environment and their wider social context without experimental pressure to behave otherwise.

This leads us to another point which highlights the importance of the ethnographic method in the study of masculinities. Namely, that the writing showcased in this volume is grounded in detailed studies of men and particular masculinities that arise in specific contexts. The data outlined in these chapters involves countless hours of interaction with interlocuters, reflecting both on the research participants' lived experiences along with those of the ethnographers during the research. The analysis of this data involves interpretation of the meanings, functions and consequences of the interactions and practices observed. By analysing the specific ethnographic data outlined in these chapters, one can identify points of tension and resistance within social words. As with almost any ethnographic research, the field site represents a space in which people's multiple identities are entwined which, ultimately, shapes the research itself (Chege 2015; Flores 2016). In ethnographic research which focuses on the study of masculinities, the challenge involves the contextualizing the articulations of men with the overarching patriarchal structure within which the participants are situated. Such research is embedded within an ethical commitment. Namely, the mapping of feminist theory onto ethnographic data in order to bring forth analysis which ultimately reveal the ways in which particular discourses reinforce or challenge the social construction of gender identities and unequal gender relations (Lazar 2007:145).

Data driving such research often complexifies the conception of men as all-powerful embodiments of the patriarchal order – whose oppression of women is rooted in a self-conscious voluntarism and misogynistic, reflexive awareness. As a wider point, this sets out a frame for how men, masculinities and patriarchies might be thought to relate to each other. This volume thus draws attention to these worlds in a range of ethnographic field-sites and aims to provide the reader with a plethora of theory and data which explores the relationship between various forms of masculinity and patriarchy, from a feminist perspective.

Furthermore, as detailed by Cornwall and Lindisfarne (2016) in their edited volume *Dislocating Masculinity*, a significant contribution in drawing together various studies on masculinities through ethnographic methods is in their comparative possibilities: 'By examining the difficulties of translating particular meanings of masculinity from one social setting to another, anthropologists challenge the existence of any apparently straightforward universal category and raise questions about the social contexts in which such categories are used' (2). Thus, the volume brings together a multitude of contexts and social relations which exemplify how masculinities are embodied, reproduced and resisted in a diverse range of social worlds.

We do not, however, intend this work to solely be consumed by anthropologists or ethnographers. Rather, we hope it will be of interest to social scientists, gender studies, feminist scholars or political activists. Our hope is that any persons interested in challenging their thinking about the multiplicity of masculinities, patriarchy and their enactment in a diverse range of contexts will find relevant material. The overall focus is thus on shaping questions and opening spaces rather than providing clear-cut or reductive answers. This is not a systematic project that articulates what post-patriarchal or various forms of ideal masculinities (which vary with time, place and power dynamic) may look like. Rather, it reflects on the grounds that make them possible or not. This is problematized further by our acknowledgement that the entanglements explore here are at every stage *personal* entanglement for us as editors as for the authors and readers. It is well known that ethnography is not a neutral, objective depiction of some state of affairs but a radically 'situated knowledge' (e.g. Haraway 1988).

The rest of this introduction sets out the sections and the chapters contained in the book. The 'existential threat' to masculinities entails a complexity of emotional and ethical response on the part of the reader. In step with an ethnographic commitment to reflexivity and holism, the study of masculinity *qua* masculinity is an act in itself that is fraught with complications. Given the scale of the issues at hand, we can at best provide a small sketch of those issues. However, we feel that any possibility of unpicking the entanglements must take account of the practical challenges of both articulating them and situationally responding to them.

Book sections and chapters

Section (1) Backlash – From margin to mainstream: As with most anti-feminist backlashes, the idea that men are facing a crisis in identity is not a novel one. However, considering the current global populist movements, which are often attributed to forms of 'toxic masculinity', such a topic has found renewed importance (Faludi 1992). From Incels (involuntary celibates) to far-right terrorists, the question surrounding 'toxic masculinity' anticipates the standard critique that feminism devalues men and masculinity, as an effective means for recruitment (Nagle 2017). While the term 'toxic masculinity' itself potentially increases receptivity to the notion that there are harmful and non-harmful forms of masculinity, its operation as an analytic tool has allowed scholars to talk in normative terms of what masculinity *should* be rather than simply describing what it appears to be; the 'non-toxic' to strive for against the 'toxic' to avoid. This section attempts to move beyond this dualism by presenting a deeper investigation into both what masculinity *means* for members of the far-right while highlighting the breadth of variety even in what is often assumed to be hegemonic.

Chapter 1, titled '*Alpha and nerd masculinities: Antifeminism in the digital sphere*', examines how masculinity is performed and understood in antifeminist digital cultures, drawing on case studies from two antifeminist sites: Return of Kings (ROK) and the Reddit forum Kotaku in Action (KIA). By navigating these digital spaces, the author highlights the paradox of a network so thematically invested in discussions of gender politics being void of any working concrete definition of masculinity. They go on to suggest that several conceptions of masculinity coexist within antifeminism, often invoked by the same actors in different situations depending on their utility.

Chapter 2, '*Before and after #MeToo': How French perpetrators of domestic violence perceive themselves as victims of feminism*, is based on ethnographic fieldwork in France and details how mandatory and/or voluntary perpetrator programmes represent a microcosm to observe the cultural and social construction of contemporary masculinities and their connections to violence. In the participants' words, the public debate spread through the media in the post-MeToo era has had an influence on the judicial system, which, in their views, benefit women at the expenses of men. The chapter analyses the attitudes of perpetrators, while bringing to light the various ways in which the #MeToo movement is viewed from a patriarchal perspective.

The interlocutors in Chapter 3, *Phantom masculinities: Brexit, absence and nostalgia in London Pubs*, believe that they are *currently* situated in a post-patriarchal Britain. Patriarchy is thus not conceived as something to be overcome or moved beyond, but as an absence that needs re-establishing, with feminism being seen as an obstacle to this process. This chapter employs Hockey et al.'s (2010) statement that 'personhood and identity emerge as relational, negotiated concepts that refer to spatially located practices' (227), while making the argument that for the interlocutors, the erosion of their spatially located practices threatens their sense of belonging, community and agency, while strengthening the belief in the absence of 'real men' in the power.

Chapter 4, *Is there a 'post-patriarchal' Indian man? An ethnography of 'new' discourses of neoliberal masculinities in India*, explores how post-patriarchal masculinities usurp the language of social justice and gender equality, whilst reproducing patriarchal male privileges in new and more insidious ways. Through fourteen months of ethnographic fieldwork with young middle-class Indian men in New Delhi, this chapter seeks to reveal the way in which neoliberal masculinities give legitimacy to men's misogyny and protect their privilege, while at the same-time hailing them as 'new' male heroes of a 'new' India.

Section (2) Normativity and diversity: In this section, we examine behaviours that are hegemonically presented as 'ideal' or 'normal' with regards to masculinity, as well as diversity within them. Where there is multiplicity, the self-evident or clear character of norms recedes and there is room for dissent, critique or manoeuvre. The chapters here probe boundaries of hegemony and question the accepted definitions of masculinity or maleness as a norm, and of identity, as fixed.

Chapter 5, *Tenuous masculinities: Situated agency and value of the Indonesian transgender men's masculinities*, draws on queer theoretical analysis while looking at the emergence of transman (transpria) as identity construction and a political movement in Indonesia. It also examines how the subjectivity of transman evolves and departs from the previous models of masculine woman, butch, priawan (an amalgam of man-pria and woman-wanita) and tomboy (Blackwood 2010). In doing so, it specifically explores how transpria conceptualize various types of masculinity, how these masculinities are differently embodied in different spaces and situations, and how their masculinities are linked to their politics to challenge hetero-patriarchal culture.

Chapter 6, *'It's the touch that is doing the talking': UK sex clubs, dark rooms and the loss of masculinity*, uses ethnographic data which explores spaces called the 'dark room in British sex clubs'. Dark rooms, often called 'back rooms' in gay and bisexual clubs, are rooms that tend to be blacked out, sometimes with mazes and tunnels. In such spaces, sexual activity usually takes place anonymously with the visual being replaced by touch, taste and smell. Through observations of dark rooms and interviews with men who visit them, this chapter examines how men seek to 'lose themselves' in the darkness, reconfiguring their sense of gender and sexuality in their pursuit of bodies and pleasures.

Chapter 7, *Misogyny, fear, or boundary maintenance? Responses to brand activism on gender diversity amongst players of Magic: The Gathering*, focuses on the original trading card game 'Magic: The Gathering' where most of the visible players, including the vast majority of the competitive 'pro players', are cis men. However, the player-base is gradually becoming more diverse, and there are suggestions that many more women play the game at home with friends or online than attend public competitive events. In this chapter, the author builds on existing work that identifies e-sports as an alternative to mainstream forms of masculine sporting competition, particularly for those who do not fit masculine sport-body norms.

Chapter 8, *It takes a lot of balls to be a lady: Drag queens, stigma and their masculine identities*, focuses on the long, successful run of the reality television series *RuPaul's Drag Race* which has provoked claims that we are living through 'the Golden Age of Drag' (Brennan and Gudelunas 2017:1). The unprecedented popularity of drag exists, however, in a patriarchal world where the stigma of effeminacy is still present. Using the work of Esther Newton and Judith Butler, this chapter investigates the masculine identity of Drag Queen performers and their ambivalent relation with success. Taking the lives and careers of Divine and RuPaul Charles as case studies, this contribution seeks to study their late-career push to 'go legit' by performing out of drag, as their male personas.

Section (3) Bodies and minds: This section explores ways in which masculinity is dynamically produced through different registers of embodied experience. A common trope of the idealized masculine body is in the physical capacity to control both self and other with the dual promise of protection from and threat of violence. Perceived deficiencies in this capacity open a compelling space to explore the 'gap' between the fictive, hegemonic body and unruly real bodies.

Chapter 9, *Sobriety, service and selfhood: Moral-existential reconfiguration of masculinity in Alcoholics Anonymous in a large English city*, investigates how Alcoholics Anonymous (AA) discourse and practice fosters particular kinds of masculinity. As members go through the AA programme, they start to experience themselves and their relationships with others in new ways – they find that they think and feel differently. This chapter explores the ways in which these new experiential capacities are structured by AA understandings of existence, being and selfhood, and how this provides the groundwork for different kinds of masculinity to unfold. With a focus on how AA discourse frames moral action, I demonstrate how AA's discursive framework belies post-enlightenment divides between the bodily/affective and the rational/objective. AA interrupts post-enlightenment understandings of existence, and in doing so, it restructures members pre-objective conception of the human subject, which restructures their masculinity.

Chapter 10, '*Unheard voices, untold stories; men with disabilities – The invisible victims of patriarchy, a study of Kolkata, Bengal, India*', focuses on how physical disability may hamper the capacity to perform masculinity or femininity in line with patriarchally inflected expectations, where specific kinds of bodily capacity are an expected part of masculinity. Specifically, physical disability in men can be seen to relegate them to a lower status making their situations more vulnerable and invisible.

Chapter 11, *An Interview with Ed Fornieles*, discusses the embodied experience of Nordic-style Live-Action Roleplay (LARP), the bodily processes involved in the making of *Cel*, a seventy-two-hour immersive role-play performance in which ten participants navigate a fictional, embodied simulation of an extremist online community, largely populated by white men. The project aimed to explore the ideologies that influence aggressive expressions of masculinity and provide an effective framework for their dismantling.

Chapter 12, *The cultural work of hormones: The story of David and testosterone*, explores ethnographic research in two UK-based private practice clinics, the daily routines of healthcare professionals and patients coming into contact with testosterone. Namely, this includes men taking testosterone for a range of needs and women taking testosterone as part of their Hormone Replacement Therapy (HRT). Capturing multiple perspectives, the author explores the intersectional complexities associated with testosterone use and how these feature in the narratives of those intimately 'getting to know' testosterone.

The conclusion reiterates the key themes of the book, drawing together strands from the different sections while considering both pragmatic and theoretical ways forward. We draw on feminist activists and scholars, and consider how, even in the wake of the direst crises, there is an impetus towards

– indeed, an imperative for – reflection and renewal. Taking the contemporary crisis in patriarchal masculinity sketched throughout the book, we look at what factors might contribute to disrupting patriarchal power structures – and how men might also benefit from this. And finally, we ask: might the global crises we have lived through in the past few years provide an opportunity to finally build a post-patriarchal world?

Bibliography

Arjini, N. (2019) Imani Perry's Liberation Feminism. *The Nation*, 29th May 2019. Available at: https://www.thenation.com/article/archive/imani-perry-liberation-feminism-beyonce-lorraine-hansberry/ (accessed 4 February 2022).

Asahina, Y. (2015) *Mainstreaming of the Right and a New Right-Wing Movement in Japan*. M.A. Diss, University of Hawai'i at Mānoa.

Atkinson, P. and Hammersley, M. (2007) *Ethnography: Principles in Practice*. London: Routledge.

Barg, J. (2022) How 'Cultural Marxism' and 'Critical Race Theory' Became Dangerously Misunderstood. Philadelphia Inquirer, 4th January 2022. Available at: https://www.inquirer.com/opinion/cultural-marxism-critical-race-theory-language-20220104.html (accessed 4 February 2022).

Baker, J.E., Clancy, K.A. and Clancy, B. (2019) Putin as Gay Icon? Memes as a Tactic in Russian LGBT Activism, in Buyantueva, R. and Shevtsova, M. (eds.), *LGBTQ Activism in Central and Eastern Europe*, 209–33. Cham: Springer International Publishing.

Barker, K. and Jurasz, O. (2019) Online Misogyny: A Challenge for Digital Feminism?. *Journal of International Affairs*, 72(2), 95–114.

Bates, T. (1975) Gramsci and the Theory of Hegemony. *Journal of the History of Ideas*, 36(2), 351–66

Beasley, C. (2012) Problematizing Contemporary Men/Masculinities Theorizing: The Contribution of Raewyn Connell and Conceptual-Terminological Tensions Today. *The British Journal of Sociology*, 63, 747–65

Beasley, C. (2015) Caution! Hazards Ahead: Considering the Potential Gap between Feminist Thinking and Men/Masculinities Theory and Practice. *Journal of Sociology*, 51(3), 566–81

Beechey, V. (1979) On Patriarchy. *Feminist Review*, 3, 66–82

Ben-Ghiat, R. (2020) *Strongmen: Mussolini to the Present*. New York: W. W. Norton & Company.

Bhatt, C. (2020) White Extinction: Metaphysical Elements of Contemporary Western Fascism. *Theory, Culture and Society*, 38(1), 27–52

Blackwood, E. (2010) *Falling into the Lesbi World: Desire and Difference in Indonesia*. Honolulu: University of Hawaii Press.

Brennan, N. and Gudelunas, D. (2017) *RuPaul's Drag Race and the Shifting Visibility of Drag Culture: The Boundaries of Reality TV*. London: Palgrave Macmillan.

Butler, J. (1990) *Gender Trouble*. London: Routledge.

Chege, N. (2015) 'What's in It for Me?': Negotiations of Asymmetries, Concerns, and Interests between the Researcher and Research Subjects. *Ethnography*, 16(4), 463–81.

Connell, R.W. (1987) *Gender and Power*. Oxford: Polity Press.

Connell, R.W. (2005) *Masculinities*, (2nd ed.). Berkeley and Los Angeles: University of California Press.

Connell, R.W. and Messerschmidt, J.W. (2005) Hegemonic Masculinity: Rethinking the Concept. *Gender & Society*, 19, 829–59

Conway, M., Scrivens, R. and Macnair, L. (2019) *Right-Wing Extremists' Persistent Online Presence: History and Contemporary Trends*. The Hague: International Centre for Counter–Terrorism.

Cornwall, A. and Lindisfarne, N. (Eds.) (2016) *Dislocating Masculinity: Comparative Ethnographies*, (2nd ed.). London: Routledge.

Crenshaw, K. (1991) Mapping the Margins: Intersectionality, Identity Politics, and Violence against Women of Color. *Stanford Law Review*, 43, 1241–99.

Crenshaw, K. (2017) *On Intersectionality: Essential Writings*. New York: The New Press.

Davis, K. (2007) *The Making of Our Bodies, Ourselves: How Feminism Travels across Borders*. Durham, NC and London: Duke University Press Books.

Dyer, O. (2021) Demonstrations Erupt in Poland after New Abortion Law Is Blamed in Woman's Death. *British Medical Journal*, 375. Available at: https://www-bmj-com.libproxy.ucl.ac.uk/content/375/bmj.n2698 (accessed 24 February 2022).

Engels, F. (1884) *Origin of the Family, Private Property, and the State*. Marxist Internet Archive, online. Available at: https://www.marxists.org/archive/marx/works/1884/origin-family/index.htm (accessed 12 June 2022).

Faludi, S. (1992) *Backlash*. Los Angeles, CA: Pub. Mills.

Flores, G. M. (2016) Discovering a Hidden Privilege: Ethnography in Multiracial Organizations as an Outsider Within. *Ethnography*, 17(2), 190–212.

Frenkel and Karni (2021), Proud Boys Celebrate Trump's 'Stand By' Remark about Them at the Debate. *New York Times*, 29th September 2020. Available at: https://www.nytimes.com/2020/09/29/us/trump-proud-boys-biden.html (accessed 4 February 2022).

Fried, S.T. (2003) Violence against Women. *Health and Human Rights*, 6(2), 88–111.

Haraway, D. (1988) Situated Knowledges: The Science Question in Feminism and the Privilege of Partial Perspective. *Feminist Studies*, 14, 575.

Hester, H. (2018) *Xenofeminism*. Cambridge: UK Medford, MA polity 2019.

Hockey, J., Komaromy, C. and Woodthorpe, K. (2010) *The Matter of Death. Space, Place and Materiality*. Basingstoke: Palgrave Macmillan.

hooks, b. (2004) *The Will to Change: Men, Masculinity and Love*. New York, NY: Washington Square Press.

Htun, M. and Jensenius, F. R. (2020) Fighting Violence against Women: Laws, Norms & Challenges Ahead. *Daedalus*, 149(1), 144–59.

Hussein, J. et al. (2018) Abortion in Poland: Politics, Progression, Regression. *Reproductive Health Matters*, 26(52), 11–14

Kutner, S. (2020) *Swiping Right: The Allure of Hyper Masculinity and Cryptofascism for Men Who Join the Proud Boys*. The Hague: International Centre for Counter-Terrorism.

Laboria Cuboniks (Collective) (2018) *The Xenofeminist Manifesto: A Politics for Alienation*. London and New York: Verso Books.

Lazar, M.M. (2007) Feminist Critical Discourse Analysis: Articulating a Feminist Discourse Praxis. *Critical Discourse Studies*, 4(2), 141–64

Lee, M. (2020) Masculinities Studies, in N.A. Naples (ed.), *Companion to Women's and Gender Studies*, Hoboken: Wiley.

Lerner, G. (1986) *The Creation of Patriarchy*. New York: Oxford University Press.

Lentjes, R., Alterman, A. and Arey, W. (2020) 'The Ripping Apart of Silence': Sonic Patriarchy and Anti-Abortion Harassment. *Resonance*, 1(4), 422–42.

Liptek, A. (2021) Supreme Court to Hear Abortion Case Challenging Roe vs. Wade. *New York Times*, 21st May 2021. Available at: https://www.nytimes.com/2021/05/17/us/politics/supreme-court-roe-wade.html (accessed 4 February 2022).

Main, T. J. (2018) *The Rise of the Alt-Right*. Washington, DC: Brookings Institution Press.

Manne, K. (2017) *Down Girl: The Logic of Misogyny*. Oxford: Oxford University Press.

Messerschmidt, J. (2018) *Hegemonic Masculinity: Formulation, Reformulation and Amplification*. London: Rowman and Littlefield.

Miller-Idriss, C. (2017) *The Extreme Gone Mainstream: Commercialization and Far Right Youth Culture in Germany*. Princeton, NJ: Princeton University Press.

Millett, K. (1970) *Sexual Politics*. New York: Doubleday and Co.

Mohanty, C. (1988) Under Western Eyes: Feminist Scholarship and Colonial Discourses. *Feminist Review*, 30, 61–88

Morgan, L.H. (1877) *Ancient Society*. Chicago: C.H. Kerr.

Moscheller, M. and Wong, W. (2021) Joe Rogan Criticized, Mocked after Saying Straight White Men Are Silenced by 'Woke' Culture. *NBC News*, 18th May. Available at: https://www.nbcnews.com/news/us-news/joe-rogan-criticized-mocked-after-saying-straight-white-men-are-n1267801 (accessed 28 September 2021).

Mudde, C. (2019) *The Far Right Today*. Cambridge: Polity Press.

Nagle, A. (2017) *Kill All Normies: Online Culture Wars from 4chan and Tumblr to Trump and the Alt-Right*. Winchester and Washington: Zero Books.

Oppenheim, M. (2022) Colombia Decriminalises Abortion in 'Historic Victory' for Women's Rights. *Independent*, 28th February. Available at: https://www.independent.co.uk/news/world/americas/colombia-decriminalise-abortion-women-reproductive-rights-b2020427.html (accessed 28 February 2022).

Ortner, S. (2014) Too Soon for Post-Feminism: The Ongoing Life of Patriarchy in Neo-Liberal America. *History and Anthropology*, 25(4), 530–49.

Pappas, S. (2019) APA Issues First-Ever Guidelines for Practice with Men and Boys. Available at: https://www.apa.org/monitor/2019/01/ce-corner (accessed 28 September 2021).

Perry, I. (2018) *Vexy Thing: On Gender and Liberation*. Durham, NC: Duke University Press.

Reeser, T. (2010) *Masculinities in Theory: An Introduction*. Chichester: Blackwell.

Singh, S. et al. (2018) *Abortion Worldwide 2017: Uneven Progress and Unequal Access*. New York and Washington, DC: Guttmacher Institute.

UN Women (2022) Facts and Figures: Ending Violence against Women. Available at: https://www.unwomen.org/en/what-we-do/ending-violence-against-women/facts-and-figures (accessed 4 February 2022).

Vieten, U. M. (2018) Anti–Gender Campaigns in Europe: Mobilising against Equality by Roman Kuhar and David Paternotte. *Journal Feminist Dissent*, 3, 257–64.

Wendling, M. (2018) *Alt-Right: From 4chan to the White House*. London: Pluto Press.

Wood, E. A. (2016) Hypermasculinity as a Scenario of Power. *International Feminist Journal of Politics*, 18(3), 329–50.

Zetkin, C., Taber, M. and Riddell, J. (2017) *Fighting Fascism: How to Struggle and How to Win*. La Vergne: Haymarket Books.

Part One

Backlash: From margins to mainstream

1

Alpha and nerd masculinities: Antifeminism in the digital sphere

Annie Kelly

This chapter examines how masculinity is performed and understood in antifeminist digital cultures, drawing on case studies from two antifeminist sites, the now-defunct blog *Return of Kings* (ROK) and the Reddit forum *Kotaku in Action* (KIA). Both of these sites represent two vastly differing formats, styles and rhetoric: the first being a far-right 'pick-up artist'-style blog, and the second a decentralized hub for supporters of the 2014 'GamerGate' campaign.[1,2] What they share in common is an explicit opposition to feminism as a political and cultural movement, encapsulated here as 'antifeminism'. Crucially, they both exist within a reactionary socio-digital network which includes far right and white supremacist hubs and commentators, all frequently collaborating and borrowing imagery, slang and content from one another. In this chapter, I argue that it is necessary to understand the internal conflicts and contradictions surrounding masculinity in these spaces, not simply to combat online misogyny, but also the mainstream language within the far right.

I will make this case through analysing two popular antifeminist constructions of masculinity, which I have termed 'nerd masculinity' and 'alpha masculinity'. Although not an exhaustive list of antifeminist approaches to masculinity, I discuss these two because of their prevalence and popularity in discourse around gender issues, including on more mainstream and legitimized platforms, such as popular films. Sarah Banet-Weiser urges in her prescient

---

[1] BuyTheMoon, "'[Feminists] did it to scientists, they did it to sports – the Gamers were the first group … that really fought back … they like to win … they were not the right group to pick a fight with" – Christina Hoff Sommers', *Kotaku in Action* (accessed 12 September 2017).

[2] 'GamerGate' was the term coined in 2014 for a digital harassment campaign against video game journalists and developers considered to be feminists, or in internet slang 'Social Justice Warriors'. The campaign organized a network using social media hashtags, forums and imageboards.

2015 essay 'Popular Misogyny: A Zeitgeist' that 'we need to contend with how, and in what ways, misogyny has shifted its media tactics and tropes in response to popular feminism' (Banet-Weiser 2015). Whilst mainstream media often focuses on particularly lurid moments of antifeminist hostility, such as 'pick-up artist' icon Roosh V's proposition to legalize rape on private property (Valizadeh 2015), little attention is paid to the less sensational styles of persuasion and recruitment strategies that everyday antifeminists espouse to great success. By engaging not simply with how antifeminist users engage in 'masculine' performance towards women, and feminists in particular, but amongst one another, we can gain a more nuanced picture of digital antifeminism's appeal to particular groups of men.

For a network so thematically invested in discussions of gender politics, there, paradoxically, does not seem to be a working concrete definition of masculinity in the cluster of antifeminist forums and websites known colloquially as 'the manosphere'. Surveying a vast amount of antifeminist digital literature detailing the essential loss of masculinity in the West (Anthony 2016), or a supposed feminist educational campaign to demean the 'inherent masculinity' of young boys (Woodall 2015), can give the reader the slightly disorienting sense that the masculinity mentioned in these spaces is simultaneously in no need of explanation and yet is so theoretically malleable it can be used to fit any issue. Although it is rarely admitted by antifeminist commentators and users, masculinity remains a contested issue even in their own sphere. While the frequently reductive, essentialist rhetoric surrounding men and manhood might suggest otherwise, there is no 'one size fits all' vision of masculinity which perfectly encompasses the antifeminist worldview. It seems more accurate to suggest that several conceptions of masculinity coexist within antifeminism, often invoked by the same actors in different situations depending on their utility. From my own observations of digital antifeminist discourse, some of the most popular usages of masculinity in such spaces use the term to mean, respectively:

1. An essential feature of national security. A nationwide loss of masculinity and subsequent collapse of patriarchy has been detailed by some antifeminists as responsible for the 9/11 attacks, the so-called migrant crisis in Europe, and even the fall of Ancient Rome.
2. An individual mastery over those around you, which a man can choose to strive towards through a constant state of self-improvement and intense

competition. This is frequently contrasted to femininity, which is denigrated as parasitic and childlike.

3. An essential trait intrinsic to all men, which is frequently embattled and degraded by powerful societal forces, especially feminism. Men who do not display this intrinsic value to the satisfaction of the antifeminist user (e.g. gay men) are frequently deemed to be either defective or 'broken' by such forces.

4. An oppressive expectation that men are burdened with. This understanding, which could be seen as strangely close to some feminist understandings of the concept, offsets such similarities by reformulating feminism as an extension of the code of chivalry, and thus responsible for men's continued victimization as a class.

This difficulty in defining masculinity is not exclusive to antifeminists alone – even from a feminist perspective, it is common to use the term as a shorthand for a more complex concept. This becomes particularly fraught when studying people's behaviour online, where so many of the embodied visual cues associated with 'naturalized' masculinities are obscured (Alsop, Fitzsimmons and Lennon 2002:172). For the purposes of this essay, I will be examining masculinity as a primarily discursive positioning tool, meaning a method for constructing one's own, someone else's, or a collective performative identity in either writing or conversation. Whilst this will necessarily be limited to online discourse for this chapter, it is not definitively so – I borrow the concept from R. W. Connell and James W. Messerschmidt's (2005) analysis of in-person interviews where participants discussed their own relationship to masculinity. Nonetheless, this position obviously requires some nuance, for as Connell and Messerschmidt (2005:842) point out,

> One is not free to adopt any gender position in interaction simply as a discursive or reflexive mode. The possibilities are constrained massively by embodiment, by institutional histories, by economic forces, and by personal and family relationships. The costs of making certain discursive choices can be extremely high.

It would be simplistic to suggest that speaking on a comment section, message board or posting an article, by virtue of anonymity, removes or nullifies such barriers. Lisa Nakamura has heavily criticized the neoliberal understanding of digital spaces that emphasizes identity, particularly race, as a superficial matter of being *seen* as this identity, an issue that disappears entirely through non-visual communication (Nakamura 2014:34). Such arguments, she reasons, position identity and subsequent identity conflicts as matters of hyper-visibility – in short race and gender are 'on' oneself and not a much more complex rooted connection to 'larger flows of labour, culture and power' (ibid.:36). I do not mean to discount these realities or suggest that widespread digital anonymity is a helpful preventative for established social hierarchies.

However, what does seem fair to suggest is that the 'costs' of our discursive choices that Connell and Messerschmidt point to are often significantly reduced in digital environments, even if the most meaningful inequalities, such as who gets access (in terms of both technology and leisure time) remain. One is not likely to face immediate, significant consequences that impact offline areas of our lives for the styles of discourse we choose for ourselves, and cases where this does happen are still rare enough to be considered newsworthy, such as the few who have faced criminal charges for extreme acts of 'trolling' (Kentish 2017). Indeed, where there are immediate and material costs for online speech, they tend overwhelmingly to be for the targets of online misogyny rather than its perpetrators. Nonetheless, it is not as if material social costs are the only factor that prevents certain men from adopting such strategies – their very appeal is likely to be dependent on how any individual user relates themselves to the world already. To give a specific example, one of my source sites *Return of Kings* frequently features explicitly racist rhetoric, such as an article that declares '[a]ny man, regardless of race, will admit that white men are at the top of the food chain in terms of sexual predilection among females the world over' and goes onto denigrate white women who sleep with Black men (Sharpe 2015). It is extremely likely that such rhetoric operates as a hidden 'cost' for Black users reading the site in a way it does not for white men, and thus the appeal of adopting the site's style of masculinity will differ depending on race. Since this chapter is concerned with antifeminist discourse and rhetoric rather than the offline lives of its participants however, it seems apt to narrow down its focus onto masculinity as a discursive performance, without discounting the multitude of personal and societal reasons users may individually feel that such a performance best fits their situational needs at that current time.

This chapter compares two different strategies that I have identified in antifeminist digital spaces. To illustrate how such strategies work in practice, I've attached them to case studies from two antifeminist sites: *Return of Kings*, which is a blog borne out of the 'pick-up artist' and sexual strategy digital network, and KIA, a forum on the popular chat site Reddit that was central to the 2014

'GamerGate' campaign primarily against feminist game journalists. It should be noted though that neither of the categories I go onto describe are exclusive to their correlated site. As befits an ideological value that is consistently shifting according to its political utility, there is regular slippage between the sites and even individual users in terms of which form of masculinity they choose to employ in their writing.

'Nerd' masculinity

With this understanding in mind, it seems appropriate to turn to a source that seems to have the most invested in maintaining the popular notion of masculinity as a fixed, largely unobtainable personality type (Alsop, Fitzsimmons and Lennon 2002:140). KIA, the GamerGate forum on the popular chat-site Reddit (known as a 'subreddit'), is described in its own sidebar as a space 'where gaming, nerd culture, the Internet, and media collide'. This collaboration of concepts euphemistically subsumes the subreddit's highly ideological position by the more hobbyist, neutral-sounding 'gaming [and] nerd culture'. This is a theme enthusiastically repeated by KIA users, who are fond of claiming the title of 'apolitical' in contrast to what they see as feminism's determination to 'politicize' video games.

This framing of the sides of this 'collision' and the presumed dominion that antifeminism has over nerd culture is not incidental. Vicky Osterweil, in a thorough longform piece for *Real Life* magazine, documented the popular cinematic image of the nerd, ever-present on our screens since the 1980s as 'a smart but awkward, always well-meaning white boy irrationally persecuted by his implacable jock antagonists' (Osterweil 2016). She argues that films like *Revenge of the Nerds* (1987) symbolically displace the 'actual categories of social struggle and oppression with the concept of the jock-nerd struggle' (ibid.). In this regard, *Kotaku in Action* is a wealth of discourse, with many lengthy and considered posts or discussions on the subsuming oppression that nerd masculinity entails. As one post muses, nerds cannot even really be seen to benefit from male privilege at all, since:

'Male privilege' is really 'gender-conforming male privilege' ('Alpha Male Privilege'). Men who are not gender conforming, be they nerds, non-macho gays, or anything of that ilk, *do not receive nearly as much in the way of male privilege*. Indeed, they receive scorn and misery. Males, for being males, get no privileges. They are only given privilege when they are perceived as living up to the male gender role. This is because society in general perceives masculinity in a Platonic fashion (an ideal to live up to), and anyone who fails to participate in the Platonic form of manhood *ceases being a man.*[3]

Here the effects of what Osterweil charts as decades of popular media using the nerd/jock binary as an appropriative parallel for civil rights reaches its natural conclusion. By the KIA user's re-classification of 'nerd' as an oppressed class (equivalent to homosexuality) and masculinity as an exclusive fixed personality type (although as we have seen this is not actually the case even in antifeminist circles), a user-base of primarily white, university-educated men are able to reinforce patriarchy by declaring their existence outside of it (Ferguson and Glasgow 2020). The antifeminist implications of male-centric postfeminist rhetoric that Tania Modleski expressed concern about in her book *Feminism without Women* (1991:5) reach a consensus in much of KIA's discourses on nerd masculinity, which concludes that liberation discourses' only valid use is for the liberation of the 'non-macho' man.

However, it is important to note that in the above KIA post, and in many others, there is an allusion to the 'dues paid' by the nerd in the oppression that he has faced. The 'scorn and misery' that the user outlines suggest that he is oppressed not simply by masculine violence but by social ostracization and lack of romantic prospects. This runs along similar lines to other antifeminist victimization narratives, such as that of the 'incel' (short for 'involuntarily celibate') community, but crucially offers users a very specific style of reprieve. What distinguishes this position is the nerd's presumed mastery of specific male-coded pursuits, in this case video games. The combination of both these discourses of alienation from wider society and technical competence in KIA can lead to posts which are striking in their semi-militaristic bravado. One such highly upvoted and recirculated post reads:

They targeted gamers.
Gamers.

We're a group of people who will sit for hours, days, even weeks on end performing some of the hardest, most mentally demanding tasks. Over, and

---

[3]   For the purposes of ethically researching digital spaces as a covert observer, I have re-pseudonymized the usernames of all forum users in the reference list and not included web or archive links. This is done on the understanding that many people use the same usernames across platforms, and it does not seem fair to immortalize a user for a years-old comment they may well regret, or even have deleted. None of their words have been altered.

over, and over all for nothing more than a little digital token saying we did.

We'll punish our selfs [*sic*] doing things others would consider torture, because we think it's fun.

We'll spend most if not all of our free time min maxing the stats of a fictional character all to draw out a single extra point of damage per second.

Many of us have made careers out of doing just these things: slogging through the grind, all day, the same quests over and over, hundreds of times to the point where we know evety [*sic*] little detail such that some have attained such gamer nirvana that they can literally play these games blindfolded.

Do these people have any idea how many controllers have been smashed, systems over heated, disks and carts destroyed 8n [*sic*] frustration? All to latter be referred to as bragging rights?

These people honestly think this is a battle they can win? They take our media? We're already building a new one without them. They take our devs? Gamers aren't shy about throwing their money else where, or even making the games our selves. They think calling us racist, mysoginistic, [*sic*] rape apologists is going to change us? We've been called worse things by prepubescent 10 year olds with a shitty head set. They picked a fight against a group that's already grown desensitized to their strategies and methods. Who enjoy the battle of attrition they've threatened us with. Who take it as a challange [*sic*] when they tell us we no longer matter. Our obsession with proving we can after being told we can't is so deeply ingrained from years of dealing with big brothers/sisters and friends laughing at how pathetic we used to be that proving you people wrong has become a very real need; a honed reflex.

Gamers are competitive [*sic*], hard core, by nature. We love a challenge [*sic*]. The worst thing you did in all of this was to challenge [*sic*] us. You're not special, you're not original, you're not the first; this is just another boss fight.

This monologue, in which enjoyment of video games is repeatedly equated with an interior resilience and industriousness, is striking in its valorization of a particular hyper-conservative ideal of masculinity. It leaves no room for vulnerability and crucially, no room for defeat. Here is where the discursive construction of geek masculinity becomes not simply a method of self-positioning, but positioning the reader as well, and therefore encouraging them to a specific course of action. The writer swiftly moves from describing the act of gaming, presumably familiar to the vast majority of his fellow KIA users, using the pluralising 'we', rather than 'I', to a more abstract future in which 'we're already building a new [media] without them'. In this rallying cry, the intended readers are simultaneously threatened with the invocation of being seen as 'pathetic' losers, and then swiftly offered a flattering alternative. In this prospect reality, geek masculinity is repackaged as explicitly for *winners*, but only if its representatives take part in the 'battle' against feminism the writer describes. Thus, the twinned perspectives of nerd masculinity – one derided and pathetic, the other valorized and triumphant, both work to perpetuate KIA's existence as a community. The only way to escape the 'pathetic' zone of geek masculinity that the user alludes to is to occupy a space which, through militant antifeminism, repackages this supposedly shared history into a collective victory.

This 'reversal' of the downtrodden geek's fortune, however, is not really a true reversal at all. In the stories that Osterweill describes, the nerd usually emerges victorious as a direct result of his derided skillset, just as the KIA poster describes. It could be suggested that the plethora of biographical films surrounding figures such as Steve Jobs and Mark Zuckerberg shows that the story of a socially alienated white male nerd who eventually succeeds is a commercially profitable power fantasy. Thus, while KIA's actual antifeminist content spans a diverse range of topics, it is an important tactic to subsume this fairly obvious ideology in 'nerd culture' in order to appropriate an already existing powerful narrative in which the order of antagonism is permanently in their favour, from a storytelling sense. Since the (implicitly white) nerd is an inherently persecuted character, it is he who is (irrationally) 'targeted' by implacable agents of feminism in the media. Feminist or anti-racist critiques of almost any media topic can be re-cast as persecution of the nerd identity, with which KIA users have a vast array of discursive options to claim, is tantamount to persecution of the individuals themselves.

Given this particular community's construction of nerd masculinity, it hardly seems surprising that it was women who bore the brunt of GamerGate's own 'revenge of the nerds'. Zoe Quinn, the campaign's first declared target, had already attracted the ire of several majority male internet communities for her video game *Depression Quest*, a free text-based simulation of depressive disorder based on Quinn's own experiences with depression. As a member of one such community wrote: 'All females are sluts and have no right to be depressed. They can just go out onto the street, lie down with their hole open and have any man come and solve all of their problems' (Whitman 2013). The figure of wicked womanhood, who (sexually) rewards other men's violence but either ignores or despises the nerd, is not simply incidental to the integrity of nerd masculinity as a valid self-positioning tool but vital to it. After all, if the nerd's lack of romantic success is not a result of women's failings, then his own victimization falls into question, and as a result so does the eventual success he is entitled to according to the familiar story-arc. As these extracts have shown, whilst much of the self-positioning of nerd masculinity may appear at first glance to be self-deprecating, it often yields a self-regard of technical competence that Judy Wajcman describes as 'central to the dominant cultural idea of masculinity' (Massanari 2015:129), and hard-won but deserved victory, often in the form of revenge upon one's persecutors.

Women staking a claim to the symbols of nerd masculinity – depression, loneliness, video game culture, even the internet – jeopardize this entire framework. To assert women's agency and humanity is to deny the nerd his birth right. It seems strangely unremarkable then, that Quinn posting comments such as the one above, detailing the harassing phone calls she received from members of the same forum, became re-calculated by KIA as her attacking 'a board for depressed men [...] over only a couple of negative comments', which in turn became a reason for harassing and stalking her. In this way, the revenge discourses of nerd masculinity are a continually self-fulfilling prophecy. While KIA's membership may have dwindled slightly since its inception in August 2014, it remains a remarkably active board. There are always new feminist figures whose perceived advances into internet culture will represent a threat to nerd masculinity's domain, and thus the cycle seems perpetually set to continue.

Alpha masculinity

What however happens to users who are unconvinced by the rote and seeming relentlessly unsatisfying prospect of imminent nerd vengeance? *Return of Kings*, a site originally marketed as pickup artist-style dating advice for men, may seem to have little relation to nerd culture hubs such as KIA, but nevertheless it starts off with much the same sexual mythos. As a collective, women's choice of sexual partners is not a grievance but a collective domination, as one article tellingly titled 'Women Have No Sense of Justice' goes on to outline:

> [I]t would seem, on the face of it, that treating women with respect – your dealings with them being governed by justice and honor – would lead to success with them. But as every American man who isn't stupid or a pussy eventually learns, this is far from true. [...] If you think otherwise, I encourage you to be that nice guy in the sweet, emotional way, and see how that goes for you.
>
> (Contrary 2016)

Here, the subtext in the earlier details of the 'scorn and misery' necessarily entailed in nerd masculinity becomes overt in the age-old common sense adage: nice guys finish last. Much like KIA, *Return of Kings* advocates a style of masculinity that is simultaneously a form of vengeance upon women and a mode of self-defence against them. ROK's model of masculinity stands in sharp contrast to KIA who seem to ideologically bound to nerd masculinity as an immutable, inherent trait in order to make the case for it as an oppressed class. ROK's discourses of naturalness and artificiality in practicing gender seem, perhaps strikingly for a site that frequently flirts with white nationalism, somewhat more flexible and even adjacent to more progressive theoretical positions on gender.

A consistently popular genre of ROK narrative is that of 'taking the red pill', a term appropriated from the character Neo's awakening in the 1999 science-fiction film *The Matrix*, in which the narrator 'unlearns' liberal beliefs and substitutes them with reactionary ideology. In doing so, he is able to become an 'alpha male', with a superior dominion not over just women but other men too. While the specific details of these stories change, the structure remains remarkably similar in that this is always shown to have an overwhelmingly positive effect on the narrator's life. Articles with subtitles like 'I was the Blue Pill King' (Sharpe 2014) typically go into excruciating detail on a past life of humiliation and subservience at the hands of women (and occasionally other men) before achieving sexual and financial self-determination through the 'red pill' philosophy. Much like the KIA's nerd vengeance mythos, a portion of this is simply a sly marketing strategy. The blue-pilled past self is depicted in language as unflattering as possible and in situations designed to underscore his shamefully low social position (being left for another man is a common trope) in order to provide a menacing reference point for the reader's potential undesirability if they do not continually revisit ROK and its brother sites. As such, these stories are not simply conversion narratives, but subtle threats to their own readership. As these articles frequently caution, even men with seemingly untaught 'swagger, great style, and supreme confidence' are in a more precarious situation than the user embarking on a red pill journey, as without 'red pill wisdom or game to go along with it your life can be still be made a living hell by a woman' (ibid.). Being truly alpha, in the sense of the word that indicates an elite precedence in an assumed hierarchy of masculine styles, necessarily entails consuming and adopting ROK's ideological frameworks on gender and culture. Similarly, it means that recognizing the constructed element to becoming a truly self-determined alpha male is integral to ROK's commercial viability. If it were not acknowledged as in some way a learned process, then the site (and the many others with similar promises on masculine self-improvement) would be, by their own admission, useless.

In order to escape this uncomfortably feminist-adjacent position of describing gender as performance, most Red Pill narratives take care to underscore that alpha masculinity is *also* the real natural state of man. As one such article, semi-paradoxically titled 'Taking the Red Pill Is One of the Hardest Things a Man Can Do' begins,

> Men have been biologically programmed for thousands of years to desire a high amount of sex, to make decisions, to fight, and to build. Everything that makes the masculine. [...] In today's world, men are being told to be sensitive (not fight), be nice (results in no sex), to work for someone else (not building), and to defer to your woman in every possible case (not decisive).
>
> (Trouble 2017)

Another article mentions a similar story, but notes that 'eventually we all come across that one [red pill] article that catches our eye and jives with every last circuit of our masculine hard drive' (Sharpe 2014). Use of the semantic field of technical circuitry to describe a biologically determined masculine independence and dominance here is a feature that seems to strike a chord with ROK writers and commenters alike, partially because of its perceptively different ideological imperatives. By shifting the discursive construction of masculinity from the rhetoric of nature and the natural world, which at least subtly also calls to the reader's mind the long-spanning discourses surrounding 'taming' nature, technical language surrounding man's true nature turns 'taming' into hacking or in computer-science slang, 'modding' (Stephens 2013:6). While 'taming' nature is, according to ROK, in men's biological programming through their need to 'build', the language of hacking suggests a risky, uncertain enterprise which crucially involves tinkering with something that does not belong to the hacker. This leads to a paradoxical binary of rhetoric surrounding gendered imperatives in ROK discourse. Women's true nature, which is promiscuous, illogical and selfish should be 'tamed' for the good of society, but hacking men's 'hardwired' biological programming is unethical, dangerous and not always likely to work. As many commenters below the line of 'taking the red pill' narratives are fond of pointing out, there was always some part of them that knew 'that something is wrong with the world, but the world convinced me that I was the problem' (Trouble 2017). Thus, alpha masculinity involves re-casting the self as an active agent in one's own engineering in order to detach from supposed societal gender norms that have not simply lost their way, but been actively and deliberately subverted.

This conspiratorial detail is therefore vital to the ideological integrity of alpha masculinity. It also connects comfortably with several strains of hard right and alt-right thought that are all too happy to provide answers for *who* exactly is responsible for 'unmanning' the apparently innately alpha male population. It is therefore not uncommon to see anti-Semitic discourses mixed in with ROK's antifeminist branding. As one commenter ruefully notes, 'The red-pill used to just be about figuring out how to get a woman to swallow your cum … Somehow it's become about saving ourselves from NWO rule [New World Order, a frequently anti-Semitic conspiracy theory detailing a secretive and powerful "world government"] and civil war' (Trouble 2017). Another user responds to him in a slightly more upbeat tone:

> Indeed! […] this [Pick Up Artist]-like attitude morphed into something more political, more vast. I think this is one of the last steps of redpilling;
> 1st manning up by putting women down from their pedestal
> 2nd reinvent one's life and give it a true masculine positive direction, and bed all women one can do.
> 3rd become aware of how the world is really ruled, by (((who))) and why
> 4th resistance against all soros's suckers, NWO and all those motherfuckers.
> 5th transmit the knowledge to the future generations

Leaving the commenter's casual mix-n-match approach to several strains of right-wing conspiracy theories aside, they make a relatively astute observation that for all its claims to self-determination, alpha masculinity's reflexive positioning of 'the red pill' relies on a seemingly perpetual state of being acted upon, even if by mostly fictional forces. Much like KIA's continual narrative cycle of nerd masculinity's vengeance and victimization, ROK offers a reprieve from its own reiterative discourses of anxiety surrounding blue-pilled men and their endless humiliation, but never a true escape. While the alpha male may be able to master his interactions with the women around him (mainly through keeping them at both an emotional and physical distance), ROK's website and comment sections are a testament to the fact that he is constantly at battle with forces very deliberately constructed to be permanently out of his control.

Conclusion

Given masculinity's clear malleability as both a positioning tool and an ideological placeholder within antifeminist spaces, it seems necessary when engaging with antifeminist usage of the word to consider both what style of masculinity they are employing, and what rhetorical strategies come with it. In direct contradiction to popular notions of masculinity as a fixed and unchanging character trait, I have tried to use this chapter as both an explanation and an introduction to a range of discursive options available to antifeminist users navigating digital space in order to demonstrate their appeal. In this context, however, 'appeal' needs to be elaborated on more broadly – in digital spaces, antifeminist masculinities do not simply operate as the reason a user visits the site in the first place, but also a reason that they keep coming back. While antifeminist masculinities might be at first surprising with the range of options they offer to readers to try out, play with and either independently or communally evolve, they also come with their own relatively punitive limits which threaten a lifetime of loneliness and humiliation if not enacted 'right'. This is a key finding to consider when viewing antifeminism as a major introductory step within the wider alt-right digital network, and in particular its significance to younger users.

Masculinity as a counter-subversive tool has a tendency to prey on its audience through both threatening their sense of identity and also offering them an ameliorative alternative. But it is crucial to stress that this is a strategy that would not have enjoyed the kind of success it has if it were not operating within a culture in which such anxieties within masculinity were not already both normalized and largely exploited. Susan Faludi, writing on the effects of globalization and large-scale economic 'downsizing' in *Stiffed: The Betrayal of the American Man* (1999), explains how economic insecurity can have a psychological impact even on the middle-class men who were least materially affected:

> A social pact between the nation's men and its institutions was collapsing, most prominently but not exclusively within the institutions of work. Masculine ideals of loyalty, productivity and service lay in shards. Such codes were seen as passé and their male subscribers as vaguely pathetic [...] Such a profound and traumatic transformation affected all men, whether they lost their jobs or simply feared losing them, whether they drowned or floated in the treacherous new currents. In the course of my travels, I would meet men amply rewarded by the quicksilver, image-based new economy, men who, nonetheless, felt, as they would say to me time and again, 'emasculated' by the very forces that elevated them.
>
> (43)

It seems little wonder to me that in this culture of seemingly faceless corporate emasculation, hegemonic masculinity tries to find space to reassert itself by creating a narrative of digital self-actualization and a clear, definable target for its promises of misdirected revenge. Women have long been the object of narrative templates for masculine self-positioning in mainstream culture – we do not have to scour the comment sections *Return of Kings*, for instance, to easily find stories in which sexual conquest dictates a hierarchy of superior to inferior manhood. But in the digital sphere the sheer availability of chances to enact these fantasies has never been higher, and the 'costs' of such choices have never been lower.

To tackle the material 'costs' of these choices by way of ending internet anonymity, as some writers and even government officials have suggested, seems to me to be an ineffective (and largely unethical) treatment of a symptom, rather than a cause. Many antifeminist contributors have always been happy to attach their real names to their brands, and this is only increasing as the alt-right network shores itself up in commercialization. The most successful responses to combat digital hate have been ones which directly seek to put pressure on the digital platforms that allow such commercialization, thereby threatening their financial incentive to do so. These tactics are exemplified by Sleeping Giants, an organization which describes itself as 'dedicated to stopping racist, sexist, homophobic, xenophobic and anti-Semitic news sites by stopping their ad dollars'. We even have proof from one of my source sites that this method works – *Return of Kings* posted a farewell post in October 2018 which essentially admitted that being 'banned from Paypal and countless ad partners', as well as comment-hosting platform Disqus, 'started a negative spiral of declining content quality, site traffic, and revenues' (Valizadeh 2018).

Nonetheless this strategy is not a totalizing solution to the growing tide of antifeminist and alt-right content online. To target digital platforms in isolation would be to treat antifeminist users as a problem external to neoliberal society rather than fully integrated within it. As the researcher of technology and politics Becca Lewis writes, internet users 'don't always just stumble upon more and more extremist content – in fact, audiences often *demand* this kind of content from their preferred creators' (Lewis 2020). It is necessary to understand this frequently less obvious appeal, and tackle both its material and cultural incentives, without summarily dismissing the behaviours of antifeminist users (and thus the consequences for their targets) as insignificant ephemera.

Bibliography

Alsop, R., Fitzsimmons, R. and Lennon, K. (2002) *Theorizing Gender*. Cambridge: Blackwell.

Anthony, J. (2016) 'What the Next 25 Years of Western Civilization Will Be Like', *Return of Kings*, 14th December. Available at: http://www.returnofkings.com/104892/a-realistic-timeline-for-the-next-twenty-five-years-of-western-civilization (accessed 10 February 2022).

Banet-Weiser, S. (2015) Popular Misogyny: A Zeitgeist. *Cultural Digitally*, January 21st. Available at: http://culturedigitally.org/2015/01/popular-misogyny-a-zeitgeist/

Connell, R. W. and Messerschmidt, James W. (2005) Hegemonic Masculinity: Rethinking the Concept. *Gender and Society*, 19(6), 829–59.

Contrary, C. (2016) Women Have No Sense of Justice. *Return of Kings*, 22nd March. Available at: http://www.returnofkings.com/30485/women-have-no-sense-of-justice (Archived 28 February 2017).

Faludi, S. (1999) *Stiffed: The Betrayal of the American Man*. New York: Perennial Books.

Ferguson, C. J. and Glasgow, B. (2021) Who Are GamerGate? A Descriptive Study of Individuals Involved in the GamerGate Controversy. *Psychology of Popular Media*, 10(2), 243–24

Kentish, B. (2017) British Man Charged after US Gamer Is Shot by Swat Police Following Hoax Terrorism Call. *The Independent*, 10th April. Available at: http://www.independent.co.uk/news/uk/home-news/robert-mcdaid-charged-tyran-dobbs-swatting-hoax-call-swat-terrorism-maryland-shot-gun-explosives-a7677071.html (accessed 23 June 2017).

Homepage. Kotaku in Action. Available at: https://www.reddit.com/r/KotakuInAction/ [archived 16 December 2016] Archive: http://archive.is/bWAXC 118Boz, 'KiA We Need To Have a Talk', Kotaku in Action, 30th October 2015 (accessed 23 June 2016)

Lewis, B. (2020) All of YouTube, Not Just the Algorithm, Is a Far-Right Propaganda Machine. *Medium*, 8th January. Available at: https://ffwd.medium.com/all-of-youtube-not-just-the-algorithm-is-a-far-right-propaganda-machine-29b07b12430 (accessed 13 February 2021).

Massanari, A.L. (2015) *Participatory Culture, Community and Play: Learning from Reddit*. New York: Peter Lang.

Modleski, T. (1991) *Feminism without Women: Culture and Criticism in a 'Postfeminist' Age*. New York and London: Routledge.

Nakamura, L. (2014) Cyberrace, in A.Poletti and J. Rak (eds.), *Identity Technology: Constructing the Self Online*, 42–54. The University of Wisconsin Press.

Osterweil, V. (2016) What Was the Nerd?, *Real Life*, 16th November. http://reallifemag.com/what-was-the-nerd/ (accessed 10 February 2022).

Sharpe, D. (2014) The Benefits of Being a Late Bloomer. *Return of Kings*, 28th July. Available at: http://www.returnofkings.com/40478/the-benefits-of-being-a-late-bloomer (accessed 10 February 2022).

Sharpe, D. (2015) The Phenomenon of White Women Who Only Date Black Men. *Return of Kings*, 16th September. Available at: https://www.returnofkings. com/70903/the-phenomenon-of-white-women-who-only-date-black-men (accessed 10 February 2022).

Stephens, A. (2013) *Ecofeminism and Systems Thinking*. New York and London: Routledge.

Trouble, K. (2017) Taking the Red Pill Is One of the Hardest Things a Man Can Do. *Return of Kings*, 8th February. Available at: http://www.returnofkings.com/114441/ taking-the-red-pill-is-one-of-the-hardest-things-a-man-can-do (accessed 10 February 2022).

Valizadeh, R. (2015) How to Stop Rape. Roosh V, 16th February. Available at: http:// www.rooshv.com/how-to-stop-rape (accessed 10 February 2022).

Valizadeh, R. (2018) Return of Kings Is Going on Hiatus. *Return of Kings*, 1st October. Available at: http://www.returnofkings.com/195790/return-of-kings-is-going-on-hiatus (accessed 10 February 2022).

Whitman, C. (2013) Depression Quest Harassment Campaign. *Storify*, 12th December. Available at: https://storify.com/SeeBeeWhitman/depression-quest-harassment-campaign (accessed 10 February 2022).

Woodall, K. (2015) Education, Emasculation and Equality: A Letter to Yvette Cooper. *A Voice for Men*, 14th February. Available at: https://www.avoiceformen.com/ feminism/education-emasculation-and-equality-a-letter-to-yvette-cooper/ (archived 24 March 2017)

2

'Before and after #MeToo': How French perpetrators of domestic violence perceive themselves as 'victims of feminism'

Cristina Oddone

In 1983, the French filmmaker Raymond Dépardon spent three months in a police station for his documentary *Faits Divers* (Dépardon 1983). During that period of time, he happened to film a short scene portraying a woman wanting to press charges for marital rape. While close-up in front of the camera, the policeman who was supposed to file the report replies to the woman (out of frame):

> You have to understand one thing, Miss, and that is that rape in France is a crime. That this boy might end up in jail for at least five years because he had sex with you and you did not agree to have sex with him (…) *You can send him to jail for five years.* That's still a lot, don't you think?[1] [...] Now, he [is going to apologise] for doing what he did to you, which may not have been very correct. And *you, you're going to apologize to him. You* made him have quite a night too, huh.

Dépardon's documentary was shot only a few years after the adoption of the French law on rape in 1980, one of the first pieces of legislation aimed at penalizing violence against women in the country.[2] The sequence is not only a good example of secondary victimization, namely, blaming the victim by holding *her* accountable for what she has suffered; it also reveals the cultural, social,

I would like to thank Pauline Delage and Sabrina Moro, as well as the book editors, for their comments and suggestions on this chapter.

[1] The extract is available at: https://www.francetvinfo.fr/societe/harcelement-sexuel/video-vous-allez-vous-excuser-aupres-de-lui-comment-une-victime-de-viol-etait-accueillie-par-la-police-au-debut-des-annees-1980_2478590.html.
[2] Rape has been sanctioned in France since 1810 (article 332 of the Napoleonic Code) but started to be considered a crime only in 1980, with the adoption of the Law No. 80-1041 of 23 December 1980 *'on the repression of rape and certain indecent assaults'* (Debauche 2011).

historical understanding of men's 'natural' right to exert control over women. For the officer, the heart of the matter is not so much assessing the victim's 'truth', but rather weighing up the resulting injury to the alleged perpetrator at risk of facing charges. Dépardon's policeman first recalls that 'in France rape is a crime' and then menacingly, yet ironically, warns the victim: 'You can send him to jail for five years. That's still a lot, don't you think?'

In 2017, thirty-four years after the shooting of *Faits Divers*, the global circulation of the hashtag #MeToo 'reaffirmed publicly just how widespread sexual assault and harassment actually are; that most victim-survivors know the offender; and, significantly, that these experiences are *routine* and *normalized*' (Fileborn and Loney-Howes 2019:2). Just like four decades earlier, the focus on sexual abuse sheds light on the continuum of male violence against women (Kelly 1988) and interrogates the pervasive and persistent structural asymmetries between genders. The #MeToo 'moment' (Boyle 2019:5)[3] also triggers conservative reactions, both online and offline, by men and women who undermine the testimonies of women-survivors and claim that 'feminism has gone too far'. By disclosing the evidence of an epidemic gendered violence, the viral #MeToo makes the conflict between progress and backlash visible again and openly challenges men's undisputed sense of entitlement.

If in the 1970s all men were brought into play as potential rapists,[4] in the aftermath of 2017 all men are called to respond to the critique to the normalization of violence. Jeff Hearn (2020) has argued that 'men are an absence presence from #MeToo; generally absent from the speaking out, but all too present, in statements, allusions and effects' (72). Katherine Boyle (2019) has examined the visibility of male celebrity abusers as a discursive strategy to distance the 'monsters' from the 'normal', as opposed to average men perpetrating violence against women. Sarah Banet-Weiser (2018) has pointed to the interconnections and intertwining of 'popular feminism' and 'popular misogyny', where the first one 'actively' shapes culture while the other is 'reactive' and determined to maintain the normative status quo (3).

---

[3]   Karen Boyle clarifies the difference between the 'Me too movement', which was founded by Tarana Burke 'as an intersectional demand for support and recognition for young women of colour who had experienced sexual abuse, as well as a statement of solidarity' (Boyle 2019:5) and #MeToo 'as a moment (which begins on 15 October 2017 and continues at the time of writing) and as a discourse' (ibid.: 8).

[4]   In 1978, a poster by the *Mouvement de libération des femmes* showed a man's face behind the caption '*Cet homme est un violeur: cet homme est un homme*' ('This man is a rapist, this man is a man') (Pipon 2013, mentioned in Pavard et al. 2020b). The image is available online at: http://arcl.fr/omeka/items/show/194.

In a moment when feminism has gained such 'spectacular visibility' (Banet-Weiser, xii), this chapter aims at analysing its cultural and political impact on a group of men compelled to participate in a programme for perpetrators of domestic violence. Based on the accounts collected during my ethnographic research on rehabilitation programmes targeted at perpetrators of domestic abuse ('perpetrator programmes'), conducted in the Grand Est region of France between 2018 and 2019, this contribution seeks answers to the questions 'what does the #MeToo moment mean to men?',[5] 'how does it affect perpetrators' representations and practices' and 'what are the links between the global misogynistic reaction to the #MeToo and male violence against women?' Although my respondents may have not felt targeted by the #MeToo, which mainly raised the issue of sexual violence, the wider general context of 'speaking up' and pressing charges against men perpetrators was indeed perceived as a threat by the domestic abusers met during my fieldwork. The first section of the chapter offers an overview of the increasing visibility of feminism in France since the years 2000s, where 'feminism' includes feminist activism, 'popular feminism'[6] (Banet-Weiser 2018) and 'institutional feminism' (Delage 2017; Herman 2016). The second section details the context and the methods of the ethnographic research on perpetrators of domestic violence in France. The third section explores and analyses perpetrators' feeling of victimhood and, in particular, their blaming attitudes towards contemporary feminism.

'La cause des femmes' in the French media, before and after the #MeToo

The global outreach of #MeToo comes about in a moment when feminism enjoys great popularity, not only in the Anglo-American context (Banet-Weiser 2018) but also in France, where *'la cause des femmes'* started to gain increased visibility since the 2000s (Dalibert 2013, 2017; Pavard et al. 2020a). According to Biba Pavard, Florence Rochefort and Michelle Zancarini-Fournel, the publication of the first national survey (Idup-Ined 2000) triggered a growing public 'outrage' towards violence against women (Pavard et al. 2020a, 2020b). French historians also recall the impact of a few strongly mainstreamed stories, including Marie

---

[5] The term 'men' refers to heterosexual cisgender adult male individuals.
[6] As discussed by Batet-Wieser, popular feminism 'focuses on media expressions and their circulation, the social, cultural, and economic conditions that provide a context for a specific version of popular feminism to emerge as highly visible' (Banet-Weiser 2018:4).

Trintignan's murder in 2003,[7] the public reactions against the filmmaker Roman Polanski who was accused of rape in 2010, and the controversies resulting from the 'DSK affair' in 2011.[8] In addition, the outcry against the unacceptable prevalence of gender-based violence in the country was partially supported by the personal engagement of women journalists, who consistently used shocking headlines aimed at drawing public attention such as 'a woman dies every four days at the hands of her partner' (Pavard et al. 2020b:271).

In particular, the case of Jaqueline Sauvage boosted awareness on domestic violence among the general public and reframed women's legitimate defence against the abuser. In 2012, the 65-year-old woman was condemned to ten years in prison for having killed her husband, who had perpetrated physical and sexual violence against her and their children over many years. Although her lawyers appealed, the sentence remained unchanged until President François Hollande gave Sauvage his full pardon in 2016.[9] Since the trials, up to and beyond Hollande's decision, the case was one of the main topics covered by the French media (Broue 2018; Lanez 2017). Several feminist associations launched demonstrations and petitions in support of the cause, and many political figures and celebrities got involved.[10] In 2018, the story was popularized by the TV series *Jacqueline Sauvage: C'était lui ou moi*, screened on prime-time television on the open channel TF1 and interpreted by the famous actress Muriel Robin, who was often at the forefront of public awareness raising initiatives. On 25 November 2018, International Day for the Elimination of Violence against Women, Robin led women's massive demonstrations coordinated by the feminist movement *#NousToutes*[11] and eventually became one of the French icons of the fight against domestic violence.[12]

Even before the circulation of the #MeToo hashtag, feminism in France was visible, popular and accessible. In 2017, the President Emmanuel Macron

[7] Marie Trintignan was a French actress, killed on 1 August 2003 at the hands of her partner Bertand Cantat, the singer of the popular band *Noir Désir*.

[8] On the affair involving Dominique Strauss Kahn (DSK), see Delphy (2001), Bertini (2012) and Falquet (2012).

[9] The documentary *Jaqueline Sauvage: victime ou coupable* traces the story of the women and the judicial case (Baillot and Liétar 2018).

[10] Including Anne Hidalgo, major of Paris, and Jean-Luc Melenchon, politician leader of the Socialist Party.

[11] 'Muriel Robin, Eva Darlan, Vanessa Demouy … stars et anonymes ont manifesté contre les violences faites aux femmesArticles in the press', *Closermag*, 25 Novembre 2018, available at: https://www. closermag.fr/people/muriel-robin-eva-darlan-vanessa-demouy-stars-et-anonymes-ont-manifeste-contre-le-903398.

[12] Muriel Robin s'engage contre les violences conjugales et signe une tribune avec 87 personnalités, *Le journal du dimanche*, 23 September 2018, at: https://www.voici.fr/news-people/actu-people/muriel-robin-sengage-contre-les-violences-conjugales-et-signe-une-tribune-avec-87-personnalites-650881; Muriel Robin: de l'humour à la lutte contre les violences faites aux femmes, *Marie Claire*, at: https://www.marieclaire.fr/muriel-robin,1320775.asp.

chose 'violence against women' as 'the great national cause' for his five-years presidency.[13] When the national version of the #MeToo, *#BalanceTonPorc*,[14] went viral, it provoked bitter resistance and controversial debates (Achin et al. 2019). While thousands of women were sharing their daily experiences of sexism, street harassment and sexual assault online, in January 2018 the newspaper *Le Monde* published a letter in defence of *'la seduction à la française'* (the French way of seducing) and *'le droit d'être importunée'* (the right to be harassed) (2018), which was signed by a hundred prominent French women, including journalists, writers and celebrities, among whom was the actress Catherine Deneuve (Pavard et al. 2020b). The open letter, which was also published by the *New York Times* (Safronova 2018), claimed the need to preserve the national way of understanding 'sexual freedom', against the supposed 'wave of puritanism' raised by the Anglo-American feminism symbolized by the global #MeToo. French feminist scholars interpreted the statement as a threat 'coming at a time when women's struggles against gender-based violence appear to have been revived' and criticized it as a 'new avatar of reactionary thought [...] to defend the status quo *So French*' (Achin et al. 2019: 7–8).

Under Macron's presidency, the State Secretary for Equality between women and men Marlène Schiappa, a former influential blogger and journalist, actively contributed to mainstreaming women's rights in the media and openly defined herself as 'a feminist' – although her 'feminism' has often been criticized as being 'neoliberal', 'capitalistic' or 'racist' (Writing JDD 2020). Following the #MeToo mobilizations, Schiappa pushed for the adoption of a new law 'to strengthen the fight against sexual and gender-based violence'.[15] In September

[13] The 'great national cause' is an official label that allows fostering awareness-raising campaigns on specific topics considered as national priorities. The label was already appointed to the issue of 'violence against women' under the Presicency of Francois Fillon in 2010. With regard to Macron's official speech, see: *'Discours du Président de la République à l'occasion de la journée internationale pour l'élimination de la violence à l'égard des femmes et du lancement de la grande cause du quinquennat'*, 25 November 2017, available at: https://www.elysee.fr/emmanuel-macron/2017/11/25/discours-du-president-de-la-republique-a-l-occasion-de-la-journee-internationale-pour-l-elimination-de-la-violence-a-l-egard-des-femmes-et-du-lancement-de-la-grande-cause-du-quinquennat.

[14] Literally 'denounce your pig' or 'rat out your pig'. As pointed out by Bibia Pavard and her colleagues, the hashtag #balancetonporc preceded the #MeToo phenomenon: 'On 13 October 2017, French journalist Sandra Muller [...] called for the naming and shaming of sexual harassers in the work place and launched the hashtag *#balancetonporc* [rat out your pig]. [...] Within a month, *#balancetonporc* had been used 496,000 times on Twitter. Women journalists, speakers, academics, and others, albeit primarily from the upper class, recounted their own experiences of harassment. Two days later, a tweet by actor Alyssa Milano, calling for an inventory of sexual assaults, led to a massive response in France where the #MeToo hashtag in English was immediately adopted' (Pavard et al. 2020b:273).

[15] *Loi n° 2018–703 du 3 août 2018 renforçant la lutte contre les violences sexuelles et sexistes*, available at: https://www.legifrance.gouv.fr/affichLoiPubliee.do?idDocument=JORFDOLE000036730730&type=general&legislature=15.

2019, she launched the *'Grenelle des violences conjugales'*, a national consultation based on local meetings and round tables aimed at adapting the institutional response to domestic violence. The publication of the first official report on the implementation of the Istanbul Convention in France (GREVIO 2019),[16] together with the conclusion of the *Grenelle* on 25 November 2019, found wide resonance in the media and kept domestic violence high on the agenda. The visibility of *'la cause des femmes'* in France has inspired a wave of activism as well as provoking conservative reactions, both in mainstream media and in social media platforms. Its impact can be observed on various levels, including in perpetrators' explanations of their acts, as it emerged from my fieldwork.

Investigating men perpetrators of domestic violence in France

Although work with abusive men has a long history (Gondolf 1985; Hearn 1998; Pence and Paymar 1993), that is to some extent connected to feminist practice and knowledge (Hester and Liley 2014; Westmarland and Kelly 2013, 2016), only recently have perpetrator programmes been acknowledged as part of a comprehensive institutional response to domestic violence.[17] From a socio-anthropological perspective, such programmes are an interesting microcosm to observe men's narratives and representations: perpetrator programmes can be framed as one of the spaces for the cultural and social construction of masculinities (Connell 1995). First of all, participants are not only 'perpetrators': they are heterosexual men socialized in a gendered heteronormative culture; their accounts can reveal attitudes, beliefs and common-sense ideas produced and widely shared in our societies. Secondly, programmes targeting domestic abusers represent a setting where men are asked to hold themselves accountable for their actions and to recognize the harm inflicted to their intimate partners and children. During the group meetings, such attitudes, beliefs and common-sense ideas towards women are openly questioned, discussed and challenged.

In each national context, perpetrator programmes can be implemented in different ways; they can be mandatory (court-ordered) or voluntary, in custodial

---

[16] The Istanbul Convention entered into force in 2014 (Council of Europe 2011) and its correct application is the object of country-specific evaluations by the Group of Experts on Violence against Women (GREVIO). On the publication of GREVIO's first report on France.

[17] Under the chapter on 'Prevention', Article 16 of the Istanbul Convention requires state parties to set up 'Preventive intervention and treatment programmes' targeting perpetrators of domestic violence and sex offenders. A transversal study of GREVIO's reports published to date shows a variety of practices in the implementation of perpetrators programmes in each country (Oddone *forthcoming*).

and non-custodial settings, and several approaches can be deployed to foster perpetrators' change. In France, since initiatives targeting perpetrators of domestic violence are considered as measures for the prevention of delinquency and recidivism, participation is to a large degree ordered by the judicial system (Oddone 2020b). This ethnographic study is based on the observation of five programmes in three different cities in the French region of Grand Est. My qualitative research combined several methods, including semi-directive interviews with professionals, direct and participant observation of group meetings, visual workshops and individual interviews with participants. Each programme lasted two, four or seven days; content and approach varied consistently from one programme to the other; each of the observed meetings gathered about ten men. Group meetings were coordinated by one or more facilitators, including social workers, psychologists, psychiatrists and legal professionals, and were aimed at eliciting a discussion among participants on their violent conducts and sexist attitudes.

During the fieldwork I met about fifty men, aged between twenty-three and fifty-seven years old, living in both urban and rural areas. Participants had committed several forms of violence against their female (ex) partners, including physical, psychological and sexual violence. Only six participants declared being 'single', while the rest was either 'divorced'/'separated' or 'married'/'in a couple'. Almost all men were also fathers, having from one to seven children. Although they had different levels of education and varying professions, about half of them did not graduate from secondary school and most of them were workers or craftsmen. The great majority of participants were French nationals, including overseas territories, while a much smaller portion were migrants coming from countries in the Balkans, in the Middle East, in North Africa or sub-Saharan Africa. Among the French nationals, most persons had a migrant background since their parents had moved to France either before their birth or when they were children or teenagers. Results presented in this chapter stem from wider research on domestic violence perpetrators in France and Italy,[18] aimed at understanding how social actors represent their acts (Becker 1998) and whether and how these representations relate to the making of their masculinities (Connell 2002; Connell and Messerschmidt 2005). This contribution will focus in particular on how French perpetrators link their individual experience to

---

[18] The research 'Masculinities and domestic violence in the context of mandatory and voluntary perpetrator programmes in France and Italy' won the call for post-doctoral research projects (IDEX – *Initiatives d'Excellence*) issued by the University of Strasbourg in 2017 and was conducted between July 2018 and December 2019 under the scientific supervision of Nicoletta Diasio.

events occurring in the public sphere, especially related to women's emancipation and quest for equality.

Who to blame? Perpetrators as 'victims of feminism'

As observed by several scholars (Checuti-Osorovitz 2016; Deriu 2012; Merzagora Betsos 2009) as well as by facilitators interviewed during this research, perpetrators often return to 'neutralisation techniques' (Sykes and Matza 1957) to minimize, justify or openly deny their violent conduct and their own responsibility. In the course of the rehabilitation programmes, once they started recognizing their acts as 'abuse', or when confronted with official records, participants produced a narrative of their own victimhood. In this section I identify three blaming strategies: 'blaming women', 'blaming justice' and 'blaming feminism'. First of all, perpetrators blame their female partners because, by rejecting a subordinate role, they would trigger men's violent 'reaction'. Secondly, they blame the judicial system, which seems to give women 'too many rights' at the expenses of men. Finally, they blame feminism, since these individual and systemic disruptions are viewed as directly related to the current global visibility of feminism and of feminist discourse. On top of outlining some recurrent features for each type of victimhood, this section will especially focus on perpetrators' self-perception as 'victims of feminism': an issue which was consistently raised during my fieldwork, conducted at the height of the #MeToo moment, between 2018 and 2019. This element comes up from the ethnographic material as particularly relevant and seems to be giving a new wider significance to the complaints of a few individual men.

Blaming women

In the first instance, perpetrators disclaimed their responsibility by blaming their partners. Women were often presented as the 'real' abusers, especially with regard to psychological violence. During previous extended fieldwork in a centre for male perpetrators of domestic violence in Italy, I observed a broad range of negative representations of their female partners. Women were described as provocative, unfair, irrational, hysterical, aggressive, instigators, selfish, opportunistic, insubordinate, and were perceived as essentially subversive of expected marital and/or maternal duties (Oddone 2020a). My fieldwork in France confirmed the same blaming attitudes towards women, as proven by the constant repetition of the sentence *'Je me suis juste défendu'* ('I just defended myself'). Participants to the programmes engaged in detailed anecdotes on what *she* either did or did not do to 'provoke the violence', by constantly 'poking' and 'haunting' the man. Accordingly, violence was often described as a 'reaction'. In men's words, 'when you are pushed to the limits', perpetrating violence is 'just' a 'natural', 'normal', 'fair' reply to women's behaviour (Oddone 2020b). Men used this blaming speech against women as a plausible justification for their violence and, simultaneously, as a strategy to discredit their partner's positions. As it emerged through the interaction with facilitators, in most cases women's 'provocations' were calls for symmetry and reciprocity in sharing domestic chores and care work or the expression of their desire for more 'space for action' (Downes et al. 2019). In men's accounts, the recurrent description of women's 'irritating' attitudes and 'subversive' conducts made them emerge, in oppositional and hierarchical terms, as the bearers of order and rationality.

Blaming justice

In second place, perpetrators represented themselves as victims of the judicial system. In France, participation to perpetrator programmes is made compulsory on the basis of a judicial decision, which can be issued at several stages, either as a pre-trial order or following judicial proceedings, as the main penalty or as a complement to the sentence.[19] Since abusers were compelled to take part to the programme, to complete it and pay for the expenses, heated debates around the doubtful legitimacy of judicial decisions often took place in the course of group meetings. A recurring expression was *'dans le couple, la responsabilité est toujours 50–50'* ('In a couple, responsibility is always 50–50'). Only through participation in a programme, perpetrators found out that certain behaviours – which they considered 'normal' or as 'common couple violence' (Johnson 1995) – are penalized by law.

As a matter of fact, in France such initiatives are also aimed at making participants understand the reasoning behind the judicial decision, as declared by professionals in charge. To this purpose, facilitators often presented national

---

[19] In France, perpetrator programmes were established by the Law of 10 August 2007 'strengthening the fight against the recidivism of adults and minors' and by the Law of 23 July 2014 'for real equality between women and men'. In particular, Article 50 of the Law of 2014 institutes mandatory 'responsibility training programs' (*stages de responsabilisation*, group sessions lasting a few days) and the 'obligation of care' (*obligation de soins*, a psycho-social follow-up imposed after the penal sentence, in the form of individual meetings or group sessions) are the two systems in place in the country for the mandatory treatment of perpetrators.

prevalence data and illustrated the legal provisions in force in the country regarding domestic violence, as a reminder of the law and to highlight that new criminal offences have been introduced over time. However, participants kept complaining about their obligation to attend the meetings and emphasized the fact that they were victims of an 'unfair' judicial system. In the perpetrators' views, the punishment was disproportionate if compared to the 'low' gravity of their acts. They mourned that their side of the story had not been heard by law-enforcement agents or by the judge during judicial proceedings. Since they were sentenced for one instance, and their violence was reduced to one single episode: they failed to see the continuum of violence against their partners, in terms of forms of abuse – ranging from coercive control to physical violence – and in terms of temporal extension of the abusive relationship – often covering years of living as a couple.

Following the initial stage, they eventually accepted to participate in the programme in good faith, since it meant avoiding a more severe sentence – including a conviction to imprisonment – but they mostly continued to disagree with the definition of *'auteurs de violence conjugale'* ('perpetrators of domestic violence'). In most cases, the police intervention and the unfolding of the proceedings were perceived as an intrusion to their 'private' life, which in their views had been triggered and allowed by their female partner. The woman's complaint was perceived as a disgrace, done instead of 'dealing with it within the family', and as a revenge caused by her resentment.

Blaming feminism

In the third place, it was interesting to observe how – in the course of the group meetings and through interaction – perpetrators reframed their individual experience, initially perceived as a 'private' individual issue, in the light of public events. Perpetrators openly acknowledged the existence of a structural social phenomenon, that was not 'male violence against women' but rather the hegemony of a feminist discourse, capable of causing substantial consequences on their personal lives – and more generally on men's lives.

On more than one occasion participants in group discussions made explicit reference to the case of Jaqueline Sauvage, whose story became popular also thanks to the actress and feminist activist Muriel Robin, as in the following account by a French man, age forty-six:

The funny thing about my case is that it wasn't my wife who filed a complaint; it was me who filed a complaint against my wife. It was my wife who attacked me with a knife in front of my child. […] So, what happened? When I filed a complaint, she ended up in custody; and the moment she was in custody, she got scared and made up her story. She started to say: [*with a whining tone*] 'He's been abusing me for ten years', 'I've been threatened for ten years', 'He's a former military', 'He has weapons', 'I'm scared', 'I fear for myself, I fear for my children', bla bla bla. And that's it, and they believed her. They believed *her*! She did not have any clinical record, not a mark, not a medical certificate, and of course *I* was sentenced for domestic violence over ten years, because there was a previous record dating from six years earlier. […] At that time [*during the judgement*], we were in the middle of the 'Jaquelin Sauvage era': it was the time when Muriel Robin would show her face on TV every single day, saying that 'Every three days a women is killed at the hands of their partner' … That's how it is.

(M., perpetrator programme n. 5, first meeting)

During the group meetings it was not uncommon to hear men openly refer to national news events that were widely covered by the French media. Perpetrators often insinuated that judicial decisions were biased because of the hyper-visibility of women's presence in the media, as in the case of mainstreamed massive demonstrations across France on the International Day for the Elimination of Violence against Women. In the following quote, collected a few weeks after 25 November 2018, a French man, age thirty-two, openly complained about the effects of such visibility both on women's attitudes and on 'the system'.

On TV we only see women's demonstrations: demonstrations for this, demonstrations for that. We hear about them *all the time*: women, women, women. Then it's normal for them to get carried away. Even at the police station I ran into two lesbians, I could tell [referring to the agents]. The system is not in our favour.

(H., individual interview with a psychologist before enrolling in perpetrator programme n.1)

According to this man, 'women are everywhere', not only on TV demonstrating but also 'taking men's place' at the police station and in court, as he learned from his own personal experience as a perpetrator of domestic violence going through the judicial system. Several comments expressed by other participants during the group meetings confirm the same perception, as in the following dialogue between two men:

J: It is not the same as it used to be, not the same women as they were before.
   Today women have more rights; it is women who have taken the power.
   Now they can even reverse the roles.
A.: There are women who take advantage of he law. They have *all* the rights.

(perpetrator programme n.2, first day)

From perpetrator's perspective, women's newfound presence in places of power and their ability to make their voice heard makes them 'get carried away', and consequently 'take advantage' of their recently gained new 'privilege'. In their narratives, French perpetrators abundantly mentioned the specifics of the '#MeToo moment' and often repeated that 'today', 'now', 'currently', 'nowadays', things have changed, and they minutely explained *how*. In particular, they described a specific temporal border, dividing time into a 'before and after the #MeToo', interpreted as a historical moment marked by feminism's unprecedented public exposure. In the following excerpt, a French business manager, age fifty-two, lingers on the burden of proof, to affirm that 'today' women do not need to provide any evidence of abuse in order to be believed.

If there is no proof, it is one's word against the other's. Afterwards, what voices are the most heard today by the judicial system? It is women's voice! [...] I will just tell you a personal story: when I actually got the criminal summon [*convocation pénale*], it was six months after the Weinstein affair. In the media we kept hearing 'Men are bastards', 'Men are mean', 'Every three days a women is killed at the hands of her partner'. [...] If we think about the evidence, I think that *today* the real question is: 'Is the burden of proof really 50–50 or there is a tendency, there is a particular social phenomenon that makes it easier for women ... ?

(N., perpetrator programme n.5, first meeting)

According to N., if women today enjoy their rights (or more rights than they used to have), this recent development leads to men ending up losing some of theirs. The perpetrator clearly evokes the 'Weinstein affair', where Weinstein – a white, privileged, powerful man – metonymically represents 'all men' and his accusation is perceived as symbolically targeting *all* male individuals. In the quote, men and women are viewed as subjects in competition rather than as equal citizens, a perception that is firmly anchored to the specific temporality of 'the #MeToo moment'. In some other cases perpetrators even made explicit reference to 2018 as the beginning of 'a feminist era' bringing severe consequences on men's lives:

Since the dawn of time, violence against women has always existed, except that now it is 2018, 2019, and [...] we are entering a feminist era, rightly or wrongly, I'm not going to say .... But now there is internet and social networks, rights have changed, gender equality and so on.

(D. perpetrator programme n.5, third meeting)

It comes from prehistory. [...] The man was the hunter, he was going to attack, the woman was more around the fire [...] it comes from far away, so, I think that some of that remains, and it's the whole history of our society [...] where nevertheless it was the man who dominated. And then we get to 2018, 2019, and we say 'Now we're going to stop, now we want complete equality' ... . But is it as simple as that? [...] I think that what is violent for men in recent years is that everything we had, everything we took for granted, is now totally questioned! I don't want to say whether it is right or wrong [...] but it is very disturbing for men who had gained specific achievements, at all levels of society, in the family circle, in the political circle, we can mention many examples [...] But there are laws today that force us to change this mentality, and it is not natural!

(N. perpetrator programme n. 5, first meeting)

Men repeatedly described the current public condemnation of sexism and male violence against women as 'just a slogan', as 'a generational effect' or as 'a fashion trend topic', characterized by 'too much exaggeration' and by 'an authentic craze' for accusing and punishing men. Furthermore, perpetrators' accounts are also rich in descriptions of the 'violence' they have experienced because of judicial decisions. They affirm that 'pre-trial detention was shocking'; 'the punishment was violent'; 'justice was violent'. The alleged abuse denounced by their partners is weighed up, eventually equated or minimized, if compared to the damage inflicted on men by the judicial system, as it emerges in the following quotes:

In our society women are a little more protected, and I can agree with that [*since women are weaker*]. But what about men? There are not many laws to protect men and men's rights

(J., age 41, perpetrator programme n.3, second day)

When you watch TV, there is always a help-line for women, you see violence against women all the time, yes, but you will never see violence against men! You never see a help-line for men! [...] Only when you are in custody or in pre-trial detention at the police station you actually see violence against men. You have to think about the sexism suffered by men too. There is certain sexism against men in France. Men have disappeared, especially battered men. What you see at the police station is real, it is not like on TV.

(G., age 32, perpetrator programme n.5, third meeting)

During the group meetings, participants shared the 'trauma' caused by law-enforcement agents or by the judicial procedure and, in their words, they realized that this kind of 'violence against men' – namely the violence of a 'biased system' against male individuals – is a common phenomenon. By expressing the feeling of being under attack, perpetrators indirectly echo the arguments of conservative activist groups such as the men's rights and fathers' rights movements – although none of the men observed were part of these organizations. Just like masculinist militants, domestic violence perpetrators omit any sociological analysis and eventually produce a reversal of the concept of 'equality': they denounce the system's discrimination against men and claim for egalitarianism (Blais 2019). They also seem to recall the #HimToo mobilization (Boyle and Rathnayake 2019), which originally arose to give visibility to men's experience as victims of abuse, but eventually went viral during the Senate Judiciary Committee Hearings for Brett Kavanaugh's nomination to the US Supreme Court. At that moment, the #HimToo hashtag was employed as an expression of solidarity towards the powerful defendant and became part of the reactive backlash against #MeToo (Boyle 2019:110).

When referring to the current feminist global 'trend', versioned with specific French features, the perpetrators I met during my fieldwork implicitly considered this 'trend' as a 'total social fact'.[20] In their views, 'the social phenomenon' deserving public attention was not the widespread extent of persistent male violence against women but, instead, the public and easy denunciation of *alleged abuse* against women. As pointed out by Karen Boyle with regard to Brett Kavanaugh's case, 'the judgment is not: did it happen?' Rather, there is an earlier judgment about the relative importance of the alleged perpetrator and victim/survivor, and the potential damage *to the alleged perpetrator* of the claim that it did (Boyle 2019:110). Along the same line, for these French abusers, women's complaints are not necessarily 'true' but they are real in their consequences,

[20] Marcel Mauss' concept of 'total social fact' was originally employed to explain the importance of 'the gift' in several societies (Mauss [1925] 1966). The feminist criminologist Tamar Pitch has successively used this notion to describe gender-based violence: a phenomenon, which is simultaneously 'event, discourse, representation, sign and symbol, changeable and at the same time persistent' (Pitch 1998: 164).

since they produce material effects on men's lives. Just like a 'total social fact', today feminism and feminist discourse have a concrete impact on a variety of practices and institutions: in particular, in perpetrators' views, they give rise to biased representations, biased policies and biased sentences. Women's visibility, exploded in the #MeToo moment, seems to reinforce perpetrators' defensive attitudes and their belief of having been wronged.

Conclusion

In a historical moment marked by an exceptional visibility of feminism, the analysis of French perpetrators' accounts encompasses connections between several contexts (offline and online, on mainstream media and on social media) and reveals a few specific displays of backlash, which seem to be consistent with global patterns. Men's comments and reactions, as expressed in a very specific offline setting – mandatory programmes for perpetrators of domestic violence – seem to echo misogynist discourses circulating on mainstream media and social networks; they reflect what Kate Manne (2018:197) has called 'himpathy', a flow of sympathy towards alleged perpetrators and an 'overlooked mirror image of misogyny', where misogyny has to be understood as 'a deep structuring force in culture and politics' with relevant political consequences (Banet-Weiser 2018: XI).

Just as the policeman in Depardon's 1983 documentary described at the start of this chapter, today domestic violence perpetrators swap responsibilities, opt for a defensive attitude and take the place of 'the victim' by representing themselves as 'victims of their women', 'victims of the judicial system' and 'victims of feminism'. During the group discussions, differences in terms of race, class, religion and age seem to be overcome in the name of a gendered complicity among (heterosexual) men. Perpetrators' discourse reveals that 'things have changed': acts that were once considered 'normal' are now denounced and prosecuted, and as a matter of fact they find themselves compelled to participate to a perpetrator programme as a complement to the sanction. Their personal stories confirm that a powerful *frontlash*[21] – a set of actions which is considered provocative and unsettling and whose success is perceived as 'threatening' (Alexander 2019) – is actually questioning men's sense of entitlement and fostering women's rights, as well as it is causing panic among 'the defenders of patriarchy' (Achin et al. 2019).

---

[21] Gloria Steinem, available at: https://www.greeneuropeanjournal.eu/were-living-in-a-time-of-maximum-dangers-and-maximum-possibilities/.

As it comes out from perpetrators' accounts, these men are angry with women for several reasons, including the fact that *women are being seen*: women's presence in public space – in the streets demonstrating, speaking on TV and on social networks, denouncing perpetrators or making alleged perpetrators resign public positions of power – is symbolically hard to bear. It does not matter if today's popular – and visible – feminism is actually challenging deep structural inequalities or not (Banet-Weiser 2018; Boyle 2019); according to perpetrators' views, in the contemporary economy of visibility, women are winning.

Beyond the differences in their own individual beliefs and behaviours, perpetrators' accounts gathered during my fieldwork also reveal the direct and interdependent relationship between misogyny and male violence. In the course of group meetings, misogynist speech is used to justify and legitimize men's violence against women in intimate relationships. Insults and accusations such as 'liars', 'lesbians' and 'thwarted women' actively shape *a witch stigma* (Oddone 2020a) which is directed not only against their intimate partners but also against those women professionals – such as female law-enforcement agents, female lawyers and female judges – that perpetrators met through the judicial system. Discursive discrediting strategies are employed as disciplinary sanctions towards women that do not comply with expected heteronormative models of femininity, or against women who take what was traditionally considered 'men's place'.

When referring to the prosecution of domestic violence as the consequence of a 'feminist trend' and as the product of a biased justice system, perpetrators explicitly evoke 'the risk of castrating conventional masculinity', as expressed by a man in the course of a group meeting. The #MeToo moment seems to encourage and legitimize women's 'revenge' to the detriment of men. The fear for this current anomia comes with the nostalgia for an idealized past when private life was kept 'private', and for an irenic 'natural' order where men used to rule over women, couples would not split up and fathers were respected. As pointed out by Banet-Weiser with regard to popular misogyny:

> Men are suffering because of women in general, and feminism in particular.
> Women are taking over space, jobs, desire, families, childrearing, and power. For
> popular misogynies, every space or place, every exercise of power that women
> deploy is understood as taking that power away from men. In this historical
> moment, popular feminism is in defence against, among other things, structural
> gendered inequalities. Popular misogyny is in defence against feminism and its
> putative gains.

(2018:5)

The analysis of abusers' accounts shows how misogyny works in practice and how discourse can successfully represent a perpetrator as the victim of his own crimes (Manne 2018). By reframing their own experience as 'victims', French perpetrators participate in the broader discursive construction of male suffering and victimhood, in the face of the category of *excess*: the *excess* in their female partners' behaviour, who do not 'stay at their place'; the *excess* of the judicial verdict, which they consider 'too severe'; the *excess* of contemporary feminism and its *excessive* visibility. Results from the fieldwork confirm that recent progress with regard to women's rights and visibility triggers a renewed, reactive misogyny also among anonymous average men. Today, men's potentially increasing sexist radicalization is not limited to masculinist activists or neo-conservative supporters, to celebrities or hyper-privileged men. The men met during this research are not politically active nor particularly privileged because of race and class. Their 'himpathetic' response, expressed in multiple forms, is a reminder of men's resilience against the cultural and political change represented by the #MeToo 'moment'. In this context, the perpetration of violence can still appear as a device to regulate the power dynamics between genders.

Bibliography

Achin, C., Albenga, A., Andro, A., Delage, P., Ouardi, S., Rennes, J., Zappi, S. (2019) Editorial. Révoltes sexuelles, *Mouvements*, 3, 7–10.

Alexander J.C. (2019) Frontlash/Backlash: The Crisis of Solidarity and the Threat to Civil Institutions. *Contemporary Sociology. A Journal of Reviews*, 48(1), 5–11.

Baillot, M. and Liétar, P. (2018) *Jaqueline Sauvage: victime ou coupable*, 80 min.

Banet-Weiser, S. (2018) *Empowered: Popular Feminism and Popular Misogyny*. Durham: Duke.

Becker H.S. (1998) *Tricks of the Trade: How to Think about Your Research While You're Doing It*. Chicago, IL: University of Chicago Press.

Bertini, M.-J. (2012) Genre et médias à l'épreuve de l'affaire DSK. Réflexions sur le commentaire en ligne, nouvel espace de construction de l'inégalité des sexes, *Sciences de la Société*, 83, 54–65.

Blais, M. (2019) Effets des tactiques antifeministes auprès des institutions oeuvrant contr les violences faites aux femmes, in C. Bard, M. Blais, F. Dupuis-Déri (eds.), *Antiféminismes et masculinismes d'hier et d'aujourd'hui*, 437–62. Paris: Puf.

Boyle, K. (2019) *#MeToo, Weinsten and Feminism*. London: Palgrave Macmillan.

Boyle, K. and Rathnayake, C. (2019) #HimToo and the Networking of Misogyny in the Age of #MeToo. *Feminist Media Studies*, 20(8), 1259–77.

Broue, C. (2018) Un an de #MeToo/Affaire Sauvage: la médiatisation nuit-elle à la justice, *Radio France Culture*, 06 October. Available at: https://www.franceculture.fr/emissions/la-fabrique-mediatique/un-de-metooaffaire-jacqueline-sauvage-la-mediatisation-nuit-elle-a-la-justice (accessed 24 February 2022).

Checuti-Osorovitz, N. (2016) L'apport de l'anthropologie clinique dans le processus de subjectiva- tion des auteurs de violence conjugale, in F. Chauvaud, L. Bodiou, M. Soria, et al. (eds.), *Le Corps en lambeaux*, 373–87. Rennes: Presses Universitaires de Rennes.

Collective (2018) 'Nous défendons une liberté d'importuner, indispensable à la liberté sexuelle', *Le Monde*, 9 January 2018. Available at: https://www.lemonde.fr/idees/article/2018/01/09/nous-defendons-une-liberte-d-importuner-indispensable-a-la-liberte-sexuelle_5239134_3232.html (accessed 24 February 2022).

Connell R. (1995) *Masculinities*. Berkeley, CA and Los Angeles, CA: University of California Press.

Connell R. (2002) On Hegemonic Masculinity and Violence: Response to Jefferson and Hall. *Theoretical Criminology*, 6(1), 89–99.

Connell R. and Messerschmidt J.W. (2005) Hegemonic Masculinity: Rethinking the Concept. *Gender & Society*, 19(6), 829–59.

Dalibert, M. (2013) Authentification et légitimation d'un problème de société par les journalistes: les violences de genre en banlieue dans la médiatisation de Ni putes ni soumises. *Epistémologies, théories et pratiques professionnelles en communication des organisations*, 40, 167–80.

Dalibert, M. (2017) Féminisme et ethnoracialisation du sexisme dans les médias. *Revue française des sciences de l'information et de la communication*, 11 | 2017.

Debauche, A. (2011) *Viol et rapports de genre: émergence, enregistrement et contestation d'un crime contre la personne*. Paris: Ecole Doctorale de Sciences Po (PhD thesis).

Delage, P. (2017) *Violences conjugales. Du combat féministe à la cause publique*. Paris: Les Presses de Sciences Po.

Delphy, C. (ed.) (2011) *Un troussage de domestique*. Paris: Syllepse.

Dépardon, R. (1983) *Fait Divers* 100 min. France.

Deriu, M. (2012) Il continente sconosciuto. Interviste a uomini autori di violenze sulle donne, in M. Deriu (ed.), *Il continente sconosciuto. Gli uomini e la violenza maschile*, 29–53. Regione Emilia Romagna: Liberiamoci dalla Violenza—Centro di accompagnamento al cambiamento per uomini.

Downes, J., Kelly, L. and Westmarland, N. (2019) It's a Work in Progress: Men's Accounts of Gender and Change in Their Use of Coercive Control. *Journal of Gender-Based Violence*, 3(3), 267–82.

Falquet, J. (2012) DSK ou le continuum entre les violences masculines et les violences néolibérales. *Nouvelles questions féministes*, 31(1), 80–7.

Fileborn, B. and Loney-Howes, R. (eds) (2019) *#MeToo and the Politics of Social Change*. London: Palgrave McMillan.

Gondolf, E.W. (1985) *Men Who Batter: An Integrated Approach for Stopping Wife Abuse.* Holmes Beach, FL: Learning Publications.

Gouvernement français (2018) *Grenelle des violences conjugales. Dossier de presse.* Available at: https://www.gouvernement.fr/partage/11289-cloture-du-grenelle-contre-les-violences-conjugales (accessed 24 February 2022).

GREVIO (2019) Violences faites aux femmes: le Conseil de l'Europe épingle la France, *Le Monde*, 19 November. Available at: https://www.lemonde.fr/societe/article/2019/11/19/violences-faites-aux-femmes-le-conseil-de-l-europe-epingle-la-france_6019684_3224.html. (accessed 24 February 2022).

Hearn, J. (1998) *The Violence of Men: How Men Talk about and How Agencies Respond to Men's Violence to Women.* London: SAGE.

Hearn, J. (2020) #MeToo as a Variegated Phenomenon against Men's Violences and Abuse: Implications for Men and Masculinities', in G. Chandra and I. Erlingsdóttir (eds), *The Routledge Handbook of the Politics of the #MeToo Movement*, 65–84. London: Routledge.

Herman, E. (2016) *Lutter contre les violences conjugales. Féminisme, travail social, politique publique.* Rennes: Presses Universitaires de Rennes.

Hester, M. and Liley, S.J. (2014) *Domestic and Sexual Violence Perpetrator Programmes: Article 16 of the Istanbul Convention.* Strasbourg: Council of Europe.

Idup-Ined (2000) *Enquête nationale sur les violences envers les femmes en France (ENVEFF).* Available at: http://nesstar.ined.fr/webview/?v=2&study=http%3A%2F%2Fnesstar.ined.fr%3A80%2Fobj%2FfStudy%2FIE0221&mode=documentation&submode=ddi&node=0&top=yes (accessed 21 January 2021).

Johnson, M.P. (1995) 'Patriarchal Terrorism and Common Couple Violence: Two Forms of Violence against Women. *Journal of Marriage and the Family*, 57(2), 283–94.

Kelly, L. (1988) *Surviving Sexual Violence.* Cambridge: Polity Press.

Lanez, E. (2017) Retour sur l'affaire Jacqueline Sauvage. *Le Point*, 19 Septembre, available at: https://www.lepoint.fr/societe/retour-sur-l-affaire-jacqueline-sauvage-29-09-2017-2160705_23.php (accessed 24 February 2022).

Manne, K. (2018) *Down Girl: The Logic of Misogyny.* New York & Oxford: Oxford University Press.

Merzagora Betsos, I. (2009) *Uomini violenti. I partner abusanti e il loro trattamento.* Milano: Raffaello Cortina.

Mauss, M. ([1925] 1966) *The Gift. Forms and Functions of Exchange in Archaic Societies.* London: Cohen&West LTD.

Oddone, C. (2020a) *Uomini normali. Maschilità e violenza nell'intimità.* Torino: Rosenberg & Sellier.

Oddone, C. (2020b) Perpetrating Violence as a Gendering Practice: An Ethnographic Study on Domestic Violence Perpetrators in France and Italy. *Violence. An International Journal*, I, 1–23.

Oddone (forthcoming) Article 16: Preventive Intervention and Treatment Programmes, in S. De Vido and A. Di Stefano (eds), *The Council of Europe Istanbul Convention on Preventing and Combating Violence against Women and Domestic Violence. A Commentary*. London: Edward Elgar Publishing.

Pavard, B., Rochefort, F., and Zancarini-Fournel, M. (2020a) *Ne nous libérez pas, on s'en charge. Une histoire des féminismes de 1789 à nos jours*. Paris: La Découverte.

Pavard, B., Rochefort, F. and Zancarini-Fournel, M. (2020b) #MeToo in France, A Feminist Revolution? A Sociohistorical Approach, in G. Chandra and I. Erlingsdóttir (eds) *The Routledge Handbook of the Politics of the #MeToo Movement*, 269–83. London: Routledge.

Pence, E. and Paymar, M. (1993) *Education Groups for Men Who Batter: The Duluth Model*. New York: Springer.

Pipon, C. (2013) *Et on tuera tous les affreux: Le féminisme au risque de la misandrie* (1970–1980). Rennes: PUR-Mnémosyne.

Pitch, T. (1998) *Un diritto per due. La costruzione giuridica di sesso, genere e sessualità*. Milano: Il saggiatore.

Safronova, V. (2018) Catherine Deneuve and Others Denounce the #MeToo Movement, *New York Times*, 9 January. Available at: https://www.nytimes.com/2018/01/09/movies/catherine-deneuve-and-others-denounce-the-metoo-movement.html (accessed 24 February 2022).

Sykes, G.M. and Matza, D. (1957) Techniques of Neutralization: A Theory of Delinquency. *American Sociological Review*, 22(6), 664–70.

Westmarland, N. and Kelly, L. (2013) Why Extending Measurements of 'Success' in Domestic Violence Perpetrator Programmes Matters. *British Journal of Social Work*, 43(6), 1092–110.

Westmarland, N. and Kelly, L. (2016) Intimate Partner Sexual Violence and Perpetrator Programmes. Project Mirabal Findings, in, L. McOrmond Plummer, J. Levy-Peck and P. Easteal (eds), *Perpetrators of Intimate Partner Violence*, 190–205. London: Routledge.

Writing JDD (2020) 'Le discours fémonationaliste indigne de Marlène Schiappa', *Le Journal du dimanche*, 14 July. Available at: https://www.lejdd.fr/Politique/tribune-le-discours-femonationaliste-indigne-de-marlene-schiappa-3980944 (accessed 24 February 2022).

3

Phantom masculinities: Brexit, absence and nostalgia in London pubs

Amir Massoumian

Introduction

Following Achilleos-Sarll and Martill's (2019) argument that existing accounts of Brexit have paid insufficient attention to the gendered rhetoric and affects produced by the Leave campaign, this chapter presents an analysis of gender amongst male Brexit voters from two pubs in Walthamstow in the summer of 2017. Contrary to feminist discourses on patriarchy, the interlocuters described in this chapter conceive it not as something to be overcome or moved beyond, but as an absence that needs re-establishing. This chapter thus explores patriarchy's felt absence amongst my participants in a sense that goes beyond an antonym of presence. For them, patriarchy's absence is felt as a corporeal, emotional and sensuous phenomenon articulated in distinctly concrete, political and cultural registers. This, in turn, opens space for its re-emergence owing to Brexit and its manifold possibilities.

Through interviews with my interlocuters I will also detail how these absences are perceived as being dialectical, with the absence of masculinity (particularly in the realm of politics) accelerating a decline in traditional values, the erosion of community, state interference in their day-to-day lives, and the perceived lack of border control, all of which reinforce and perpetuate the aforementioned 'absence' of masculinity. Though the data for this chapter has been collected from my doctoral research, the choice of these specific pubs and their locations is that most of the relationships with my interlocutors' stem from my master's thesis: 'We want our country back': Attitudes towards immigration in London pubs. It is from familiarity with research participants and the locations themselves that I was able to collate these findings. The choice of field-sites came from the fact that these pubs were situated in some of the most ethnically diverse spaces in London, along with being associated with high levels of the leave voters.

Phantom pains

The concept of 'phantom pains' is outlined in *An Anthropology of Absence* as a symptom that arises in soldiers with nerve damage and post-traumatic disorders, who then go onto experience the lingering presence of their amputated limbs (Bille, Hastrup and Sørensen 2010:3; Meyer and Woodthrope 2008; Wade 2003:518). The authors point to the fact that 'phantom pains' are not solely present in individuals with neurological conditions but can also occur due to a sense of loss where people, places or memories have either been 'obliterated, lost, missing or missed, or that have not yet materialised' (Bille, Hastrup and Sørensen 2010:3). Absences can thus possess materiality, are emotionally and ontologically 'real', and affect people's daily practices and experiences (Meyer and Woodthrope 2008:103). Through narratives, commemorations, bereavement, nostalgia, depictions of past experiences and visualizations of future scenarios, absences are articulated into being (ibid.). This articulation can conjure forth past experiences that disrupt what is considered normative, creating at once counter narratives to dominant modes of intersubjectivity. An example of this can be found in Stuart Hall's (2019) *Identity and Diaspora*:

> People like me who came to England in the 1950s have been there for centuries; symbolically, we have been there for centuries. I was coming home. I am the sugar at the bottom of the English cup of tea. I am the sweet tooth, the sugar plantations that rotted generations of English children's teeth. There are thousands of others beside me that are, you know, the cup of tea itself. Because they don't grow it in Lancashire, you know. Not a single tea plantation exists within the United Kingdom.
>
> (70)

In such writings, as well as much of Hall's work, remembrance and depictions of the past become tools to combat narratives of white nationalism formed around romanticized understandings of British colonialism and Empire. To highlight the absence of 'a single tea plantation' is to contextualize the commonwealth, immigration and the power relations which explain the presence of the Other; in the words of Ambalavaner Sivanandan, echoed by Ian Sanjay Patel: *We're Here because You Were There* (2021). The affirmation of such remembrance, however, is often faced by counter-narratives founded on the absence of alternatives: the absence of order, communal life and national sovereignty. These absences and disappearances have become rhetorical devices conjured by populist parties in the UK who have triumphed at the polls in recent years (Martin and Smith 2014). While the study of politicians and their utilization of today's discontentment in the UK are well documented (Muller 2017; Thorleifsson 2019; Winlow, Hall and Treadwell 2016), this chapter engages with the articulations of their supporters around two types of absences they believe to have been 'amputated' from British politics: an 'absence' of masculinity and a perceived 'loss of order'. Loss of order, particularly when relating to the changing of gender norms or essentialized divisions between sexes, often views this order as what is supposedly 'normal', 'natural' and sometimes even inevitable (Bourdieu 2007:8). Demands for changes to be made in the realms of gender threaten this supposed order of the world along with the perceptions, thoughts and actions of those who are invested in it (ibid.) Osgerby (2006) in his genealogical description of masculinities notes:

> The nineteenth century 'man of character' was marked out by his temperance and reserve, along with his ardent sense of civic duty and a devotion to hard-working industriousness. As the twentieth century progressed, however, notions of a masculinity defined by work and abstinence were undermined by an aggregation of social and economic changes. The reconfiguration of labour markets, the transformation of gender relations and the rise of mass consumption together unhinged many of the traditional certainties that had been at the heart of dominant conceptions of manhood.
>
> (9)

The consequence of the perceived fraying of what Osgerby calls 'traditional certainties' was a consensus that emerged in Western Europe amongst far-right movements in the turn of the twentieth century, calling for 'the torn fabric of society' to be 'mended' (Mosse 1999:181). A consequence of this was that new traditionalism, prosaic, normative forms of masculinity were reaffirmed to rejuvenate this return to order (ibid.). Indeed, such masculinist discourses, which are remnant of Mosse's description of a society in need of 'mending', are re-entering the political realm. Adherents of right-wing populist movements in European countries rail against the perceived threat of what they call (depending on the context) 'gender ideology', 'gender theory' or 'genderism' (Kovats 2018). Examples include the German right-wing populist party Alternative für Deutschland (AfD), which has provisional plans to cut funding for gender studies in universities and attempts of the British government to attack the 'woke' agenda and label such organizations as a threat to free-speech and democratic values (Hirsch 2020). Other examples include Hungary, where the Prime Minister Viktor Orbán pushed to ban gender studies in universities outright in October 2019, along with cases in Sweden and Italy where gender-related conferences were met with death threats from far-right groups (Apperly 2019).

Anderson (1991:6) defines the nation as 'an imagined political community – and imagined as both inherently limited and sovereign'. He goes onto highlight that it is 'ultimately this fraternity that makes it possible [...] for so many millions of people, not so much to kill, as willingly to die for such limited imaginings' (ibid.:7). Slootmaeckers (2019:243) notes that by Anderson referring to the nation as a 'fraternity', he alludes to the gendered structure of nationalism as well as the potential role of masculinities within the construction of the nation. The feelings of an absence relating to this fraternity, along with the far-right's symbolic invocation of 'crisis masculinities', have been known to provide key propaganda tools in targeting white men (Davey and Ebner 2017). Such messaging focuses on the notion that on the global stage, they are the real victims – and that by joining them, there is a potential for reclaiming those very privileges that have been taken away from them unfairly (Gartenstein-Ross and Grossman 2009; Kimmel 2003, 2017; Kimmel and Ferber 2000[1]).

In the British context, Gardners (2017:6) describes how the Brexit vote managed to reinvigorate both a sense of imperialist nostalgia, while at the same time reinvigorating an image of true 'Britishness' or 'the people' in a populist sense. The binary between the truly 'British' and non-British was reflected in the simple question of 'Leave' or 'Remain'. The pro-Brexit campaign promise was that that UK borders, which symbolically reinforce this binary, would be 'finally under control' (Follis 2017:9). Such nationalist tropes have no hesitation in isolating and making an object of analysis of what they claim are culturally specific groups and reducing wider social systems to more manageable sub-units based on shared 'ethnic' traits (Houston 2009:27). Appadurai's (1996:165) work on the politics of nostalgia certainly rings true in the context of British nationalism, particularly the claim that it is one of the 'central ironies of the politics of global cultural flows', since it is 'nostalgia without memory', both

---

[1] The term 'crisis masculinities' refers to forms of masculinity that emerge out of the intensification of social changes in terms of gender roles (usually against patriarchal norms) which embody a desire to return to patriarchal norms either lived or imagined (Kimmel 2003).

'imagined communities' and perceived 'ethnic identities' linked to a collective past have very real-world consequences (Anderson 1983:6; Jenkins 2008:27).

A common strategy for challenging this sort of Imperial or masculinist nostalgia is through presenting counterclaims from the same arena. The view of a singular, homogenized past glossed as a monolithic 'history' at the level of specific claims as well as the wider domain. The quote from Stuart Hall above foregrounds the voices of those otherwise invisible in such pictures. Their absence in such nostalgic stories is repeated considering the incredulity of their descendant's presence in modern Britain. For masculinities in particular, scholars such as Connell (1995:33) and Osgerby (2006) produce genealogical accounts where masculinity is shown to not be a 'stable object of knowledge' but plural, situated, constructed, negotiated, re-negotiated in daily practices, and differs greatly throughout time. With close scrutiny, history-as-history and gender-as-gender cannot be univocally mobilized in support of a rose-tinted, patriarchally imperial past. In both cases then, history, or the facts derived from historical accounts, is used to affect political change in the present. Right-wing narratives of a 'traditional masculinity', 'natural' gender-roles and a conflict-free past are thus resisted through historical analyses which problematize their homogenizing, oversimplifying character.

This approach is unsurprisingly common amongst scholars and commentators with expertise on these historical accounts. However, commentators on Brexit have often laid the failure of the Remain campaign on its inability to capture personal experiences of voters, but rather to rely only on information formulated through expertise, as expressed in Clarke and Newman (2017)'s article which echoes the well-known sentiment of Leave campaigners 'People in this country have had enough of experts'. Thus, a purely corrective approach often misses the nature of engagement with nostalgic stories. While it may somewhat work to mitigate the spread of historical inaccuracies of a 'golden past' it makes assumptions about people's reasons for believing or disbelieving it. This chapter posits an alternative and complimentary approach, drawing on Hockey et al.'s (2010:227) statement that 'personhood and identity emerge as relational, negotiated concepts that refer to spatially located practices'. Consideration of the situated personhoods of these individuals is as critical as critiquing the content of the claims they make or the beliefs they hold.

A sense of this discontent several years ahead of Brexit is felt powerfully in Les Back's (2009:3) book chapter 'London's Finished'. He sketches the sense of disenfranchisement and dissatisfaction amongst English white men in South-East London, capturing the melancholic frustration they feel at the state of their city. Their nostalgic commitment to a past vision of their communities and disquiet at demographic shifts evokes Raymond Williams's statement that 'nostalgia for a lost "golden age" recurs throughout history; it is a way of talking about social life providing a vocabulary for moral judgment that is situated in time' (Williams 1973). One of Back's interlocutors stated that:

> London's finished. I don't know what my mother would say if she was alive. She wouldn't believe it. In her day people lived in very close ... it was all very local. People knew each other and invested in each other. Now they don't invest around here, they're sending their money to Africa and Pakistan. You see around here. The Pakis the people they've got working for 'em. You never see the same person in there twice, they're all illegal and they're paying 'em £20 a day. I am not joking you come back next weekend see if you recognise anyone else.
>
> (Les Back 2009:2)

In the accounts that follow, I wish to demonstrate how this 'finishing' or 'end' of London articulated in 2009 has been utilized by the Brexit campaign. This sense of loss and absence of 'proper' masculinities goes some way to explaining the popularity of figures like Nigel Farage. For many of these men, he becomes an identifiable figure that represents eroded values and spaces as well as points to the possibility of their re-emergence. This speaks to the spectral nature of such patriarchal imaginings; imaginings which meant that it did not indeed have to be the end of London – that through sheer force of will there was a chance for the reinvigoration of a phantom limb.

'There used to be a pub there'

> I hear people say we have to stop and debate globalisation. You might as well debate whether autumn should follow summer ... the character of this changing world is indifferent to tradition. Unforgiving of frailty. No respecter of past reputations. It has no custom and practice. It is replete with opportunity, but they only go to those swift to adapt, slow to complain, open, willing and able to change.

Former Prime Minister Tony Blair – 2005 Labour Party conference
    In line with his determination to align the Labour Party with liberal-centrist values, then-UK Prime Minister Tony Blair saw the EU as a vehicle to strengthen the UK's relationship with other European countries, improve

its economic performance and bolster the UK's international role in the face of rapid globalization, all the while utilizing forms of naturalizing language (anything other than this strategy would be to debate whether 'autumn should follow summer'). In light of the shifts orchestrated by Blair's government, the Conservative party became split on the 'Europe question', and efforts by successive leaders, from John Major to David Cameron, to form consensus on the matter failed (Martill and Staiger 2018:6). While the reasoning for right-wing antagonism towards Blair is multifaceted, I argue that the above statement made at the 2005 Labour conference effectively summarizes the rationale behind the hostility: an 'indifference to tradition', lack of respect for 'past reputations' and a 'distaste for custom and practice'.

Utilizing this discontentment, successive leaders were able to capitalize on latent Eurosceptic attitudes among the British population and, more specifically, within the Conservative party itself. Brexit can therefore be traced back to the elite politics of the political right in the years since the global financial meltdown of 2008–9, which saw the banking and wider financial system in profound crisis. Following this history, it comes as no surprise that the consequences of this event are utilized in the broader strategy of right-wing populists who insist that established government institutions have become corrupt or unresponsive to ordinary people (Balthazar 2017; Koch 2016, 2017) and, in the case of the UK, consistently laying the blame on transnational organizations such as the EU while calling for a return to 'tradition(s)' of the past (Knight 2017).

While the feeling of being 'left behind' often coincides with economic or social neglect, in the context of my field study of Walthamstow pubs, what seems 'left behind' is in fact the material stability that local establishments such as the pub represented. The electric signs for pharmacies, barbers and the newly furnished fast-food outlets presented themselves as a sharp contrast to the pub I will be describing in this chapter. In front of the pub's entrance lies a blackboard with the evening's football match-up lined out in chalk. The decor and building itself has not changed in fifty years, says Mark, a 66-year-old pensioner, who explains to me his life-long tradition of coming to the pub:

'I've been coming to this very same pub for about 40 years now. You could say I'm part of the furniture! A lot has changed around here, but I can always come here for a pint with the regulars.'

'We love our local' chimes in Tom (61) 'All my best mates come here; it's like a small community, everyone knows each other, and there's this sort of common respect that you can't really get anywhere else … I guess it is a British thing, isn't it?'

Throughout interviews with my interlocutors, the pub is consistently referred to as a space which provides a unique feeling of community. The very word 'local' to describe the pub is testimony to the sense of continuity, regularity and order that the field-site provides for the 'regulars' who frequent the establishment (Watson 2004:204). Specifically, Mark's feeling of being 'part of the furniture' coincides with Tilley and Cameron-Daum's analysis on how the body and space are 'entangled in a network of material and social relations' which provide both affordances and constraints for the performance of 'identities that always occur in particular material and cultural contexts' (2017:7). Through almost all interactions, the identity of the pub as relating to their own identity as Englishmen was apparent. Despite things changing in their area, the cultural significance of 'a British thing' (meeting the 'regulars' in the pub for a drink) highlights the importance of the pub space as a site of consistency and reliability for these men – where a pint is always waiting.

As Fox notes:

> Although the pub is very much part of the English culture, it also has its own 'social micro-climate'. Like all drinking-places, it is in some respects a 'liminal' zone, an equivocal, marginal, borderline state, in which one finds a degree of 'cultural remission' – a structured, temporary relaxation or suspension of normal social controls (also known as 'legitimised deviance' or 'time-out behaviour'). It is partly because of this caveat that an examination of the rules of English pub-talk should tell us a lot about Englishness.
>
> (Fox 2008:35)

It is intriguing that Fox, in the above of analysis of English pubs and their relationship to 'Englishness', utilizes the word 'liminal' to describe the pub. Anthropologically, the use of the word 'liminal' is often in reference to rituals and the fact that rites of passage are antithetical to existing social structure: 'liminal entities are neither here nor there; they are betwixt and between the positions assigned and arrayed by law, custom, convention, and ceremonial. As such, their ambiguous and indeterminate attributes are expressed by a rich variety of symbols in the many societies that ritualize social and cultural transitions' (Turner 1967:359).

In the context of the pub space, the structure which reflects the brutalities of urban living intertwined with expectations of productivity and industriousness are relaxed to provide a liminal space between work and home life (Mingay 1998). While this description of the pub outlines a more idyllic context of life in the late twentieth century where labour and 'free time' have a clear divide for white working-class men, the circumstances for the participants outlined in this chapter do not reflect so neatly upon this dichotomy. This is not solely down to neoliberal market logics weaving their way into all other facets of daily life (Elmore and Elmore 2016), but rather a reflection of the men in this chapter being retired and having never lived outside of the area. During the start of my fieldwork in 2016, the haphazard and unpredictable nature of ethnographic research was eased due to their almost clockwork routine of meeting in the pub from lunchtime onwards, which made them one of my first key set of participants. I mention these details in order to situate the participants of the ethnography as contrasting what is described by Fox and Mingay. The pub, for them, is not a liminal space between the domain of work and the private space of home but is in fact a static point and nexus of familiar relations in contrast to the ever-changing acceleration that is perceived to be going on outside. Mark, one of my participants, says:

> There used to be a pub down this road called The Apollo, another one further down from that ... I can't remember the name. But anyway, both closed down and what's replaced them is a shisha cafe and an Indian takeaway. Now that tells me nobody was going to those pubs. Another thing it tells me though, is how quickly things are changing around here.

The details to the changes signify an intertwining of market forces and the consequences of immigration replacing the 'native' (the pub), the absence of which is replaced by the 'foreign' (shisha cafe and Indian takeaway). Andrew (63) confirms these changes in explicitly demographic terms:

> I can remember in 1972 the first Indian child coming to our school. If you look at the photographs from my years, there's ... I still remember his name ... Rahul Canubar, everyone adored him and he was a wonderful lad, originally Gujarati, everyone was fascinated by him, but if you looked at that picture, it might as well have been in the 1930s in terms of demographics. Very much white, completely white configuration. It's now 80 per-cent ethnics at the very same school that I used to frequent, and of the white branch half of those would be Irish travellers. I often see it on the buses now, I am the only white person on the bus.

> When I was working, you had your job, your wife and kids, and a very British way of life. As soon as the clocks hit five, everyone knew where to find me. Right here. Catch up, relax, have a good time and head home.

Ethan (67) tells me, 'mass immigration, right, changed all of this. If you have someone who's willing to work longer hours for less pay … people like myself had to change everything'.

Mark: It was around 1981 when I saw this happen, changed everything.
Ethan: and that was back in our day! Nowadays, nobody can put a lid on it. It's
    completely out of control.

While the mood during these interviews was melancholic, I had a sense that my curiosity about their lives and thoughts produced a certain cathartic effect. At the start of my interactions with them, each of my interlocutors would wait eagerly to be the next to speak their mind on how things were the summer of the Brexit vote. The invocation of the absent pubs, the memory of the bodies who frequented the pub who now no longer exist or have changed their tastes, the 'white' school and the ultimately 'British way of life' are all founded on memory and nostalgia; a constant back and forth between the past and the present, all the while indicating that 'something' has been lost.

The potential friction that I expected my presence to have caused was slowly subsided by the feeling that an ethnographer intent on listening to them was a welcome novelty. It became clear that pride in Britain's past invoked by the Leave campaign was enticing precisely due to its insistence that the affective links to the past are ontologically valid, worthy of respect, and have potential to be recovered. The discontentment's presented here are somewhat typical of research into Brexit voters. As demonstrated by Wilson (2020) almost all research on Brexit 'addresses one key theme that has remained central to Brexit: the perceived loss of, and the need to take back, control' (50). The hope, or potential, of regaining this 'something' is a facet of right-wing populist parties which propagate the idea that trust in the nation state is the best defence against this loss, and that it is only one's nationality that can provide warmth and stability in the globalized world (Mudde 2007).

Smoke and broken mirrors

'You're probably too young to remember the smoking ban, but it really bent a lot of us out of shape' Mark explains to me. 'We never had a say in the matter.'

While waiting for him to say more on the issue, I sense that he takes my silence as a sign of judgement and says 'you might think it's a small thing and that I'm being daft, but these things always start like this. Making me go outside for something I used to be able to do inside at my own choice is the first step.'

'Do you remember the reason given? For the ban I mean?' I ask

'The EU of course ... Brussels said "jump!"' he says while putting a cigarette filter in his mouth 'we are a castrated nation, Amir ... ' he mutters begrudgingly 'we have to listen.'

The context of my conversations with Mark, Tom and Ethan, regardless of the weather, has always been in the backyard of the pub under a garden umbrella. As chain smokers, the smoking ban regulations have meant that their social space has been allocated outside the pub. The perceived bio-political intrusion into their daily lives is one of many examples of the way in which an external entity, namely the EU, is deemed to take away agency from their hands. What is important to note here is that the 2006 smoking ban was not put in place by the EU but was a parliamentary decision as a result of the Health Act which made it illegal to smoke tobacco in public places, such as restaurants, shops or pubs, due to the strains on the NHS. My intention here, as mentioned in the introduction, is not to point out an inconsistency or belittle a position, but rather to illustrate the feelings of my interlocutors towards the EU as an outside entity responsible for changes that they do not like. With respect to gender, scholars such as Achilleos-Sarll and Martill (2019:16) argue that the campaign for Britain to leave the EU and the subsequent Brexit process have been dominated by discourses surrounding masculinity where 'gendered discourses invoked during the campaign which (re-)produced, and (re-)articulated masculinity in old-new ways'. Former research on Brexit has not fully accounted for the role played by gendered discourses in the campaign itself, or how these will likely come to affect the outcome of the Brexit process (ibid.). This section will articulate how the narrative of a loss of masculinity is perceived to have brought about the circumstances for such intrusion into their lives with Brexit being perceived as reinvigoration of this masculinity in the political realm.

'It's been one thing after another, telling people what to do, how to live. People from outside of this country telling the people inside how to live' Ethan tells me, while expanding on what Mark had said.

'When you stand back and look at it a lot is changing, and fast. We were on a steam engine with nobody in charge. No train driver just speeding down. There's a push against that now and I'm proud to be a part of it. You can feel it, honestly, a sense of people finally saying "no"'

Mark: They're only in it for themselves, and it has a trickle-down effect.
You look around these days and you see it everywhere. Everyone out for
themselves with blinders on. But I don't blame them, I really don't. When
you don't have strong capable leaders in charge, who have love, and I mean
really love, the country, things begin to [inaudible]

Amir: So do you see that in somebody like Farage?

Ethan: Maybe. I don't see myself in any politician, it's like looking into a
broken mirror … I've never voted for them, never will. We have nothing in
common. I'm just a regular bloke, but saying that, I do think he's more in
touch than the others

Mark: you'd at least have a pint with him

Ethan: you'd definitely have a pint with him

Mark: But no, I don't think so. I don't think it's his job either. I think UKIP's
role is to whip the conservatives into shape. Because frankly … right now
…

Ethan: 'bunch of Jaffa's' *laughs*

Mark: Cameron was absolutely spineless. You had men in the past who
actually stood for something, I mean, they weren't Churchill, but they
actually believed in something … dignity. When you look at Nigel, you get
the sense he's been in the business, knows how things work, knows how to
get things sorted.

Ethan: Time and time again we were told that it's crazy to think Leave would
win … well … here we are! I guess you can count on him for that. Tells you
something doesn't it?

While transcribing this interview on my way back from the field site, I had to
Google the term 'Jaffa' as I'd been too embarrassed to ask what it meant. Curious
to find out what was so comical about the term, I found out it referred to a
seedless orange – the inference being that the Tory party was filled with infertile
men. Throughout the above interview, terms such as 'castrated nation', 'spineless'
are contrasted to 'strong capable leaders' and 'men in the past who actually stood
for something', failed masculinities of the present in contrast to the idealized
men of the past. West and Zimmerman (1987) argue that gender is performative
and relational, in the sense that individuals are constantly producing and
trying to live up to gender norms in order to meet the expectations of others.
In short, individuals expect to be judged and 'held accountable' according to
gender norms. Failure to uphold this norm, the 'inability to sustain or properly
take up a gendered subject position' particularly in the realms of politics and
conflict, provides a ripe context for what MacKenzie and Foster (2017:207) refer

to as 'masculinity nostalgia' the 'longing for ideal types of masculinity that are linked both to the past and to security, power and order'. Nostalgia theorists note that nostalgia is not simply about looking back in time; rather, it can involve idealizing and mythologizing history (often with a male lens) (Ritivoi 2002), hence Mark's invocation of Churchill as the ultimate symbol of leadership and masculine prowess. MacKenzie and Foster (2017) further argue that that masculinity nostalgia mythologizes a time of patriarchal power, authority and gender certainty: 'the yearning for an idealized, secure and peaceful time in which gender roles were presumed to have been clear and uncontested, and a quest to reclaim patriarchal power and authority' (208).

Farage's successful task of equating of Britain's EU membership with a lack of control had fostered a Brexit discourse fixated on the law of market logics and values linked to success in the 'businessman's world', or as Mark put it, the ability to 'get things sorted'; a successful businessman, according to the discourse, equates to a successful leader; someone who 'can get the job done'. Getting the job done in this case aligns with the neoliberal policies responsible for the rapid shifts in the spatial realities of the participants, the market and corporate world which represent distinctly masculinized spaces, within which 'competitive individualism, reason and self-control' are idealized (Hooper 2001). The lack of masculinity in the realm of politics is juxtaposed to the gendered arena of business where 'men, operating within a hegemonic normative code, have thought to possess the appropriate skills, knowledge, and temperament to design and maintain the institutions of the state, while most women – assumed to be irrational, fragile, and dependent, – have tended to be relegated to supporting roles as low-grade clerks, cleaners, tea ladies, and wives' (Lovenduski 2005:147).

It is important to note, however, that the type of masculinities perceived in the world of business and politics, which are seen to be all too willing to put in motion the changes my interlocuters see as being destructive are only in alignment with what can fill the 'absence' when coupled with right-wing tropes of traditionalism and anti-immigration. By daring to address tough 'masculine' topics like immigration, insecurity and economics (Fourest and Venner 2011) figures such as Farage give evidence that they 'have balls', presenting themselves as 'tough, daring and decisive' (Moffit 2016), establishing a clear 'link [...] between populism [...] masculinity and heteronormativity' (Norocel et al. 2016:66). Ethan's statement of being 'a regular bloke', combined with saying that Farage is 'more in touch than the others', showcases the astute rhetoric of populist leaders who must appear ordinary, 'providing a sense of a direct connection with the "substance" of the people' (Müller 2016:34).

Conclusion

This chapter presents different articulations of patriarchy's absence – absence not simply meaning the opposite of presence, but as a corporeal, emotional and sensuous phenomenon articulated in distinctly concrete, political and cultural registers. For the sake of this chapter, this sense of absence is invoked specifically by Brexit in relationship to a particular embodiment of white, working-class masculinity. In his book *The Theory of Absence*, Fuery (1995) argues that absence can be divided into 'primary' absence and 'secondary' absence. Primary absence is defined as 'absence-in-itself', as existing outside of any relation to presence, meaning that there is no potential for anything other than its absence (2). Secondary absence is defined by its relational connection to presence. This means that absence and presence become inherently intertwined: 'something is absent because it is not present, but the significant detail is that the absent something is figured as potentially present' (ibid.:1). The argument can be made that because cultural ideals of hegemonic masculinity[2] are virtually unobtainable for men, masculinity in this context is therefore always something of a secondary absence; a yardstick by which male gendered subjects mirror themselves unto but can ultimately never achieve (Alsop et al. 2002).

I argue that this unattainability of an ideal of hegemonic masculinity is precisely what makes its spectral nature fitting to the experience of my interlocuters. When Ethan says: 'time and time again we were told that it's crazy to think Leave would win', there is the trusted belief in the impossibility of an occurrence in light of things being 'completely out of control'. Brexit thus managed to legitimize and reinvoke these expectations (against all odds), promising the opportunity for a halt of the influence of outside forces into their everyday lives. This intrusion manifested as a figurative form of castration by the political elite; the forceful removal of masculine agency and potency by external meddling. The masculine prowess that is perceived to be portrayed by politicians such as Farage provided a coherent picture which resonated with the cultural, physical and material expectations that powerfully influenced my interlocutors' conceptualizations of a past Britain; a world that they continued to engage with, but which was perceived to be forever lost to time.

---

[2] Hegemonic masculinity here is understood as the pattern of practice (i.e. things done, not just a set of role expectations or an identity) that allow men's dominance over women to continue. Hegemonic masculinity embodies the most honoured way of being a man, and it requires all other men to position themselves in relation to it (Connell and Messerschmidt 2005).

The overall claim of this chapter is precisely in this insistence on a patriarchy that is desired, but not altogether present. A wish or yearning for a return to an imagined past, which promises a Britain which ultimately lies in the imaginings, nostalgia and conversations of those who feel their desires to be as unheard ('crazy') and as absent as the structures they see disappearing. Mahmood (2020:141) argues that the difference between what is spectral and incarnate is 'not to be found in a metric of the real. Both are "real" in the sense that social constructs and ideologies are real. Rather, the distinction matters tactically and analytically'. Thus, it is important to note that patriarchy carries with it a spectral element whose desirability rests in the potential for its social, cultural and material resurgence. In the context of this chapter, a longing for this return was invoked in the Brexit referendum, where it was believed that the severing of the UK from the EU could reflect an ability to reintegrate a connection to this lost, nostalgic past.

Bibliography

Achilleos-Sarll, C. and Martill, B. (2019) *Toxic Masculinity: Militarism, Deal-Making and the Performance of Brexit* in Dustin, M., Ferreira, N. and Millns, S. (eds.), *Gender and Queer Perspectives on Brexit*, 15–44. London: Palgrave Macmillan.

Alsop, R., Fitzsimons, A. and Lennon, K. (2002) *Theorizing Gender*. Cambridge, UK: Polity Press in association with Blackwell.

Anderson, B. (1983) Old State, New Society: Indonesia's New Order in Comparative Historical Perspective. *The Journal of Asian Studies: Review of Eastern and Southern Asia and the Adjacent Pacific Islands*, 42(3), 477–96.

Anderson, B. (1991) *Imagined Communities: Reflections on the Origin and Spread of Nationalism* New York: Verso.

Appadurai, A. (1996) *Modernity at Large*. Minneapolis: The University of Minnesota Press.

Apperly, E. (2019) Why Is Europe Far-Right Targeting Gender Studies?. *The Atlantic*, 15 June. Available at: https://www.theatlantic.com/international/archive/2019/06/europe-far-right-target-gender-studies/591208/ (accessed 11 February 2022).

Back, L. (2009) Researching Community and Its Moral Projects. *21st Century Society: Journal of the Academy of Social Sciences*, 4(2), 201–14.

Balthazar, A.C. (2017) Made in Britain: Brexit, Teacups, and the Materiality of the Nation. *American Ethnologist*, 44(2), 220–4.

Bille, M., Hastrup, F. and Sørensen, T. F. (2010) Introduction: An Anthropology of Absence, in M. Bille, F. Hastrup and T. F. Soerensen (eds.), *An Anthropology of Absence: Materializations of Transcendence and Loss*, 3–22. New York City: Springer.

Bourdieu, P. (2007) *Masculine Domination*. Cambridge: Politiy Press.

Bronislaw, M. (1922) *Argonauts of the Western Pacific: An Account of Native Enterprise, and Adventure in the Archipelagoes, of Melanesian New Guinea*. London: G. Routledge & Sons.

Clarke, J and Newman, J. (2017) People in This Country Have Had Enough of Experts. Brexit and the Paradoxes of Populism. *Critical Policy Studies*, 11(1), 101–16.

Connell, R. W. (1995) *Masculinities*. Cambridge, UK: Polity Press.

Connell, R. W. and Messerschmidt, J. W. (2005) Hegemonic Masculinity: Rethinking the Concept. *Gender & Society*, 19(6), 829–59.

Davey, J. and Ebner, J. (2017) *The Fringe Insurgency: Connectivity, Convergence, and Mainstreaming of the Extreme Right*. London: The Institute for Strategic Dialogue.

Elmore, J. and Elmore, R. (2016) Human Become Coin: Neoliberalism, Anthropology, and Human Possibilities in No Country for Old Men. *The Cormac McCarthy Journal*, 14(2), 168–85.

Evans-Pritchard, E. E. (1940) *The Nuer*. New York: Oxford University Press.

Follis, K. (2017) Maritime Migration, Brexit and the Future of European Borders: Anthropological Previews/Námořní migrace, brexit a budoucnost evropských hranic očima antropoložky. *Český Lid*, 104(1), 5–32.

Fourest, C. and Venner, F. (2011) *Marine Le Pen: [biographie]*. Paris: Bernard Grasset.

Fox, K. (2008) *Watching the English the Hidden Rules of English Behaviour*. London: Hodder & Stoughton.

Fuery, P. (1995) *The Theory of Absence: Subjectivity, Signification and Desire*. Westport: Greenwood Press.

Gardner, A. (2017) Brexit, Boundaries and Imperial Identities: A Comparative View. *Journal of Social Archaeology*, 17(1), 3–26.

Gartenstein-Ross, D. and Grossman, L. (2009) Homegrown Terrorists in the US and UK: An Empirical Examination of the Radicalization Process. *FDD Center for Terrorism Research*, 11.

Green, S., et al. (2016) Brexit Referendum: First Reactions from Anthropology. *Social Anthropology*, 24, 478–502.

Hall, S. (1990) Cultural Identity and Diaspora, in Rutherford, J. (ed.), *Identity, Community, Culture, Difference*, 222–37. London: Lawrence and Wishart.

Hirsch, A. (2020) Boris Johnson Does Have a Strategy on Racism after All. It's Called a 'War on Woke', *Guardian*. 17 June. Available at: https://www.theguardian.com/commentisfree/2020/jun/17/boris-johnson-racism-woke-tories (accessed 11 February 2022).

Hockey, J., Komaromy, C. and Woodthorpe, K. (2010) The Matter of Death. Space, Place and Materiality. Basingstoke: Palgrave Macmillan.

Hooper, C. (2001) *Manly States: Masculinities, International Relations, and Gender Politics*. New York City: Columbia University Press.

Houston, C. (2009) An Anti-History of a Non-People: Kurds, Colonialism, and Nationalism in the History of Anthropology. *The Journal of the Royal Anthropological Institute*, 15(1), 19–35.

Jenkins, R. (2008) *Rethinking Ethnicity: Arguments and Explorations.* London: Sage, 80.

Keskinen, S., Norocel, O. C. and Jørgensen, M. B. (2016) The Politics and Policies of Welfare Chauvinism under the Economic Crisis. *Critical Social Policy*, 36(3), 321–9.

Kimmel, M. (2003) Globalization and Its Mal(e)contents: The Gendered Moral and Political Economy of Terrorism. *International Sociology*, 18(3), 603–20.

Kimmel, M. (2017) White Men as Victims: The Men's Rights Movement, in Michael Kimmel (ed.), *Angry White Men: American Masculinity at the End of an Era*, 99–134. New York, NY: Nation Books.

Kimmel, M. and Ferber, A.L. (2000) 'White Men Are This Nation:' Right-Wing Militias and the Restoration of Rural American Masculinity. *Rural Sociology*, 65(4), 582–604.

Knight, D.M. (2017) Anxiety and Cosmopolitan Futures: Brexit and Scotland. *American Ethnologist*, 44(2), 237–42.

Koch, I. (2017) What's in a Vote? Brexit beyond Culture Wars. *American Ethnologist*, 44(2), 225–30.

Kováts, E. (2018) Questioning Consensuses: Right-Wing Populism, Anti-Populism, and the Threat of 'Gender Ideology'. *Sociological Research Online*, 23(2), 528–38.

Lazar, M.M. (2007) Feminist Critical Discourse Analysis: Articulating a Feminist Discourse Praxis. *Critical Discourse Studies*, 4(2), 141–64.

Leach, E. R. (1954) *Political Systems of Highland Burma: A Study of Kachin Social Structure.* New York, NY: ACLS History.

Lovenduski, J. (2005) *Feminizing Politics.* Cambridge, UK: Polity Press.

MacKenzie, M. and Foster, A. (2017) Masculinity Nostalgia: How War and Occupation Inspire a Yearning for Gender Order. *Security Dialogue*, 48(3), 206–23.

Mahmud, L. (2020) Fascism, a Haunting: Spectral Politics and Antifascist Resistance in Twenty-First-Century Italy, in Maskovsky, Jeff and Sophie Bjork-James, (eds.), *Beyond Populism: Angry Politics and the Twilight of Neoliberalism*, 141–66. Virginia: West Virginia University Press.

Martill, B. and Staiger, U. (Eds.) (2018) *Brexit and beyond: Rethinking the Futures of Europe.* London: UCL Press.

Martin, K. and Smith, K. (2014) UKIP and the Rise of Populist Politics. *Anthropology Today*, 30(3), 1–2.

Meyer, M. and Woodthorpe, K. (2008) The Material Presence of Absence: A Dialogue between Museums and Cemeteries. *Sociological Research Online*, 13(5), 127–35.

Mingay, G. E. (1998) *Rural Life in Victorian England.* Thrupp, Stroud, Gloucestershire: Sutton Pub.

Moffitt, B. (2016) *The Global Rise of Populism: Performance, Political Style, and Representation.* Stanford, CA: Stanford University Press.

Mosse, G. L. (1999) *The Image of Man: The Creation of Modern Masculinity.* Oxford: Oxford University Press.

Mudde, C. (2007) *Populist Radical Right Parties in Europe.* Cambridge: Cambridge University Press.

Müller, J.W. (2017) *What Is Populism?* New York: Penguin Books Ltd.

Müller, J.W. (2016) *What Is Populism?* London: Penguin Random House.

Osgerby, B. (2006) *Playboys in Paradise: Masculinity, Youth and Leisure-Style in Modern America*. Oxford: Berg.

Patel, I. S. (2021) *We're Here because You Were There: Immigration and the End of Empire*. La Vergne, TN: Verso.

Ritivoi, A.D. (2002) *Yesterday's Self: Nostalgia and the Immigrant Identity*. Lanham, MD: Rowman & Littlefield.

Slootmaeckers, K. (2019) Nationalism as Competing Masculinities: Homophobia as a Technology of Othering for Hetero- and Homonationalism. *Theor Soc*, 48, 239–65.

Tilley, C., and Cameron-Daum, K. (2017) *Anthropology of Landscape: The Extraordinary in the Ordinary*. London: UCL Press.

Thorleifsson, C. (2019) *Nationalist Responses to the Crises in Europe*. London: Routledge.

Turner, V. (1967) *The Forest of Symbols: Aspects of Ndembu Ritual*. Ithaca: Cornell University Press.

Victor, W.T. (1969) *The Ritual Process: Structure and Anti-Structure*. Chicago: Aldine Publishing Company.

Wade, N. J. (2003) The Legacy of Phantom Limbs. *Perception*, 32, 517–24.

Watson, G. (2004) Make Me Reflexive – But Not Yet: Strategies for Managing Essential Reflexivity in Ethnographic Discourse. *Journal of Anthropological Research*, 43(1), 204.

West, C. and Zimmerman, D. H. (1987) Doing Gender. *Gender & Society*, 1(2), 125–51.

Winlow, S., Hall, S. and Treadwell, J. (2016) *The Rise of the Right: English Nationalism and the Transformation of Working-Class Politics*. (1st ed.). Bristol: Bristol University Press.

Williams, R. (1973) *The Country and the City*. New York: Oxford University Press.

Wilson, T. M. (2020) Anthropological Approaches to Why Brexit Matters. *Ethnologia Europaea*, 50(2), 7–15.

Wodak, R. and Meyer, M. (2009) Critical Discourse Analysis: History, Agenda, Theory and Methodology, in R. Wodak and M. Meyer (eds.), *Methods of Critical Discourse Analysis* (2nd ed.). 1–32. London: Sage.

4

Is there a 'post-patriarchal' Indian man? An ethnography of 'new' discourses of neoliberal masculinities in India

Shannon Phillip

Introduction

Neoliberalism in India has substantially shaped the politics of gender, space, youth, class and media (Gooptu 2009, 2013). This expansion of neoliberalism[1] has fundamentally changed the landscape of the country, with a shift towards urbanization and an 'enterprise culture' which emphasizes individual self-actualization. All these work towards the creation of what is seen as a 'new' India with 'new' citizens. As several scholars have argued, these processes are heavily gendered; with new discourses emerging about the 'new' Indian woman (Broisus 2017; Gooptu 2013) as well as 'new' Indian masculinities (Philip 2018). In this chapter I explore how shifts in Indian media and the arrival of global capital has seen an emergence of self-identified 'new' men with what are characterized as 'new' discourses and ways of thinking, many of which claim to be 'post-patriarchal' in character. I critically study these emerging discourses amongst young middle-class Indian men, based on my ethnographic fieldwork in India, exploring how these 'post-patriarchal' masculinities usurp the language of social justice and gender equality while reproducing patriarchal male privileges in new and insidious ways. In addition, I seek to reveal the ways in which these neoliberal masculinities give legitimacy to men's misogyny and protect their

---

[1] Neoliberaism for this paper is a process of economic, social and political shift which favours private capital and individual responsibilization for economic success in an allegedly free market (Gooptu 2013).

privileges, whilst at the same-time hailing them as the 'new' male heroes of a 'new' India.

The patriarchal context of India has been well documented within Indian feminist scholarship (see Ray 2012 for an overview of this vast field). This chapter argues that in the highly patriarchal context of India, the discourse of being a 'post-patriarchal' man is highly problematic as it allows for the reproduction of patriarchy in seemingly apolitical and novel ways. I ethnographically show that 'new' Indian men try to position themselves as protectors of Indian women while at the same time exerting great control and power over them. Hence in a patriarchal society like India it becomes important to ask 'what does "post-patriarchy" mean and what does it stand for?' While critical for the realization of gender justice in India, this chapter also explores the contradictory ways some men and boys engage with gender justice projects.

Methodology

The data for this chapter comes from my qualitative and long-term ethnographic fieldwork in New Delhi, India, from 2016 to 2018, for my doctoral research at the University of Oxford, UK, as well as follow-up conversations through social media platforms and visits to Delhi to meet my informants. The data comprises ethnographic observations, semi-structured interviews with over forty young middle-class men and twelve women, analysis of media and digital sources, as well as key informant interviews with non-governmental organizations (NGOs) and women's organizations in New Delhi. Methodologically, this chapter privileges ethnographic descriptions of the life-worlds of young Indian men and how they negotiate neoliberal masculinities as a discourse. In order to do, so the chapter begins by looking in detail at the 'New Thinking' campaign in India which influences young men in Delhi and is a highly prominent media campaign in contemporary India. The next section builds on this empirical example and critically analyses the patriarchal ways in which women's respect, and the idea of honour, is constructed in India. The next section, then, critically asses men's 'new' thinking about how these patriarchal framings of women play out in Indian social contexts and the paradoxes of being 'post-patriarchal' in a highly patriarchal country. Finally, the chapter looks at the masculinities discourses between 'new' men and 'traditional' or 'old thinking' men and their assessments of the many social and gendered inequalities in contemporary Indian society, and offers some concluding remarks.

The 'New thinking' of Indian men

Raj, a twenty-seven-year-old Indian male respondent, had a cricket t-shirt made with his mother's name 'Ratna' on the back. He showed me a photo of himself wearing this t-shirt with great pride and told me that it was inspired by the Indian cricket team and their campaign at the time called '*Nayi Soch*' or 'New thinking'. This 'New thinking' campaign was a major media campaign that continues to have wide appeal in India amongst young middle-class Indian men (TNN 2016). It had Indian cricket team players wearing t-shirts with their mothers' names on the back for several cricket matches that were broadcast on national television. It appealed to a broad section of young and older men in various parts of the country from a myriad of social, caste and class backgrounds. The campaign began due to the high levels of violence towards women being reported in the Indian media at the time, and was an attempt to engage more men in gender equality work. One particularly inspiring cricketer for my respondents was the Indian cricket team captain Virat Kohli, who had his mother's name 'Saroj' printed on his t-shirt. This was seen as a significant change from his normal cricket shirts which carried the word 'Kohli', his paternal surname. In unpacking the various discourses surrounding the 'New thinking' campaign, I argue that this media campaign, which specifically aimed to create a 'new thinking' amongst Indian men, provides us with an interesting empirical example to think about aspects of neoliberal masculinities in India. Particularly given the wide appeal of cricket and sports for Indian men (Osella and Osella 2006) such a campaign meant that young male respondents like Raj emulated the messages promoted by the campaign.

Raj explained to me that he really valued the 'New thinking' campaign and took its message seriously. He told me that he wore this t-shirt several times to various cricket matches and other social events. He explained: '*It's a great thing the Indian cricket team are doing, ... I think it's a great idea, it's really what India needs .... People have to show more respect for their mothers and women in the country.*' According to Raj, the 'New thinking' campaign symbolically marked the importance of women and celebrated them. He explained: '*Ratna is my mother's name and I got a t-shirt with her name specially because of the campaign. In India we always put our father's name everywhere, but it is important to remember our mothers too.*' Raj also talked about how much he respected Virat Kohli for wearing his mother's name on his t-shirt and explained that this act symbolized that Virat Kohli was a 'new thinking' man who respected women and therefore was a good role model for other Indian men. In turn, Raj wanted to be seen as a 'new thinking' man who respects women. Several of my other respondents in Delhi also talked about this campaign as an important and positive step towards symbolically creating gender equality in a country they believed to be highly unequal in gendered terms.

Within the patriarchal context of India, feminist scholars have argued that the social institutions of arranged marriages and the social privilege enjoyed by fathers and sons more generally (Desai 2016; Ray 2012) privilege men and place women in a subordinate position. Hence the fact that the 'New thinking' campaign directly engages with the issue of familial identities and their symbolic meanings is significant and has multiple dimensions. In keeping with bureaucratic, social and legal procedures in India, women take the names of the patriarchal households they are marrying into, in line with many patriarchal contexts around the globe where wives take their husband's surname (see Ray 2012 for a broader overview of gender and bureaucracy in India). However, in India, this has added significance, as several scholars have spoken about how women are conceptualized as '*paraya dhan*' or 'someone else's' wealth and how this leads to such practises as paying dowries to the groom's family (Ray 2012). It was striking that Aditya, another male respondent, explained that he was helping his newly married sister change her name on legal documents to that of her husband and that this was 'natural' and 'required' given that she now 'belonged' there and that she was somehow no longer part of 'his family'.

This is why Virat Kohli, as well as my informants like Aditya and Raj, used the first names of their mothers, Saroj and Ratna, on their t-shirts, rather than their pre-marital last names which are no longer are legally or socially recognized. In this way, this idea of 'respecting women', which is one of the stated aims of the 'New thinking' campaign is very much from within a patriarchal structure, rather than from a position of challenging the patriarchal framing of women, their identities and their lives. It is striking, for example, that I could not find Saroj Kohli's pre-marital name anywhere on the internet, even though she has several articles written about her. After her arranged marriage, the only legally and socially rendered identity she has is of being the wife within the context of her marital home. Such a framing of women through a patriarchal lens then raises further questions as to the relationship between respecting the mother figure and women more generally and framing around Indian masculinities.

Patriarchal 'respect' for women

The discussion of gendered ideas about the 'respectability' of women in India can help us contextualize this discussion about mothers and their names and marriage practices. The figure of the mother, highlighted by the 'New thinking' campaign and its followers, has a long trajectory of sociological thinking in the Indian social context, with the idea of 'Mother India' as well as ideas around sexual virtue and purity (Menon 2012). However, the specific identity of women to be respected in the 'New thinking' campaign is the mother figure rather than a girlfriend or a wife. Within the patriarchal institution of heterosexual arranged marriage in India and South Asia more generally, women's position and sexuality are reduced to producing children and sustaining the patriarchal family along appropriate class, caste and social lines (John and Nair 2000; Menon 2012). Women's bodies and sexualities, as several feminist scholars have argued, are disciplined and controlled by social forces and the institutions of arranged marriage in India that seek to limit and contain them (ibid.). The figure of the mother thus becomes the epitome of female sexual virtue within a patriarchal context – one which other women are encouraged to aspire to and emulate.

As Indian feminists have long argued, young women in India have their sexualities controlled and limited by their families in order to appear 'attractive' on the 'arranged marriage market' with their sexual virtue intact (see John and Nair 2000 for a detailed discussion). The power of this discourse on sexualities is so great that unmarried young women found (or even suspected) to be dating or having sexual relationships outside of marriage are deemed 'fallen' women, even amongst urban and purportedly liberal spheres of the Indian middle-classes (Trivedi 2014). Several studies have shown that women who do in fact date and have sexual relationships with men before marriage have to use a whole range of social strategies to manage and negotiate their relationships and sexual lives in order to maintain the appearance of social honour and respectable femininity (see Krishnan 2015; Iyer 2017 for more examples). Likewise, other scholars have demonstrated that women found engaging in sexual pre-marital relationships are often referred to and abused, using terms for sex workers or 'fallen women' more broadly (Menon 2012). Sex workers in India, for example, are regularly thought of as 'fallen women' who have an active sexuality beyond the prescribed norms of hetero-patriarchy in India (ibid.). The only appropriate sexual and social role for women is that of a loving and caring wife in a patriarchal family; to be sexually faithful, subordinate mothers worthy of patriarchal respect. Furthermore, in this context, married women without children are seen as 'barren' or even 'not women at all' (Ray 2012).

The 'New thinking' campaign frames the idea of respecting women only within the narrow framework of the patriarchal mother figure. It presents this idea of 'respecting women/mothers' as new; however, as feminists have long argued, being a 'respectable mother' has ostensibly been the only socially sanctioned model of femininity amongst the middle classes in India (Ray 2012). Such dominant tropes about respecting women as mothers limit and discipline women so they do not pose a challenge to gendered biases or norms in Indian society (see Menon 2012 for more). Thus the 'New thinking' campaign, rather than respecting women in any new way, reproduces the norms of women's patriarchal respectability as mothers and operates through patriarchal logics that Indian feminists have long been fighting against.

What is also interesting in the politics of gendered and social order of names is that women do not really have autonomy, as their positions almost exclusively emerge from within patriarchal relationships. A girl child born within a patriarchal Indian family has to adopt her father's names rather than her mother's. Indeed, amongst the respondents I worked with, it was striking that I never met anyone born out of wedlock in India and all the young men and women came from tightly knit arranged-marriage families where the family used the father's name. A girl child is born into a family with her father's name and then becomes a wife and takes on her husband's name and then becomes a mother and all her children have her husband's family name. Hence patriarchal power and privilege becomes institutionalized at birth and gets further enmeshed and framed within a patriarchal social and gendered order across the life cycle. As scholars of Indian masculinities have argued, these patriarchal structures privilege men, their names, families and lives and continue to frame women in and through relationships with men (Chopra, Osella and Osella 2004; Philip 2015, 2017).

The literature on Indian masculinities also points out that the role of young men in patriarchal India is about 'protecting' mothers and sisters to ensure their sexual purity and to make their sexualities align with the demands of the arranged marriage which privileges men. As Kira Hall (2009) points out, swearing at and insulting other men in India is often done indirectly by commenting on the 'impurity' of women who are seen as being under their protection. For example, sisters' and mothers' names are frequently used as an insult in everyday contexts by Indian men in their use of the words such as 'motherfucker' or 'sisterfucker' in Hindi which are aligned with the patriarchal system in India where men act as guarantors of women's sexual purity (ibid.). These are understood as the ultimate insults that one man can give to another, challenging the purity of his mother or sister and as a result suggesting the inability of the man to carry out his masculine duty. Discursive insults like 'sisterfucker' draw their power from their heavily gendered social context and, as scholars point out, young men and women are intricately involved in managing the 'brother-sister' bond in complex ways (see Iyer 2017 for a more detailed discussion on brother-sister naming practices). Likewise, the son is deemed to be the protector of the mother and so an insult using the term 'motherfucker' is aimed as much at the son's inability to protect his mother as at her allegedly fallen status and immoral sexual practices.

In this way, Raj, Aditya, as well as several other respondents who support the 'New thinking' campaign do so from the safety of a patriarchal framing of women rather than a position that challenges gendered inequalities or deeper power dynamics between men and women. Raj and Aditya would often use insults like 'sisterfucker' and 'motherfucker' without reflection on their gendered significance, whist also arguing for the staunch respectability of the 'mother figure' articulated in 'New thinking' campaign. As I have argued, new thinking is not so new after all. There is in fact a stronger rearticulation of the idealized mother figure, supported by the validation of new masculinities which are then claimed to be 'new' thinking. This then raises interesting questions about how these discourses about 'new' thinking relate to wider discourses about of masculinities and men in India.

'New' versus 'old' thinking men

Amongst the young middle-class men I worked with, the significance of the 'New thinking' campaign is closely linked to their own sense of being male citizens of an allegedly modern and new India. This is the idea of a neoliberal India; one which seeks to become increasingly attractive as an investment destination for global capital and where 'development' has come to mean neoliberal economic growth rather than a socialist model of the state (Gooptu 2013). In this context, the 'new' young Indian male citizens seek to correct the negative international and local media attention on India as a patriarchal and violent space for women with regressive gender norms (Brosius 2017). It becomes important to look at changing masculinities discourses amongst young middle-class men like Raj and Aditya who are at the forefront of creating the image of a neoliberal India as an allegedly 'post-patriarchal' country where women are respected and gendered violence does not belong. For example, Raj told me that he believes that as a young, modern Indian man he must respect women and that wearing the t-shirt bearing his mother's first name represents one way of doing so. As such, Raj thinks of himself as the type of man who begins to define a 'new' India where women are not discriminated against. In his comments he further explained that 'India needs more men like me' because he believes the high level of violence experienced by women in India can only be stopped by more 'New thinking' men who can demonstrate their respect for women.

These ideas were reflected by several young male respondents who said they thought of themselves as 'post-patriarchal' men – without actually giving up any of their patriarchal power over women and their privileged place in the gendered social hierarchy. Kunal, for example, explained that he was a 'feminist man' and this was a term he had found on the internet which really resonated with him in keeping with the image of a 'new' India. He added that he considered himself to be a 'feminist' because he deeply respected women and thought of them as 'equal' to men. For Kunal, a discourse of respect and equality towards women meant that he felt he was in touch with 'new' India as well as a new idea of masculinity which moves away from the 'old' ways of being a man. These new ideas of masculinity for him were reflected in the 'New thinking' campaign where young men could use the symbolic discourse of gender equality without actually creating any real shift in the power dynamics. Rather, they could signify a commitment to equality by simply donning a t-shirt with their mother's name on it. In practice, Kunal remained an extremely controlling boyfriend to the women he was dating and would cat-call women regularly when we would 'roam' around the city, enjoying the power and privileges afforded to him by local forms of patriarchy. Yet Kunal also argued that his speech and ideas about gender and women's abilities and inabilities were very different to those of his father and other men of an older generation. For him, the 'old' India was a patriarchal India, but the 'new India' was a free and liberated space defined by campaigns like 'New thinking' which promoted respect for women. The age-gender matrix (Harris 2012) is at play here to define young men like Kunal and my other informants as 'new' Indian men by drawing a distinction with older men, in terms of both their age and modes of thinking. In other words, a 'new' India for 'new thinking' men like Kunal becomes allegedly 'post-patriarchal' through rhetoric and symbolism.

However, as I have demonstrated, this discursive shift does not actually imply a shift in thinking or a shift in power relations between men and women. Rather it masks the effects and inequalities that are foundational to the Indian patriarchal order. What is also of interest is that young men like Kunal told me that there were 'biological differences' between men and women which meant that they were not the same. Kunal argued that this biological difference was a positive thing. He explained that because men and women were 'designed' to have different roles in society, and that their roles were in 'balance' and in accordance with 'nature'. In elaborating his idea of 'difference', he suggested that men and women are different, but should be equal in, and through, their differences. He argued that there are several things that women cannot do and several other things that men cannot do. He gave the example that men cannot give birth to children and thus, for him, it was an indication that both 'men' and 'women' were fixed to their biological roles which then also justified their social roles. This idea further meant that women were 'naturally' more caring and that men were somehow 'less caring'. In this biological determinism, Kunal and several other young men are confident about their 'modern', 'feminist' selves which promote the idea of 'equality' between men and women, but crucially while respecting what they see as their natural differences. Indeed, as Butler (2006) has long argued, this sense of biological determinism is central to maintaining what she calls the 'heterosexual matrix' that ties gender, social roles, reproduction, bodies and desire in linear and narrow ways. For a young man like Kunal, then, the body is a fixed biological entity that has a strong and defined gendered basis. This biological determinism furthermore defines the social lives of various bodies. For Kunal inequality comes from disrespect for women's bodies, yet it is seemingly accepted as 'natural' that women cannot do everything that men can.

This dualistic idea of respecting women as 'equal but different' was often framed by respondents as unique to 'new' thinking in India. According to Raj, 'old thinking' viewed women as inferior and not as equal. To him and men like him, this idea of 'old thinking' is directly opposite to the idea of 'new thinking'. As I have argued elsewhere (Philip 2017), these ideas of 'old' and 'new' become a marker of crucial difference for such young men from the generation of their fathers or older men who embody more explicitly patriarchal language. For Raj, his new thinking was demonstrated both through his use of these new discourses and his father's reported lack of access to it. In keeping with the shifts of a 'new' India (Philip 2018), fathers and other older men start to embody the old, patriarchal India whereas these young men become new, feminist men who enact a discourse of gendered equality without ever compromising their gendered power or privileges. In this way young men like Raj, Aditya and Kunal begin to think of themselves as 'modern' and 'better' young men who do not discriminate against women. At the same time, they talk about older Indian men of a previous generation as uneducated, unmodern and uncivilized – serving as an explanation for why India has sometimes been seen as oppressive to women. In this post-patriarchal narrative of 'new men' and their 'new' thinking, there is a clear use of feminist language and discourses. Yet this occurs without awareness of or taking responsibility for the power, privilege and entitlements enjoyed by young men in the local patriarchies of India.

Masculine power and control

This idea of young men creating a sense of masculinity for themselves in opposition to that of their elders while also maintaining male power and control is well theorized in the literature on masculinities and patriarchy in India and elsewhere. In male-dominated gender orders or patriarchy, masculinity often exists in contrast with a complementarily subordinate femininity (Connell 2005; Osella and Osella 2006). In order to be accepted as a legitimate 'man', regular acts that are culturally, legally, socially and historically intelligible need to be performed by individuals (Butler 2006). For Butler, 'intelligible' bodies are bodies that fit within the heterosexual matrix in keeping with local gendered norms (ibid.). Thus masculinities are always an ongoing social process which involves complex building and rebuilding, consolidation, representation and enforcement (Hearn 1998; McDowell 2011; Srivastava 2007). In the Indian context, masculinities are produced in and through various changing localized social structures, histories and cultural formations resulting in multiple cultures of masculinities (Srivastava 2004, 2007). The fragmented nature of the cultural sphere in India, compounded by regional, linguistic, historical and religious differences, means that there is no centralized or singular idea of masculinities; rather there are multiple ways of being a man and multiple cultures of masculinities from wherein men enact their masculinities (Connell 2005). Thus it is important to view the 'New thinking' campaign and the comments of my respondents from within these changing cultural and gendered spaces as moving and evolving discourses and ways of being a man, rather than as static or fixed. Indeed, my argument does not suggest that young men are necessary anti-feminists or are violent towards women; however I am critical of new discourses of post-patriarchal masculinities that are emerging in India and the changing cultures of masculinities and their discourses where post-patriarchal language is used and co-opted without any shift in patriarchal power dynamics.

At the same time, it is important to highlight how young men like Raj and Aditya have begun thinking about women and their relationships with them given the many public and media discussions about gender currently taking place in India. The violent rape and murder of a middle-class young woman, subsequently dubbed 'Nirbhaya' or 'the fearless one', on a moving bus in Delhi in 2012 has seen men engaging with issues of gender equality and gendered violence (Brosius 2017). A crucial 'silence' Nair and John (2000) once argued exists around issues of gendered violence now seems to have been broken. Several young men told me that they had been part of the protests that emerged in Delhi and across India after the Nirbhaya incident and it encouraged them to take more action for gender equality. Nonetheless according to several of my middle-class young informants, the violence experienced by women was caused by 'old thinking' men with their 'patriarchal' ideas, or by 'uneducated' men. My respondents never questioned their own masculine power, privilege or gendered inequalities within their own contexts. Caste scholars in India also pointed out the disproportionate media attention and youth mobilization around the Nirbhaya case and the relatively much smaller attention given to the high levels of rape and violence experienced by Dalit and poorer women in India. Suraj Yengde (2019) argued that caste-based gendered violence in India has been systematically under-addressed in India or often simply ignored. Yengde's work also points out the tendency amongst Indian middle-classes to suggest caste and gendered biases as 'problems' of the past, that do not exist in a 'new' India (Yengde 2019:33).

Through my ethnographic fieldwork with young men, I often saw first-hand how young men like Kunal and Raj showed extremely controlling behaviour towards their sisters and girlfriends, as well as their cat-calling of women on the streets and sending unwanted and often explicit photographs to women they had crushes on. The young men participated in various forms of gendered violence while maintaining their 'feminist' credentials. As I have tried to demonstrate, we must be careful when we see these discourses celebrating 'new' men and look at them critically within their social and gendered context. Rather than taking men's words at face value, through ethnographic enquiry and long-term engagement, I have tried to show the paradoxes and contradictions in what men say and think about themselves and what they actually do.

The comments and discourses of 'post-patriarchal' young men must be considered critically and within their social context. The seemingly feminist language of young Indian men and their claims of a new masculinity do not readily translate into a safer social and spatial context for women. There are parallels in other countries – indeed as South African feminist scholar Pumla Gqola (2015) has argued, Black women in South Africa in particular have been framed as 'unrapable' by legal and social discourse, even though they experience extremely high levels of gendered violence, including rape. Gqola points out that the particular racialized construction of Black femininity and its corresponding masculinity means that in South Africa today it is very difficult to find and convict a man of rape because allegedly all men in South Africa claim to 'respect' Black women. According to Gqola, in this way it becomes a discursive impossibility to either rape a Black woman or find a patriarchal and oppressive man in South Africa. Gqola goes on to state that this points to a context where men espouse feminist language and terms such as 'equality' and 'gender justice', yet this never leads to a deeper shift in power relations or a real reduction in the high levels of violence women experience from men. Likewise, the threat to Black women's bodies in South Africa become impossible to articulate and make visible because of the patriarchal forces at play in shaping and creating those discourses. In the Indian case too, it is important to analyse and compare the discourses of 'new' and 'old' masculinities as well as their ideas of gendered inequalities which can mask oppression and deep-rooted biases towards women while using the language of progressive feminism.

Conclusion

Young middle-class men's ideas of masculinities in contemporary neoliberal India are constructed through a discourse that allows them to actively label themselves as feminist men, or as I would argue 'post-patriarchal' men. There is a deliberate attempt to construct a 'modern' masculinity which arguably appears to be 'post-patriarchal' while masking deep gendered inequalities and biases towards women and failing to acknowledge the key role of power relations. As several feminists in India have pointed out, patriarchy is rife and perhaps more powerful than ever in neoliberal India, while there has been an emergence of new language and discourse around equality (Philip 2017). I have tried to demonstrate in this chapter that patriarchy in fact powerfully operates amongst young men in new and complex ways through discourses of 'modernity' and 'new thinking' entangled with the idea of neoliberal India. I have demonstrated that patriarchal masculine entitlement and control over women takes on new forms even as it deploys progressive language. We as feminist scholars and activists must be able to continually and carefully reflect on the practices that underpin and accompany these discourses rather than uncritically celebrating them as a shift in gender norms. Yet at the same time, it is important to acknowledge the progress and change that the Indian feminist movement has made in the country (Menon 2012), while also looking at the great need to further engage men and boys in critical reflection and deeper changes. While the discourses of 'new masculinities' at play in contemporary India may create the façade of a 'post-patriarchal' man, he remains strongly patriarchal in new and complex ways.

Bibliography

Brosius, C. (2017) Regulating Access and Mobility of Single Women in a 'World Class'-city: Gender and Inequality in Delhi, India, in Gerhard, U., Hoelscher, M., Wilson, D. (eds.), *Inequalities in Creative Cities*, 239–260. New York: Palgrave Macmillan.

Butler, J. (2006) *Gender Trouble: Feminism and the Subversion of Identity*. New York and London: Routledge.

Connell, R.W. (2005) *Masculinities* (2nd ed.). Cambridge: Polity.

Chopra, R., Osella, C. and Osella, F. (2004) South Asian Masculinities: Context of Change, Sites of Continuity, Women Unlimited, an associate of Kali for Women, New Delhi.

Desai, M. (2016) Gendered Violence and India's Body Politic. *New Left Review*, 99, 67–83.

Geetha, V. (2007) *Patriarchy (Theorising Feminism)*. Kolkata: Stree.

Gooptu, N. (2009) Neoliberal Subjectivity. *Enterprise Culture and New Workplaces: Organised Retail and Shopping Malls in India, Economic and Political Weekly*, 44(22), 45–54.

Gooptu, N. (ed.) (2013) *Enterprise Culture in Neoliberal India: Studies in Youth, Class, Work and Media*. (1st ed.). London and New York: Routledge.

Gqola, P.D. (2015) *Rape: A South African Nightmare*. Auckland Park, South Africa: MF Books Joburg.

Hall, K. (2009) Boys' Talk: Hindi, Moustaches, and Masculinity in New Delhi, In Pia Pichler and Eva Eppler (eds.), *Gender and Spoken Interaction*, 139–162. London: Palgrave Macmillan.

Harris, C. (2012) Gender-age Systems and Social Change: A Haugaardian Power Analysis Based on Research from Northern Uganda. MICROCON Research Working Paper, vol. 65.

Hearn, J. (1998) *The Violence's of Men: How Men talk about and How Agencies Respond to Men's Violence to Women*. London: Sage.

Iyer, P. (2017) 'Due to All This Fear, We're Getting Less Freedom': Young People's Understandings of Gender and Sexual Violence in New Delhi, India. *Gender and Education*, 47(6), 222–39.

John, M. and Nair, J. (2000) *A Question of Silence? The Sexual Economics of Modern India*. London: Zed.

Krishnan, L. (2015) Social Exclusion, Mental Health, Disadvantage and Injustice. *Psychology and Developing Societies*, 27(2), 155–73.

McDowell, L. (1999) *Gender, Identity and Place: Understanding Feminist Geographies*. Cambridge: Polity.

McDowell, L. (2011) *Redundant Masculinities?: Employment Change and White Working Class Youth*. Malden, Oxford and Carlton: John Wiley & Sons.

Menon, N. (2012) *Seeing Like a Feminist*. New Delhi: Published by Zubaan in collaboration with Penguin Books.

Osella, C. and Osella, F. (2006) *Men and Masculinities in South India*. London: Anthem Press, London.

Philip, S. (2015) Making Men and Masculinities Visible: A Macro Level Enquiry into Conceptualizations of Gender and Violence in Indian Policies. *NORMA*, 10(3–4), 326–38.

Philip, S. (2017) Caught in-between: Social Developments and Young Men in Urban India. *Journal of Gender Studies*, 27(3), 362–70.

Philip, S. (2018) Youth and ICTs in a 'New' India: Exploring Changing Gendered Online Relationships among Young Urban Men and Women. *Gender & Development*, 26(2), 313–24.

Ray, R. (2012) *Handbook of Gender*. Oxford: Oxford University Press.

Srivastava, S. (2004) *Masculinity and Its Role in Gender-Based Violence in Public Spaces*. New Delhi: Centre for Equity and Inclusion.

Srivastava, S. (2007) Modi-Masculinity: Media. *Manhood and 'Traditions' in a Time of Consumerism, Television & New Media*, 16(4), 331.

TNN (2016) Indian Team Appreciates 'Nayi Soch', Sports Jerseys with Mothers' Names. *The Times of India*, 29th October. Available at: https://timesofindia.indiatimes.com/sports/new-zealand-in-india-2016/top-stories/Indian-team-appreciates-Nayi-Soch-sports-jerseys-with-mothers-names/articleshow/55130376.cms (last accessed 13 May 2021).

Trivedi, I. (2014) *India in Love*. Delhi: Aleph Book Company.

Yengde, S. (2019) *Caste Matters*. Gurugram: Penguin Random House India Private Limited.

Part Two

Normativity and diversity

5

Tenuous masculinities: Situated agency and value of the Indonesian transgender men's masculinities

Alvi A. H. and Hendri Yulius Wijaya

Introduction

Since mid-2015, Lesbian, Gay, Bisexual and Transgender (LGBT) people have attracted an unprecedented level of negative attention from the state and the public in Indonesia (Wieringa 2019; Wijaya 2020). The press reported and conflated LGBT individuals with 'abnormality', 'immorality', 'outcome of Western influence' and 'threat to the nation-state' (Listiorini 2020; Yulius 2017). This anti-LGBT sentiment has made the term 'LGBT' itself become 'a part of the everyday vernacular of many Indonesians' (Wijaya 2020:3) and is increasingly used as a catchall to refer to any person with non-normative genders and sexualities. The media coverage patterns and reports signal that the anti-LGBT hysteria mostly targeted gay men and transgender women. This observation then became an impetus for Alvi, one of the authors of this chapter, to raise an important question about the existence and subjectivities of transgender men, specifically in a broader landscape of Indonesia's gender and sexuality politics.

Since early childhood, Alvi has felt that he is a 'man' inside. Unsurprisingly, due to his biological sex, his family and society used to categorize him as a 'woman'. For instance, he longed to wear a medical doctor or police uniform in school art events instead of a traditional costume commonly worn by female students. Equally, he also preferred to wear short trousers and a white t-shirt to skirts. Having struggled with this inner sense of not belonging to the female identity led him to seek a new language to fully capture his embodied identity and experiences. In his twenties, around 2004, Alvi moved from his hometown, East Java, to Jakarta, Indonesia's capital city, and eventually joined a lesbian community and later, PLUSH, a grass-roots LGBT organization in Yogyakarta. His participation in the latter organization is where and when Alvi heard the term 'transman' for the first time. Since then, he has increasingly been confident to identify as a transgender man. Recalling this critical shift in his life experience, Alvi also noticed a significant growth and expansion of transmen movements in Indonesia during the same year, demonstrating how 'transman' or *'priawan'* – a local term for a transgender man[1] – as an identity category and political movement has become increasingly prominent in local queer politics.

Visibility does not always automatically bring acceptance, either from the non-queer or from the queer community. During Alvi's tenure in a non-governmental organization working on human and women's rights, colleagues often accused him of 'not being manly enough' because of his unmasculine voice, among other things. At the same time, the lesbian and feminist community that Alvi belonged to also began to question his motivation to embrace being a transman as his new identity. These hostile voices seemed to assume that Alvi's identity preference was motivated by long-standing and uninterrogated male privilege. In other words, Alvi was misrepresented as a 'woman' who utilizes a transman identity to access male power in a patriarchal society.

Drawing on the personal experience and observations above, Alvi and Hendri, the second author, have written this chapter to examine how Indonesian transmen understand, enact and negotiate their identities in everyday life. We introduce the term 'tenuous masculinities' to describe how transmen's masculinities are always at risk of denial and rejection. Consequently, they require constant re-enactment to convince people that their masculinities are authentic enough. In Alvi's words, such a personal attempt is supposed to be 'a lifetime journey'.

This chapter seeks to locate transmen's masculinities within a broader ecosystem of gender and sexual politics in Indonesia in order to reveal how the existing pathways to social and legal recognition from the state and society might drive transmen to embrace 'toxic masculinity' in order to prove themselves worthy of male identity. Furthermore, we also challenge the medical imperative: a successful transition and societal acceptance of trans bodies often require a bodily transformation through medical interventions (Puar 2017b), including sexual-reassignment surgery and hormonal therapy, among others. Instead, our

---

[1]   We recognize that there is still a debate ongoing within the community as to which term is more suitable to describe transman identity/experience. It is not the purpose of this chapter to intervene into this debate, and all our interlocutors identify themselves as 'transman'.

chapter highlights the pivotal role of 'social transitioning' in helping transmen navigate the social world.

Nevertheless, attention to dominant gender norms does not necessarily discount the agency of transgender individuals. Indonesian transmen strategically enact and negotiate their masculinities in everyday life in order to gain acceptance from families and society in general. Through these quotidian negotiations, this social process also enables transmen to share time and space with other people, inviting their immediate communities to better understand their gender identity and sexuality.

Written during the COVID pandemic, we unfortunately could not conduct the fieldwork to interact with the community directly. Instead, we organized two focus group discussions (FGD) – the first involved four Indonesian transmen[2] aged between twenty and forty-five, while the second involved three non-transmen allies. Almost all our key informants have participated in, or at least have encountered, LGBT and feminist movements. They were based in Yogyakarta, Jakarta and South Sumatra. We accompanied these FGDs with a discourse analysis of Indonesia's transmen organizations' publications to provide historical and contextual background in analysing our primary data.

Drawing on the concept of 'queerly ordinary' (Cavalcante 2018:171) and a sociological framework of 'masculinities' (see, for example, Connell 2005; Messerchmidt et al. 2018; Schilt 2018), we wish to invite more critical discussions on transmasculinities from two particular perspectives. First, as it emerged throughout our participants' narratives of lived experiences, the 'queerly ordinary' helps to unpack how the Indonesian transmen 'mobilise and enact queerness in ways that work for them within the limitation and structures of their world' (Cavalcante 2018:172). We pay attention to individuals' agency in navigating their social worlds without overlooking influences from the social structures that concomitantly shape their various navigation strategies. Second, by looking at situated masculinities, we hope to demonstrate the 'intersection of structural theories and empirical analysis' (Schilt 2018:68), highlighting the connections between 'the structural constraints, the emerging possibilities, [and] the contextual lives', of transgender people, exploring and revealing their agency (ibid.).

For the reasons above, this chapter challenges commonplace assumptions about the 'masculine/superior' and 'femininity/ inferior' binary. It is understood

---

[2] Because he could not attend the FGD, one of the key informants responded to our questions by email.

that masculinity would not exist without femininity (Connell 2005:68), and the patriarchal gender relations set a polarization between men and women: men with their masculinity exert dominance over women with their femininity (ibid.:74). However, beyond the gender binary, positioning the key informants neither automatically empowered nor oppressed, we situate trans-agency as a constant improvization and negotiation depending on the social worlds they inhabit (see Cavalcante 2018:176). Echoing the power of queerly ordinary, Susan Stryker (quoted from Skidmore 2017:177) also aptly explains, 'People with trans identity could describe themselves as men and women too – or resist binary categorization altogether – but in doing either they queered the dominant relationship of sexed body and gendered subject'.

Indonesia's transman identity

While non-normative genders and sexualities could easily be found in various historical and cultural practices of ethnic groups in the country, trans, gay and lesbian identities emerged during the late 1970s during the authoritarian 'New Order' era (1966–98). The term *'waria'*, an amalgam of the terms *'wanita'* (woman) and *'pria'* (man), was introduced by Governor Jakarta Ali Sadikin in 1978 (Boellstorff 2007:78–113) to refer to 'men who express their gender more like women'. As the media began to report and discuss gay and lesbian life in the late 1970s and the early 1980s (Boellstorff 2005), people with same-sex desires also simultaneously began to name and channel their attraction into those identities.

Although homosexuality was not explicitly perceived as 'a particular threat' to national identity (Wijaya and Davies 2019:154), gay and lesbian Indonesians saw their sexualities as a form of sickness and abnormality and didn't seek to defend their identity rights. Entangled within the New Order's gender regime that idealized traditional gender norms and the heteronormative family principle (Suryakusuma 1996), many gay and lesbian Indonesians eventually entered heterosexual marriage, which 'was understood as a primary marker of adulthood … and ideal citizenship' (Boellstorff 2005; Wijaya 2020:53). However, this marriage entry is not to say that gay and lesbian people stopped forming same-sex relationships outside of the institution of marriage.

Coterminous with the emerging global development of LGBT and sexual and reproductive rights in the 1990s was an influx of foreign funding from international humanitarian organizations for the gay, lesbian and *waria* community in Indonesia. This support enabled local gay and *waria* communities and organizations to promote HIV/AIDS prevention. Importantly, starting from the early 2000s, the use of the terminology 'LGBT' and 'LGBT rights' had prominence within activist circles.

Alongside the increased visibility of the LGBT movement in public, previously suppressed conservative Islamic forces emerged. During the New Order, President Suharto repressed Islamic politics to curb any potential opposition to his power (Robinson 2015; Wichelen 2010). After the end of the New Order, Indonesia's democratization from the authoritarian regime (1998–present) enabled conservatives to take advantage of the new environment of increased democratic freedom (Robinson 2015; Wijaya and Davies 2020).

Ironically, the democratic landscape, alongside the rise of conservative Islam, witnessed a significant increase in the number of attacks and open verbal vitriol towards LGBT Indonesians, including the forced cancellation of Q! Film Festival, a queer film festival, in 2010 and other subsequent LGBT-related events (Paramaditha 2018). This was mainly driven by the religious vigilante group, the Islamic Defenders Front (*Front Pembela Islam, FPI*) (Davies 2015; Wijaya 2020). Despite the challenges, the LGBT movement did not stop organizing events and advocacy.

However, the language of human rights and LGBT identity politics continued to be a fertile ground for queer activists and the queer community to articulate and name their subjectivities. Such an observation is particularly relevant to detect the shifting boundaries between lesbians, '*tomboi*' and transgender men. On the one hand, the term '*lesbi*', a local term for lesbian, has been used since the 1980s to refer to 'same-sex attraction between women and to masculine women who have women lovers' (Blackwood 2008:490). On the other hand, the term '*tomboi*', also widely used in the queer community, refers to 'gender behaviour ... [rather than] necessarily to connote sexuality' (ibid.). In an interview with a participant who is a long-standing ally of the Indonesian LGBT movement, we were told that in the past, the term '*Laki-Laki Harry Benjamin*' (man of Harry Benjamin) was also used by some community members, signalling the creative use of the American sexologist's name to label a transgender-man-related disposition before it is called as such. Indeed, it is necessary to acknowledge how '*tomboi*' (and other masculine female identities) are understood and inhabited in multiple ways by various subjects. For example, older butches saw themselves as 'possessing a male soul in a woman's body' (Wieringa quoted from Blackwood 2009:456), and *tombois* understood themselves as men while performing masculinities differently in different times and spaces (ibid.; Blackwood 2010).

At this juncture, the category 'transgender' was less likely to have had circulated in the Indonesian queer community.

Since the late 1990s, lesbian activists, especially in big cities like Jakarta, began to receive funding from international organizations, as well as engaging in discourses on gender and sexuality from the global LGBT movement. The arrival of the term 'transgender' eventually replaced the category of *tomboi* (Blackwood 2008:497), showing the flexible characteristics of the category itself when it is redefined transnationally. Jakarta-based activists increasingly merged *tombois* into the transgender category, since the *tombois*³ saw themselves as a man or frequently thought to become a man (ibid.:495–6). In other words, lesbians, including butch lesbians,⁴ are still classified as women, while female-to-male (FTM) transgender people are not (ibid.:497; Yolandasari 2015:90).

As Barry and Reay (2010:10) write: 'Despite this emerging landscape, it is vital to avoid collapsing different forms of non-normative genders/sexualities into the transgender label, assuming that every subject experiences and feels the same embodiment and subjectivity.' In line with this argument, we are invited to 'resist transgender as a master category for all aspects of trans history'. In a similar vein, Jack Halberstam (2018a:143) proposes to carefully look at 'the surprising continuities and unpredictable discontinuities between gender variance that retains the birth body (for example, butchness) and gender variance that necessitates sex reassignment'.

While it is challenging to locate the words history precisely, researchers suggest that the label 'transgender man' (*trans laki-laki/transpria*) or '*priawan*', an amalgam of the terms '*pria*' (male) and '*wanita*' (female), has been widely used since 2010 (see Agustine, Sutrisno, and Candraningrum 2015:74). In February 2015, the first national transmen association, The Indonesian Transmen Association (*Persatuan Priawan Indonesia or PPI*), was founded to connect Indonesian transmen across the archipelago and advocate public policies that recognize the existence and needs of the transman community.

As the most recent publication from PPI would suggest, the emergence and circulation of the transman category is deeply linked to the adoption of the international framework of Sexual Orientation, Gender Identity, Gender

---

³ While used among Indonesian female with same-sex desire or lesbians (Blackwood 2008), this term has also been deployed generally to address women with masculine mannerisms regardless their sexual orientation. In the context of female with same-sex desire, 'tomboi' might proceed the other terms like 'transman'.

⁴ In Indonesia, they are often called '*butchie*' or '*butch*'. 'Butch' is different from 'tomboi', as the latter is specifically used in lesbian relationship to address female with masculine mannerisms.

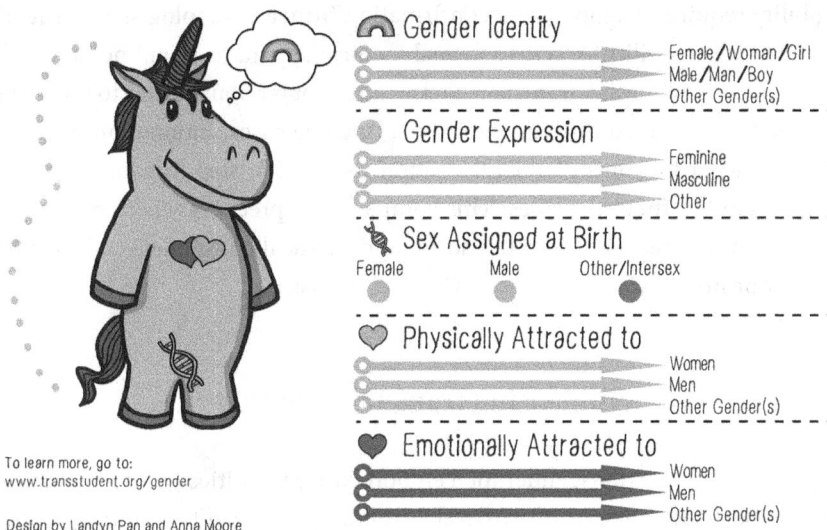

Figure 1 *The Gender Unicorn is used regularly by queer activists to show SOGIESC. 2015, Trans Student Educational Resources under Creative Commons License.*

(Source: https://transstudent.org/gender/)

Expression, and Sexual Characteristics (SOGIESC) (ibid.). Having been adopted by Indonesian queer activists since the mid-2010s (Wijaya 2020:183), this concept enables the split of these four gender/sexuality components.

It subsequently allowed subjects to embrace 'transman' as a 'gender identity' while simultaneously disconnecting themselves from the presumption of same-sexual orientation that often equates 'masculine female/women with gender variance' with lesbian identity. Following such conceptualization, it is now possible to be a transman who harbours sexual attraction towards men. Meanwhile, the term 'butch' is now considered a form of gender expression, since butch women still see themselves as women. This repositioning of butch might be read as both continuities and discontinuities of female masculinity variance, especially among women with same-sex desire or lesbians, in the Indonesian context. At the time of writing, the SOGIESC framework has been increasingly disseminated by queer activists to fellow activists across the country.

Central to trans identity is the idea of 'transition'. Medical transition, particularly gender-confirmation surgery and hormonal therapy, is not the only means to achieve this recognition. Frequently, the medical and legal transition eligibility requires diagnoses and confirmation from a psychologist, and equally, the financial capability. Access to formal medical apparatus might not always be accessible for Indonesian transmen. Some individuals obtain access to hormones informally through community networks. In some cases, Indonesian transmen prioritize what they term 'social transition' as the first step to gain acceptance from society for their identities. This complexity is precisely where performing masculinities is necessary and has social and political consequences, leading to whether or not they are identified as 'proper' transmen.

Inhabiting transman identity

To understand how transgender men embody their identities is to recognize 'the connections between the micro-level of bodies, personalities, and emotional experience and the macro-level of cultures, institutions, and societies' (Connell quoted in Ferree 2018:15). In this context, discussions of trans bodies and subjectivities depart from the language of identity itself. Halberstam (2018b:9) positions language as 'a shifting ecosystem', referring to how labels and categories also conjure new possibilities and subjectivities. Equally importantly, they may be inhabited differently by different individuals. Some transmen might take up '*butchie*' or '*tomboi*' identity before embracing 'transman' identity, although their masculine feelings and subjectivities might not always be fully captured by those non-transman labels.

Our participants, Hakan, Ophie and Zefan, already felt 'different' since their childhood. Growing up, they preferred masculine expressions. At around four years old, Zefan chose the role of 'father' when he played a 'family roleplay' with his elder sister. At a roughly similar age, Ophie also began to feel like a 'boy', wished to be treated like one and asked to wear male outfits instead of the female ones. Recounting his experience, Zefan asserted that his transman friends also took up the male role when playing with dolls when they were still children, conveying that non-normative gender expressions/identities existed since birth. However, as the term, 'transman' did not exist during that period and people were not yet familiar with gender diversity, some of them, in this case, Ophie and Hakan, had to settle with the term '*tomboi*' that was often attached to them by people around them. It is no surprise that they did not feel comfortable with that kind of treatment. For instance, in his youth, Hakan knew that the '*tomboi*' label was commonly used to signify a particular gender identity, that is a woman (with masculine expressions). Instead, Hakan felt that he had always been a man who is attracted to women, seeing this attraction as something 'normal'. Hakan also believed that it would be wrong if he fell in love with a man, since it would position him as a homosexual. Looking back at this experience, he admitted that such view was homophobic. Similarly, Ophie also felt uncomfortable when he was initially labelled as 'butch' or '*tomboi*': 'But, at that time, I didn't know what the right label was [for my subjectivity]. Once I knew there is the transman identity, I felt "fit in". Zefan and another participant, Wahyu, found the transman identity through social media, where they discovered information about transman communities and events. From this encounter, they finally found the right label to describe their selfhood after inhabiting a non-transman identity for some time.

Inhabiting the transman identity, however, did not stop their struggles. This is where the importance of 'transitioning' process lies. According to most participants, generally, there are two types of transitioning – medical and social. While both seem like two distinct aspects, the relationship between the two can be more complicated in practice. To start, Wahyu believes that social transition is more important and more difficult than the medical one in this context. To him, the social transition is a lifetime journey to gain social acceptance. As a transman who was transitioning socially, Wahyu argued that people around him are also simultaneously transitioning side-by-side with the trans person. Similarly, coming out to his mother as a transman, Hakan admitted how his mother was also 'transitioning' to understand and accept him fully as a man. He continued, 'Although we have lived together for around twenty years, she knew the outer and the inner side of me, but she still does not fully understand my feelings. Thank God, she accepts me the way I am.' Central to these accounts is the queerly ordinary, in which immediate communities are queerly touched by new experiences and encounters with trans people that might offer new gender perspectives beyond traditional gender norms. Developed by Andre Cavalcante, the queerly ordinary approach proposed the middle ground between queer theory's anti-normativity stance and the lived experience of queer subjects, 'challeng[ing] the queer/normal binary, blurring the boundaries between the two' (Cavalcante 2018:176). Critical with the social norms, in the anti-normative vein, queer theory inadvertently constructs an ideal queer subject that is always aware of and thus consistently resist sociocultural norms (Puar 2017a:24). Yet looking at a 'lived queerness' (ibid.:176) rather than an abstract theorization, the queerly ordinary approach shares a commitment to locate queerness in everyday life, opening up ways of inhabiting normative spaces while simultaneously queering it.

Although social transitioning is essential, some informants also saw how some aspects of medical transition might help them go through social transition. For instance, Ophie and Zefan underwent some aspects of medical transition – in this context, hormonal therapy – to ease the social-transitioning process. In a similar vein, Ophie shared a similar view that coming out as a transman is not always adequate to make people respect his identity and won't absolve people from identifying him (as a female person). Furthermore, he expressed that having a bigger body and a more masculine-sounding voice would boost his confidence with his transman identity, and people would be more likely to respect his identity. Hakan, who has not undergone medical transition, admitted that such transition would help him become like a 'real' man according to his own perception. With this kind of approach, he constantly educated himself that becoming a man must not always embody stereotypical masculine expressions, for example, a man must not always have a beard.

While the above accounts perhaps show how some transmen feel the need to have a male body as part of identity affirmation, it does not mean that they don't critically assess their preference of masculinity. Even, as stipulated in Hakan's and Ophie's account, the ways they attempt to define and inhabit male bodies show the multiple means of attaching masculine meanings to particular bodily aspects, from body size and deeper voice, and rejecting some others, such as Hakan's self-reflective attempt to dislodge the centrality of a beard to masculinity.

After highlighting the critical role of medical transition for social acceptance, Hakan admitted that he still needs to deconstruct his thoughts on masculinity that might perpetuate traditional gender stereotypes. Wahyu and Zefan also shared similar observations. Both criticized forms of the 'toxic masculinity' they saw in the community, which sustained the competition among transmen to reach the ideal male body, and equally, the sexist treatment towards cisgender women (discussed in more detail later).

Notably, the decision of whether or not to do a medical transition also intersects with the person's aspiration in life. Working as a civil servant in the public health sector, Wahyu aspired to build a career there. Most of his colleagues were female and did not understand trans identity. This situation was where his negotiation played a critical role. When his colleagues identified him as a 'tomboi', Wahyu did not see it as an issue. He did not want to force his identity upon his colleagues, and consequently, he accepts and strategically navigates the workplace without confrontation. Positioning social acceptance as a critical factor that would help him succeed in his career, Wahyu did not want to undergo a medical transition at the time of writing. He argued that nowadays, medical transitioning is easier when you have money. To him, social and family acceptance is more challenging and a long journey for trans people. All the above accounts demonstrate the agency of the transgender men through the diverse ways of inhabiting transman identities.

Attaching value to masculinity

Parallel to the multiple ways that transmen embody their identities is how they imbue meanings and values to masculinities. Here, masculinities are not merely a gender performance that aligns with transman identity. Instead, these masculine expressions are also performed to give oneself a particular 'value' in the immediate community to gain acceptance. The ability of transman individuals to express masculinities and their identities is entangled with access to economic resources. It can work on two levels. First, performing well at the workplace and being willing to compromise or accept labels like '*tomboi*' are a means to secure economic independence. Second, being financially independent can help provide a sense of security to express transman identities and reduce the risk of being disowned by family. To illustrate, the following accounts aim to signal transmasculinities' relational character, particularly on how they intersect with paid work and economic value.

As a government civil servant in the public health sector, Wahyu was responsible for health-related campaigns in his office. Since most of his colleagues were middle-aged women, Wahyu strategically positioned and used his masculinity to take over some 'heavy' tasks, like hanging posters along the streets, nailing posters on the wall or moving hospital beds. His colleagues often called him '*adek bujang*' – a local term for 'little brother' at the workplace. In the interview, Wahyu made it clear that he did not come out as a transman to his colleagues, and this decision was shaped by his aspiration to build a long-lasting career in the sector where he worked. Consequently, his colleagues often still addressed him as '*tomboi*', recognizing how his masculinity was attached to a 'female' body. Believing that such conduct was not fair to him, Wahyu, however, tried to understand and strategically navigate it. He remarked that maybe there would always be uncomfortable words for him, but he must negotiate with them. For him, these people are in the process (of understanding him), while he is also in the process (of understanding himself). As previously explained, the trope of 'side-by-side transitioning' is rehearsed here to highlight the effects of transmen's presence in their immediate communities.

While uncomfortable with the '*tomboi*' or 'strong woman' (*cewek gagah*) label, Wahyu was not angry. Instead, he continued to perform well at work, wanting people to recognize his capabilities instead of his non-normative gender expressions/identities. Working in a female-dominated workplace, Wahyu placed a 'productive value' on masculinity, elucidating the advantages of masculinity that might increase social acceptance and an individual's value in specific settings despite their non-normative identity.

Wahyu's masculinities worked in two ways. On the one hand, he became someone who was relied upon by his colleagues. On the other, his colleagues in turn accepted his non-normative gender expressions. For instance, when his departmental colleagues decided to design and wear office uniforms that took the form of long dresses, surprisingly, they decided not to make Wahyu do the same. According to Wahyu, one of his colleagues remarked, 'Why don't we just give Wahyu the clothing material? Not everyone wants to wear a long dress.' Wahyu was touched by this, revealing how his masculinity was recognized, and equally, accepted by his colleague.

Social acceptance gained through good work performance is not entirely new in the cultural politics of queer Indonesians. Gay and trans Indonesians also practise similar strategies (see Boellstorff 2007; Hegarty 2017b). In brief, through the idea of '*prestasi*' (achievement), gay individuals and transwomen attempt to show their productivity and contributions to society to reduce the negative stigma attached to queer identities (ibid.). In Wahyu's account above, his gender identity, along with his excellent performance, leveraged his supposed-to-be marginalized status to a respectable one in the workplace.

Equally importantly, the productive value flowing from masculinities should not obscure the relationship between economic capital and the freedom to express masculinities. A pertinent example comes from Zefan who had started medical transition through hormonal therapy and now lived alone in Yogyakarta, the same city with his grandmother and uncle in Yogyakarta. Living far from his parents, Zefan did not tell his parents about his trans identity in the early phase of transitioning. As a Christian, his coming-out episode to his parents was facilitated by his pastor, who told his parents that Zefan was a transgender man. Nevertheless, it seemed that he was not too worried about what his parents and family would say about his identity. When we asked him how he expressed masculinities at home vis-à-vis in public space, Zefan did not particularly see any differences. He said that his parents once asked him why his voice changed when he visited his hometown during the Christmas holiday, but he did not face explicit stigma from his grandmother. She did not problematize even his clearly visible tattooed hands. In the Indonesian contexts, while being tattooed is not an exclusively male domain, it is often still perceived as 'a masculine domain that draws on ideals of rebellion and naughtiness as part of its appeal' (Hegarty 2017a:136). Zefan continued, 'I am independent economically … I no longer rely on my parents.' It can be inferred that economic independence potentially allows him to express his transmasculinities openly and, to live independently. Put differently, economic resources can provide a buffer when unexpected things occur, such as being disowned by one's family and kicked-out of the family home. During our discussion, Zefan eventually stated that he does not care about what his parents and big family say about him, since he is already independent economically.

This is not to suggest that Zefan did not suffer from economic discrimination. In the past, he was rejected by several institutions just because of his transman identity. In one case, his employment was cancelled a day before his official start day. However, his current employer and some co-workers all know that he is a transman, while treating him daily as a 'cisgender man'. This is because having undergone physical transitioning, during a job interview, he must explain why his appearance – i.e. having a beard and a bass voice – is different from his personal/identity documents which still identify himself as 'female'. Such 'discrepancy' could hinder transmen from getting accepted into formal employment or would put pressure on them to wear 'female' dress to obtain the job.

While economic independence can serve as a buffer for trans subjects, it is also critical to acknowledge that not all transmen can easily access such economic independence. Moreover, when a transman can access employment, he might strategically navigate his masculinity to the point that he capitalizes on such masculinity to gain acceptance and respect, as demonstrated by Wahyu's experience.

Based on the accounts above, the sociological analysis of gender must incorporate a situated approach that considers the meanings and values transmen give to their masculinities in particular situations. Agency to challenge social norms potentially intersects with other aspects, including economic independence (cf. Messerschmidt and Messner 2018:45; Schilt 2018:67–8).

Evaluating masculine performances

While highlighting transmen's agency in navigating everyday life, most trans and non-trans ally interviewees articulated the asymmetrical understanding of masculinity's fluidity across the community. Using the popular term 'toxic masculinity', they revealed how some transmen in both online and offline circles often embrace and portray prevailing masculine stereotypes to prove their male identity by objectifying cisgender women through, for example, making sexist jokes[5] and 'using' women for sex. However, these practices should not be simply perceived as an 'individualized' problem detached from existing dominant sociocultural norms. Without any intention to generalize, in public discourse, normative masculinity (or cisgender masculinity) is often mediated through 'hypermasculinity'. Pam Nilan (2009) observes that popular media plays a crucial role in promoting hypermasculinity as the ideal aspiration for men. In this context, hypermasculinity is mediated through the images of bearded devout Muslims, criminal or gang members, and secular, cool, yet sensitive figures (ibid.:328–9); these images signal masculinity to be expressed through 'physical strength, cunning, bravery, sex drive, and aggression' (ibid.:329). These images are indeed not exhaustive; yet they have become aspirations for men that influence the societal view on masculinity (ibid.). In other words, masculinity is a set of ideals demanding to be achieved and enacted in daily life, although it seems that none can truly achieve them.

Norms pertaining to masculinity clearly affect transmen's lives. Legal, medical and social acceptance usually requires transmen to perform masculine expressions that align with societal expectations of being a proper 'man'. Stef M. Shuster (2021) shows how medical apparatus granted access to surgical and hormonal interventions when the trans patients expressed their gender identity closely aligned with traditional gender norms. This observation demonstrates the roles of inhabiting traditional gender norms in enabling trans people to be accepted as 'proper' subjects. The following is our interlocutors' experiences and strategies in inhabiting multiple forms of masculinities and challenging what they call 'toxic masculinity'.

When he started identifying as a transman, Zefan still had long hair and was challenged by his trans peers, 'How come a transman keeps his hair long?' A similar response from peers was also addressed to Wahyu, who loved

---

[5] According to the discussion with the participants, the sexist jokes revolved around the objectification of cisgender women, including deliberately using women for sex and sorting women into the stereotypical category of virgin (*perawan*) and widow (*janda*) as a basis to choose them for sex.

getting body treatments, which is culturally considered as a 'feminine' activity. Nevertheless, Wahyu himself did not see it as detrimental to his trans identity. In countering such accusations, which are shaped by the prevailing gender norms, Wahyu argued that body treatment was his specific way to enjoy 'me-time' and equally, to look after his own body. Through this perspective, not only did Wahyu attach a particular meaning to, and disassociate a self-care activity from a gendered stereotype, but he also highlighted that transman's masculinities are contingent, and equally, plural. In their lived experiences, transmen might follow some aspects of cis-normative masculinities, while rejecting the others. What makes it 'queer' is the multiple masculinities that might emerge from such combinations and permutations of masculine aspects in a trans body. As such, masculinities are not prescribed as universal norms that must be followed by all transgender men. Both transman's and cisgender men's masculinities, Wahyu asserted, are supposed to be strongly related to each person's self-understanding. Putting it differently, a common wish amongst our interlocutors seems to be that transmen could perform masculinities that they feel comfortable with instead of following the masculine norms in their society.

Intriguingly, while both Zefan and Wahyu were comfortable enough with their selfhood, they also voiced their concerns about the ways that many transmen they know attempt to follow traditional masculine gender norms to gain social acceptance as a 'proper man'. Such compliance may have something to do with the risks of rejection and denial faced by transmen that potentially structure their feelings. Echoing this sentiment, Ophie wrote to us saying that cisgender heterosexual men have an excessive pride in their sense of self that is difficult (for transmen) to imitate.

In some online transman community groups, most of the participants also recognized the 'competition' among the members to embody this 'ideal' masculine self. A *Facebook* group of transmen, for instance, often became a site for its members to show the progress of their 'physical' transitioning. Having been asked many times about access to hormones, and the process he had undergone, by some members, Zefan admitted that he was uncomfortable with those questions. He continued to say that not only were such questions invasive, but they could also trigger 'gender dysphoria' in him since they seemed to strive for an ideal masculine body and selfhood. Equally concerning are the other forms of 'toxic masculinity' expressions verbally and visually circulated on social media outlets. Both Wahyu and Zefan witnessed that in a transman only *Whatsapp* group, some members not only distributed photos showing the progress of their muscle growth and beards but also incited discussions around drugs to increase sexual energy and performance (*obat kuat*) and have multiple irresponsible romantic relationships with women (*mainin/mempermainkan perempuan*). Most of the participants used the term 'toxic masculinity', as a way to not only signal their familiarity with this concept, but also to show their agency in distancing themselves from particular aspects of traditional masculinity norms deemed patriarchal, while claiming the others perceived as less antagonistic to gender equality.

Understanding the pivotal role of societal gender norms in shaping transmen's structures of feeling and gender performance avoids blaming transmen when they imitate those toxic masculine expressions. One of the allies, Renate, argued that in the past, the tendency to adopt toxic masculinity might be driven by the need to comply with the existing regulations for legal and medical transition. In the past, to change sex/gender identity (*jenis kelamin*) on identity cards, one had to obtain approvals or testimonies from medical and psychological sources affirming their current identity and showing proof that they had lived as a woman/man according to societal norms. Adherence to the prevailing social norms became an entry to gain eligibility for identity recognition. Furthermore, from our interlocutors' experiences, the risk of being rejected as a 'proper' transman pressured them into embodying normative masculinity. Here, while recognizing transmen's agency in navigating social norms, it is also critical to acknowledge that in some contexts individuals cannot always entirely resist prevailing structures.

Since most of our interlocutors have participated in the Indonesian LGBT movements, they saw the practical values of the SOGIESC framework to disrupt adherence to toxic masculinity. The split between 'gender identity' and 'gender expression' enables the possibility that 'one's actions do not or should not always determine one's identity' (Wijaya 2020:189). For instance, it is now possible for 'a person [to] identify as a woman but have more masculine mannerisms' (ibid.:188). With this understanding, Zefan, Hakan and Wahyu might have conveniently navigated the societal pressure to adopt normative masculinities, since their trans identities did not need to be stabilized through compliance with those norms. Nevertheless, Renate highlighted that not all transmen across Indonesia could access the SOGIESC information due to uneven access to technology, among other reasons. This 'asymmetrical information' (ibid.: 201) prompted activists 'to reach out to fellow activists and other stakeholders and sensitize them with SOGIE[SC]' (ibid.).

The adoption of SOGIESC has helped to inaugurate new understandings and possibilities of embodying gender and sexual identities in the way that a transman identity (an inner sense of selfhood) must not always be fully aligned with normative masculine norms. Our interlocutors see their masculinities as more situated and fluid. Hakan saw that 'transman' is an identity that merges masculinity and femininity together in one body, while Wahyu was not afraid that having body treatment would reduce or increase his perceived level of femininity or masculinity. Lastly, Zefan said he did not have to follow cismale gender expressions in order to be treated as a 'man'.

Conclusion

This chapter does not aim to offer a generalized account of transmen's lived masculinities in Indonesia. Instead, it attempts to open conversations about the subjectivities, agency and strategic resilience of trans communities without simply perpetuating the oppressed vis-à-vis empowered binary, and equally, the binary of normative vis-à-vis subversive queer subjectivity (see Cavalcante 2018; Savci 2021; Tang 2017). A more situated and grounded exploration of the trans lived experiences is essential to properly understand how such individuals inhabit their identities while simultaneously navigating everyday life. Put differently, our interlocutors show: 'the ordinariness in queerness, and queerness in ordinariness' (Cavalcante 2018:176), through which they dwell in normative and ordinary lives while at the same time 'queering' them. Equally importantly, we want to show that trans feelings and experiences are valid to guide all of us to understand their lives. By recognizing such validity, we would like trans individuals to be able to confidently embrace their selfhood and identity – what is popularly known as 'coming in' in the Indonesian context – and perceive the multiple ways of being transgender.

We have identified three implications from this research. First, rather than seeing masculinity as a singular and fixed disposition, it is more pertinent to see it as a contingent and relational expression inseparable from the social settings. Specific time, place, the people we interact with and our aspirations may shape how we enact our gender expressions (see, among others, Abelson 2019; Messerschmidt and Messner 2018). This type of understanding might help us avoid the easy conflation between masculinity and superiority. Second, multiple subjectivities under the umbrella term of 'transmen' may help to situate gender expressions and relations in a wide variety of social contexts. Thus, it is necessary to be conscious of, and attend to, both similarities and differences across Indonesia's transmen subjects. Third, without dismissing the existing heteronormative system, we wish to show that agency and resilience can be exercised in quotidian practices.

This chapter does not interrogate the relationship between religiosity and trans identities (see, among others, Kuggle 2013; Rodriguez 2019) or between trans identities and material life (i.e. economy and labour) in great detail (see, for example, Hegarty 2017b). We acknowledge this study's limitation, thus inviting other scholars and activists to continue this exploration on the relational and situated characteristics of masculinities.

Acknowledgements

The authors would like to thank Ingrid Irawati Atmosukarto for introducing us to this project, and also to all our interlocutors: Wahyu, Ophie, Hakan, Zefan, Renate, Ryu and Frida.

Bibliography

Abelson, M. J. (2019) *Men in Place: Trans Masculinity, Race, and Sexuality in America*. Minnesota: Minnesota University Press.

Agustine, S., Sutrisno, E.L. and Candraningrum, D. (2015) Diri, Tubuh, dan Relasi Kajian atas Transgender FTM (*Female to Male*) di Jakarta [Selves, Bodies, and Relations: A Study of Female-to-Male Transgenders in Jakarta]. *Jurnal Perempuan [The Indonesian Feminist Journal]*, 20(4), 48–74.

Blackwood, E. (2008) Transnational Discourses and Circuits of Queer Knowledge in Indonesia. *GLQ: A Journal of Lesbian and Gay Studies*, 14(4), 481–507.

Blackwood, E. (2009) Trans Identities and Contingent Masculinities: Being Tombois in Everyday Practice. *Feminist Studies*, 35(3), 454–80.

Blackwood, E. (2010) *Falling into the Lesbi World: Desire and Difference in Indonesia*. Honolulu: University of Hawaii Press.

Boellstorff, T. (2005) *The Gay Archipelago: Sexuality and Nation in Indonesia*. Princeton: Princeton University Press.

Boellstorff, T. (2007) *A Coincidence of Desires: Anthropology, Queer Studies, Indonesia*. Durham and London: Duke University Press.

Connell, R. (2005) *Masculinities* (2nd ed.). Berkeley and Los Angeles: University of California Press.

Cavalcante, A. (2018) *Struggling for Ordinary: Media and Transgender Belonging in Everyday Life*. New York: New York University Press.

Davies, S.G. (2015) Surveilling Sexuality in Indonesia, in L.R. Bennett and S.G. Davies, (eds.), *Sex and Sexualities in Contemporary Indonesia*, 29–50. London and New York: Routledge.

Ferree, M. M. (2018) 'Theories Don't Grow on Trees': Contextualising Gender Knowledge, in J.W. Messerschmidt, P.Y. Martin, M.A. Messner and R. Connell (eds.), *Gender Reckonings*, 13–34. New York: New York University Press.

Halberstam, J. (2018a) *Female Masculinity*. 20th anniversary edn. Durham and London: Duke University Press.

Halberstam, J. (2018b) *Trans*: A Quick and Quirky Account of Gender Variability*. Oakland: University of California Press.

Hegarty, B. (2017a) 'No Nation of Experts': Kustom Tattooing and the Middle-Class Body in Post-Authoritarian Indonesia'. *The Asia Pacific Journal of Anthropology*, 18(2), 135–48

Hegarty, B. (2017b) The Value of Transgender: *Waria* Affective Labor of Transnational Media Markets in Indonesia. *TSQ: Transgender Studies Quarterly*, 4(1), 78–95

Kugle, S. S. (2013) *Living Out Islam: Voices of Gay, Lesbian, and Transgender Muslims*. New York: New York University Press.

Listiorini, D. (2020) Online Hate Speech. *Inside Indonesia*, 26 January.

Messerschmidt, J. and Messner, M.A. (2018) Hegemonic, Nonhegemonic, and 'New' Masculinities, in J.W. Messerschmidt, P.Y. Martin, M.A. Messner and R. Connell (eds.), *Gender Reckonings*, 35–56. New York: New York University Press.

Messerschmidt, J. et al. (2018) Introduction: The Editors, in J.W. Messerschmidt, P.Y. Martin, M.A. Messner, R. Connell (eds.), *Gender Reckonings*, 1–12. New York: New York University Press.

Nilan, P. (2009) Contemporary Masculinities and Young Men in Indonesia. *Indonesia and the Malay World*, 37(109), 327–44.

Paramaditha, I. (2018) Q! Film Festival as Cultural Activism: Strategic Cinephilia and the Expansion of a Queer Counterpublic. *Visual Anthropology*, 31(1–2), 74–92.

Puar, J.K. (2017a) *Terrorist Assemblages: Homonationalism in Queer Times—Tenth Anniversary Expanded Edition*. Durham and London: Duke University Press.

Puar, J.K. (2017b) *The Right to Maim*. Durham and London: Duke University Press.

Reay, B. (2020) *Trans America: A Counter-History*. Cambridge: Polity Press.

Robinson, K. (2015) Masculinity, Sexuality, and Islam, in L.R. Bennett and S.G. Davies (eds.), *Sex and Sexualities in Contemporary Indonesia*, 51–68. London and New York: Routledge.

Rodriguez, D.G. (2019) The Muslim *Waria* of Yogyakarta: Finding Agency within Submission. *TSQ: Transgender Studies Quarterly*, 6(3), 368–85.

Savci, E. (2021) *Queer in Translation: Sexual Politics under Neoliberal Islam*. Durham and London: Duke University Press.

Schilt, K. (2018) From Object to Subject: Situating Transgender Lives in Sociology, in J.W. Messerschmidt, P.Y. Martin, M.A. Messner, R. Connell (eds.), *Gender Reckonings*, 57–70. New York: New York University Press.

Shuster, S.M. (2021) *Trans Medicine: The Emergence and Practice of Treating Gender (forthcoming)*. New York: New York University Press.

Skidmore, E. (2017) *True Sex: The Lives of Trans Men at the Turn of the 20th Century*. New York: New York University Press.

Suryakusuma, J.I. (1996) The State and Sexuality in New Order Indonesia, in L.J. Sears (eds.), *Fantasising the Feminine in Indonesia*, 92–119. Durham and London: Duke University Press.

Tang, S. (2017) *Postcolonial Lesbian Identities in Singapore: Re-thinking Global Sexualities*. London: Routledge.

Wichelen, S. (2010) *Religion, Politics, and Gender in Indonesia: Disputing the Muslim Body*. Oxon: Routledge.

Wieringa, S. (2019) Is the Recent Wave of Homophobia in Indonesia Unexpected?, in G. Fealy and R. Ricci (eds.), *Contentious Belonging: The Place of Minorities in Indonesia*, 113–32. Singapore: ISEAS Publishing.

Wijaya, H.Y. (2020) *Intimate Assemblages: The Politics of Queer Identities and Sexualities in Indonesia*. Singapore: Palgrave Macmillan.

Wijaya, H. Y. and Davies, S.G. (2019) The Unfulfilled Promise of Democracy: Lesbian and Gay Activism and Indonesia, in T. Dibley and M. Ford (eds.), *Activists in Transition: Progressive Politics in Democratic Indonesia*, 153–70. Ithaca: Cornell University Press.

Yolandasari, A.R. (2015) Penyebab atau Penyembuh? Kekerasan Seksual terhadap Lesbian, Biseksual, dan Transgender *Female-to-Male* di Indonesia [Cause or Remedy? Sexual Violence against Lesbians, Bisexual, and Female-to-Male Transgenders in Indonesia]. *Jurnal Perempuan [The Indonesian Feminist Journal]*, 20(4), 86–96.

Yulius, H. (2017) 'Moral Panic and the Reinvention of LGBT. *Indonesia at Melbourne*, 17 May.

6

'It's the touch that is doing the talking': UK sex clubs, dark rooms and the loss of masculinity

Chris Haywood

Introduction

Globally, sex clubs have emerged as an increasingly visible aspect of people's recreational sexuality. In the UK alone, it is said that over one million people have visited a sex club in the last year (Green 2020). Sex clubs have traditionally been perceived as 'Swinger' or 'Swap' clubs: clubs that cater for communities that advocate Consensual Non-Monogamy in heterosexual relationships (CNM). However, somewhat ironically, this representation of sex clubs (hetero) normalizes the diversity of predilections and practices that take place in clubs. Sex clubs offer a range of sexual appeals, for example Greedy Girls, BDSM, Black Cock Fan Clubs, Fet Nights, Young Guns and mums, TV and TG admirers, BBW's and Curvy Girls and Bi Nights. These are not clubs that employ sex workers, nor are they lap dancing clubs or 'strip clubs'. Rather, these are clubs run with the primary purpose of facilitating consensual sex, primarily between anonymous likeminded people. It is argued that the increasing visibility of sex clubs in the UK, from around twenty-three in 2001 to over forty-three in 2020 (Haywood 2022) connects with the growth of a 'neo-liberal disposition in which our sex life is supposed to raise our self-esteem' (Kaplan 2020:219). In short, sexual pleasure/leisure is becoming infused with self-regulation and entrepreneurial sexual citizenship that is underpinned by a neoliberal ethic of sexual choice and responsibility (Haywood 2018a). I argue that this intricate relationship between sexual consumption and commodification is both reinforcing and problematizing traditional gendered heterosexual relationships and the corresponding patriarchal power relations that are often embedded within them. More specifically, this chapter argues that an interplay between spaces within the sex club, namely the 'dark room', and formations of alternative erotic subjectivities that exceed the limits of masculinity and heterosexuality have the potential to dislodge and unsettle patriarchy.

Existing work on men and masculinities suggests that heterosexual competence is central to men's articulation of patriarchal power. More specifically, as Stick and Fetner (2020:4) argue, 'Sexual behavior is central to the construction of masculinity, with masculinity effectuated through the control of women's bodies in intercourse and sexual conquest' (Bird 1996; Grazian 2007; Hyde et al. 2009). Furthermore, it is argued that men incorporate the tropes of traditional heterosexual masculinities, such as sex as conquest (Hollway 1989; Hunter 2010), the sexual objectification of women (Calogero and Tylka 2014; Seabrook et al. 2018) and homophobia (Diefendorf and Bridges 2020; Moss 2001) into developing forms of sexual recreation. Other research on masculinity and heterosexuality suggests that there is a shifting relationship between them, which, in turn, may be destabilizing the key components of patriarchy. For example, Hamlall's (2018) discussion of young Black men in South Africa points to a more complex picture of young men negotiating their masculinities in romantic and heterosexual relationships that are based on 'mutual respect and monogamy'. In effect, men's heterosexual masculinities are 'reflective of a broader set of understandings that could not be reduced simply to gender oppression, patriarchal dominance, and reinforcing hegemonic masculine values' (Hamlall 2018:317). Similarly, Scoats's (2020) research on threesomes suggests that there is more willingness among young men to engage in same-sex practices as part of Male/Male/Female threesomes. In this instance, Scoats attributes the expanded boundaries of heterosexuality to a collapse in the one-time rule of homosexuality, which sees a disconnection of masculinity from homophobia (see also Branfman et al. 2018). While the seemingly progressive nature of masculinities appears to be problematizing the heterosexual structures that hold patriarchy in place, it has been suggested that the diversity of men's sexual practices may be a means to reinforce patriarchy. For example, Reynolds (2015) highlights how men seeking to have sex with men reinforce their heterosexual masculinity by seeking 'buds' and 'no homos'. Such language, it is argued, is 'directly linked to heterosexuality and androcentric discourses of hypermasculinity' (ibid.:220). While the above approaches have much to offer in exploring the (im)possibilities of post-patriarchy, they depend upon understanding men's gendered and sexual selves through the concept of 'masculinity'. As a result, this chapter argues that we need to consider how in some instances, a patriarchal masculinity is an inadequate term to understand and explain men's gendered and sexual subjectivities. More specifically it is argued that there are ways of being a man that are not dependant on a patriarchal framing.

The chapter critically explores patriarchal masculinity by reporting on a research project that explores high risk sex in hard-to-reach places. Too often the theoretical, analytical and often political responsibility of understanding patriarchy has been through an examining of women's experiences. While such work is pivotal, this chapter firmly shifts this focus on men, to make their role in high-risk sex central. There are limits on focusing on men, but it does so in order to make visible men's responsibility and role in risky sexual practices in heterosexual contexts. Furthermore, current concerns about sexual health tend to focus on recreational sex between men (MSM) (Hess et al. 2017; Pérez, Santamaria and Operario 2018). There is very little research that explores older heterosexual men and their contribution to high rates of sexual infections. The project explored in this chapter initially began by exploring high-risk sex in heterosexual sex clubs by conducting interviews with twelve men recruited from online sex club forums. The interviews, conducted over the phone, not only enabled the researcher to employ ethics protocols such as informed consent, but it also supported men's self-disclosure. After obtaining full institutional ethical approval, the interviews were supplemented by thirty-five episodic on-site covert ethnographies involving eighteen sex clubs in the UK. Episodic ethnographies refer to a short, time-limited immersion into the cultural worlds of participants (Adler 2019). Sex clubs market themselves on their discreteness and anonymity offered to patrons within the club. The covert nature of the ethnographies was not only necessary to secure access to the club, but it also interestingly supported the anonymous and the non-intrusive ethos cultivated by clubs and their participants (see Haywood 2022 for a fuller discussion of the ethical challenges). Importantly, the names, identities and geographical locations have been adjusted in this chapter to protect the clubs and participants.

The ethnographies also presented specific challenges to the researcher that not only involved developing strategies to remember and recall encounters, but also because their body became subject to the voyeuristic gaze of men and women in the clubs. Wood (2021:737) usefully highlights that 'not only do we take up space and use our bodies in the field in particular ways, but the very nature of our bodies shapes the ways in which the research site is experienced by the researcher and the research relationships that are developed in the field'. As a result, the ethical responsibility to the participants in the research brought into focus the ethical responsibility of the ethnographer to themselves. Often wearing nothing more than a towel, and on occasion having to remove that, the ethnographic practice was very much concerned with being unintrusive. These ethnographic experiences combined with the interview data employed thematic analysis to unpack men's experiences (Braun and Clarke 2006). The remainder of this chapter explores the resulting analysis on how dark rooms disrupt masculinities by problematizing sexual competence as a performance and second, on how dark rooms enable men to go beyond their heterosexual masculinities and experience a post-patriarchal or more specifically a post-masculine erotic subjectivity. First, the chapter provides a short summary of sex clubs and the dark room.

Sex clubs in the UK

Although sex clubs have a strong online presence, it is difficult to physically find them in England. They can be found in rural locations on the edges of suburbia, situated on industrial estates, or sometimes on the backstreets of run-down estates. Housed in factory units, renovated pubs or reclaimed retail premises, their presence is often underplayed via discreet signage or obscure entrances. Beyond the initial reception (where you pay) and the social area (where you drink), sex clubs offer a number of 'playrooms' where sex takes place. For example, there are dry spaces, such as the couple's room, the dungeon, the mirrored room, the glory hole room, the cinema room or the schoolroom. These rooms often mimic classic 'pornscapes' with highly theatrical and grandiose interior designs; generally black-painted MDF boards or black plastic mattresses with red and purple velour drapes. One of the overriding features of the 'playrooms' is their strong visual dynamic, with observer windows, two-way mirrors, viewing booths, peepholes and open doors. In some rooms, chairs, chaise lounges and couches surround play areas, for others to watch and/ or extend the sexual activity. Importantly, this architecture of visual pleasure contributes to an economy of desire, with women (single or within a couple), black bodies, young bodies and toned bodies being ascribed sexual capital. Green's (2014) notion of the sexual field captures the ways that a collective set of values and judgements are in place which promote an economy of desire. Green argues that 'structures of desire eroticize and assign value to certain bodies, affects, and practices while rending others neuter or undesirable' (28). The club ethos, its marketing and promotion, its formal rules, and patrons, collectively assign sexual capital to particular bodies, creating status hierarchies. Those bodies with erotic capital often have the power of selection, choosing who joins them, and who chooses them to join in sexual play. Men and women secure erotic capital through racially inflected heteronormative assumptions of women as sexually insatiable, Black men as hypersexual, men with toned bodies as sexually vigorous and younger men as sexually resilient (able to have orgasms in quick succession).

One of my first encounters in a club involved watching a woman having sex with three men. Although I was intrigued by how she demanded each man to give her the kind of sex that she wanted, it was the attending queue of men waiting to be selected to pleasure her, and the criteria of selection, that were revealing: 'I'm looking for young black cocks, you fat old bastards can get out.' Within the formal rules of the all the clubs visited, women's control in all sexual encounters takes precedence. This is often enforced through regular visits to rooms from security personnel, through CCTV and a policing by club-goers themselves. However, although consent is formalized in the club, we must be careful not to assume what women's pleasure and consent is experienced and lived out. Although there is little research on how sex clubs facilitate and shape women (or men's) sexual encounters, there is work on women who are involved in NCM. For example, Bentzen and Træen (2014) highlight how women were often the ones who have the authority to reject or accept approaches from other men and women in clubs. However, Wolkomir (2020) suggests that in the context of soft swing activities, women appeared to engage in activities that appeared to be driven by men's fantasies, such as women's same sex activities and use of sex toys. However, in hard swap situations women advocated their sexual liberation and rights to sexual pleasure. In response, Wolkomir suggests that women are simply re-enacting a masculine sexuality. One of the most interesting accounts of women's engagement in NCM is Wagner's (2009) autoethnography that documents her engagement in sexual encounters as a process of re-negotiating her own femininity. Rather than presenting NCM encounters as a negative or positive experience, Wagner documents the difficulties of trying to leave behind societal expectations that insist on understanding of women's sexuality as passive. Such research reminds us that when discussing men's experiences of the dark room, we should not conflate men's understanding of consent, pleasure and erotic diversity, with those of women, trans communities and a range of other club goers.

There is one space in the clubs where sexual acuity has little purchase and erotic hierarchies break down. This is the dark room. Often located at the back of the club, in a cellar or in the attic, dark rooms tend to be disconnected from the visual rhythms of a club. It should be added that not all dark rooms are the same. Some have sophisticated mazes where the doors close in on themselves and you are unable to go back through; others are simply a room with no lighting, whereas in others you might find glory holes with bars as walls. Fundamentally, the dark room is different from other rooms in the club as through the use of darkness, it suspends visual cues and the informal rules and responsibilities of sexual engagement that predominate in the club. Richters (2007:287) succinctly points out that, in relation to the dark rooms in gay clubs, 'The darkroom is a world of sensation, of touch, smell, taste. Its ideals and values and, crucially, its interactional rules, are different from those of the visible world'. In a similar way, Bersani (2002) uses the concept of social personality to capture how anonymity works in the context of the gay bathhouse:

> The gay bathhouse is especially favorable to ideal cruising because, in addition to the opportunity anonymous sex offers its practitioners of shedding much of the personality that individuates them psychologically, the common bathhouse uniform – a towel – communicates very little (although there are of ways of wearing a towel ...) about our social personality (economic privilege, class status, taste, and so on).
>
> (28)

For Bersani, the gay bathhouse enables the relinquishing of identity through the loss of clothes, suggesting that the gay bathhouse is a space where the self is left behind. This means that naked bodies offer little information about 'social personalities' such as 'economic privilege, class status, taste, and so on' (ibid.). Payne (2014) argues that Bersani's account is limited as bodies that mingle involve more complex forms of subjectification that are not simply based on the 'shedding' of social personalities. In many ways, Payne is correct, in that the loss of clothing does not simply mean the collapse of hierarchies; instead, the absence of clothing results in the emergence of new economies of the body. In the sex club, new economies of the erotic circulate around the length and girth of the penis, body shape, breast size, age, height, piercings and tattoos. However, this chapter argues that dark rooms in sex clubs have the potential to have a transformative effect on men and their masculinities; dark rooms are spaces where men engage in processes where masculinity, both as a descriptive and as an analytical concept, has little purchase.

Beyond masculinity and heterosexual performance

As indicated above, much work on men and sexual practices tends to frame men's (hetero)sexuality as predatory and driven by the need for the sexual conquest of women in order to consolidate their masculinity. Importantly, homosocial environments 'compel' men to demonstrate their heterosexual competence in order to prove their masculinities (Sweeney 2014). More recently, such competence has been articulated through performance. Montemurro and Riehman-Murphy (2019) suggest that 'as cultural scenarios shift to focus more on performance than accomplishment of the act of sex itself, boy's/men's focus may be less on who initiated first sexual experiences and more on their skill'. This resonates with observations in the sex club, where the emphasis tends to be on men being asked by other men and women to demonstrate their sexual skill, for example through relentless fucking, enabling women to orgasm and squirt, and cuckolding and humiliating other men. James explains what sexual skill looks like:

> In the main playrooms in clubs, the erotic side isn't there for me, apart from in the dark room area. You will be getting in a room, one of the main playrooms, where a guy is attempting to be a stud and showing off how good he could be, and couples that go and just want to be with a stud.

For James, a stud is someone who can control their orgasms under direction from women or a couple. What is interesting is that couples use the stud for their own sexual satisfaction; a similar point is made by Adam:

> You get the scenarios: 'Right, OK. I want to just stick it in and hang on in there as long as you can, and I'll tell you when you come out and then I want you to cum on my tits'. It might be a quick experience, and quite often in a swingers' club, it can be that way. But quite often I found that women want that, they don't want a guy to last for a long while. If a woman is wanting multiple guys, then she wants on with one, then off with that one, and on with the new one, and that's the way I've seen it. But I haven't seen it in dark rooms, I also haven't seen someone fucking for ages, because it's been a question of a touching and feeling, fucking without worrying, 'does this look good?'

The description of encounters in the main playroom resonates with visual representations that are akin to conventional pornographic tropes. In many ways, sexual skill in the main playrooms tends to be closely connected to the performance of masculinity. However, Adam points to erotic experiences in the dark room that move away from a skill-based performance. During interviews, men suggested that the dark rooms facilitated an erotic space liberated from the pressures and expectations of heterosexual masculinities. For these men the dark room produced a different kind of erotic experience. As David points out:

> No, I just, I think that performance just goes out the window. I think it will have been there, yeah, in the rest of the club, but in the dark room everything just goes out the window. You can't hide in the dark room. And if it doesn't happen, it doesn't happen, if you can't perform you can't perform, it's not the end of the world. Does that make sense?

There is an interesting juxtaposition here with how performance and conventional heterosexual masculinity, in spaces that are designed to maximize being seen, operate as a form of hiding. In contrast, darkness becomes revelatory where the truth of desire becomes visible and not hidden away behind a performance. This suggests that men feel that they can be their true selves in the dark room as there is no pretence. Even though sexual encounters take place in shadows, the feeling of it being 'real' means that the context produces an experience that is felt and understood, in their view, as raw and unfettered. Thus, the dark room enables a particular configuration of masculine subjectivity that is not bound to the 'rules of masculinity' present in the rest of the club.

An interesting theme emerging here is that as heterosexual masculinity becomes less connected to cultural imperatives that locate masculinities within patriarchal structures, structures that operate through gendered bodies and aesthetics, men appeal to different forms of gendered subjectivity. Existing work suggests that when men 'lose' their masculinity, they are often unable to demonstrate their maleness as a result of their helplessness, vulnerability, lack of control, physical ability and lack of emotional management; examples include wounded soldiers (Hoyt et al. 2011), medical interventions (Zaider et al. 2012) or sexual assault (Mathews et al. 2018). In essence, loss is often framed because of injury, where a lack of masculinity results in anxiety, fear and depression. The dark room provides an alternative reading of loss: the perceived loss of masculinity becomes a productive, liberating experience. Thus, it is argued that the possibility of the post-patriarchal can be found not in a new liberated progressive masculinity or a feminist-focused masculinity, but rather in the spaces where masculinity becomes undone and rendered incomprehensible. Furthermore, connected with this loss of identity is also a loss of control and managing the socio-sexual scenario. Existing research on gay and lesbian dark rooms suggests that gender and sexuality operate in particular ways. Hammers (2009) talks about how different kinds of sex club encourage both bounded and non-bounded sex. In gay bathhouses sexual practices are presented as bounded, anonymous and focused. For example, Sowell's (1998) discussion of gay men's use of sex clubs points out that men don't talk until after they have finished having sex. They suggest that because of this there is a distinction between sex and intimacy, with talking being understood as producing intimate encounters. Hammers suggests that this contrasts with the lesbian bathhouse, where sexual interaction is verbalized and more socially focused.

The dark room in the heterosexually focused sex club combines both features. While in the dark room there is a lack of socializing, this is not cold transactional sex. In many ways the dark room is treated as a bounded and closed space of anonymity and unknowability. However, rather than creating a transactional sexual encounter, it produces the build-up of a charged erotic intensity. As in the case of dogging, the silent and non-verbal nature of the interaction does not lend itself to cold, calculated sex (Haywood 2018b); rather it adds to the erotic experience of the encounter. As James suggests, not talking adds to the excitement and the intensity embedded in a theme of not knowing:

> I think it's … nine times out of – I mean, people just don't speak there and that's part of the thrill, they just don't speak. Which I quite – I quite like that, you just … You know, like it's … Yeah, because when you don't speak, you don't whether it's a man or a woman … which is what it's all about, you know. But … yeah, so you just … You know, for me to switch the lights out, it's so much more fun.

Ricco (2002:7) suggests that individuals, as bodies-of-desire, forfeit their individual subjective selves as they are reconstituted as parts of a collective assemblage, in which personal identities are exchanged for anonymous positions within a multiplicity of desiring bodies. Or, as Todd Reeser (2017) has argued, by combining masculinity and affect, we can open up the possibilities of masculinity and even gender itself in a transformative manner. More specifically, the process of the 'discharge of emotion' 'temporarily decomposes or composes masculinity' (Reeser and Reeser 2017:111). Importantly, the letting go of a heterosexual masculinity is embedded in the erotic discharge. The implication here is that the dark room provides the *mise en scène* for the disruption of men's gendered subjectivities. As Canham (2009:91) suggests, 'Control is a central aspect of the Western hegemonic masculinity script'. However, as masculinities become redundant in the dark room, the gendered relationships and attendant relations of power become problematized:

> I think naturally the blood pumps through your body a lot quicker so you are much more turned on. I think it's a known, I think you can literally feel the veins pumping because you just don't know, you know, and you do not know whether it's a guy who's got your cock in his mouth or if it's a woman.

It is argued that the absence of knowing and the lack of control begin to reconfigure how we make sense of men's gendered and sexual subjectivities. For example, Holmes et al. (2017), in the context of the glory hole, argue that faceless sex encounters occur between bodily rather than through identities that have depth. Holmes et al. suggest that with a lack of identities, there is also a lack of shame or intolerance. Instead, we need to think about the role of 'surfaces, intensities, and flows' (ibid.:181) as ways of understanding gendered and sexual subjectivities. In this sense, bodies become meaningful according to the context in which they are assembled through their relationships with other bodies, the architecture of the space and the lack of visibility. In the sex club, darkness enables men to explore a form of erotic subjectivity that is not bounded by the cultural norms of heterosexuality and masculinity.

Post-masculinity eroticism

In the previous sections it was argued that the dark room enables men to explore a gendered and sexual subjectivity that is not governed by the cultural scripts associated with masculinity. This section argues that the dark room, because of the lack of social and cultural codes of masculinity and its attendant heterosexual identifications, enables men to engage in an alternative, erotic subjectivity. As a result, this chapter explores what men's erotic subjectivity means in the dark room. Below, David highlights that he sees himself as a very visual person, but that the dark room facilitates a sexual desire that stands outside potential forms of objectification:

> David: It's a sort of place that's different for me because I'm a very visual
>   person ... I see someone that's attractive and that sort of thing ... sights and
>   seeing are a massive thing for me so the dark rooms are different. It's like
>   stuff happens in your mind for a different reason.
> Chris: So that's really interesting, isn't it? Because you said that you're really
>   visual and I get that. So how is the dark room different?

David: I think it's just the not knowing or your mind sort of runs away with who it might be or it could be anybody wanting anything, doing anything. I think it's that, that goes through your mind, that runs away with it for me.

Here the mind becomes personified, running towards erotic limits that in many ways become a form of defensiveness within the interview, to take up an alternative way of engaging with desire. In this way, the dark room enables men to differently organize a sense of their sexual self that becomes immersed in a gendered and sexual liminality. Taylor (2013) talks about how subjectivity is itself a form of self-relation, a mechanism through which individuals make themselves and gain the status of a subject, creating the possibility of liberation. This, however, is different from subjective freedom, as the normative rules and laws that enable a liberated subject to remain in place. In response, she argues for 'desubjectifying' (where desubjectification entails constituting, understanding and relating to oneself in ways other than as a subject)' (ibid.:89) and instead suggests the need for a 'disobedient self-relation characterized by refusal, curiosity, and innovation – a desubjectifying mode of self-relation' (ibid.:94). Desubjectifying oneself is a form of being which recreates a different kind of relationship that one has with oneself. Thus, the dark room is a space of empowerment where the conventions of patriarchal or even post-patriarchal identifications become unfastened from everyday subjectivities. The unknown possibilities of the dark room enable men to relinquish the everyday strategies that are employed to make manhood and instead immerse themselves into circuits of desire that circumvent heteronormative narratives that configure men and their desires. Gavin explains what this might look like:

But the dark room leaves a totally different experience. When you're just sort of in somewhere and you can't see anything but then someone's hand just brushes you in an erotic area, and your dick is going up or whatever then it can be a tingle, an electric shock like you don't get at other times, and I know that I have been to one or two gangbangs, and to be honest, I can't raise a smile these days because it's so mechanical. You know it's not ... it isn't a buzz anymore, and nowadays, it tends to be that these things are not ... they're not spontaneous exciting things, they are an organized thing and the woman that's doing it is not getting anything out of it. And in the dark room, it's a mind game for both of you in that you think that she really, really wants you for you in the back your mind, and she is there, just sort of thinking, I'm just having a wet dream.

Here Gavin demonstrates how the dark room can open up the fluidity of desire, with him transcending traditional positioning as the subject of desire and as a result exceeding the limits of masculinity. In short, in the dark room, men imagine fucking women, other men and themselves. They introject the female, male and homosexual 'Other' as their subjectivity, oscillating between and thus beyond, being the subject and object in the erotic encounter. This is where the self gets lost, replaced or reinforced; Gavin suggests that it is more of a dreamlike scenario. Some might argue that single men are simply acting out an intensified predatory opportunist heterosexuality. However, there is also a sense that the experience of the dark room is similar to gay cruising, in that it 'resists moralities and norms prescribed by heterosexuality, by performing multiple forms of sexual pleasure with multiple, often unknown partners' (Gove 2000:2).

In the dark room, it is argued that the heterosexual masculinities circulating around the sex club unravel as the 'individualizing, interiorizing, subjectifying and objectifying forms and functions of "desire", "sex" and "sexuality"' (Siisiäinen 2018:39) become disaggregated. In this context, 'masculinity' offers little currency as a means of self-identification or performance. Rather, according to Ricco (2002:10) the dark room is a place for 'exile and escape': when freed from visuality, dark rooms join 'desiring bodies with desiring bodies'. He goes on, 'One is attracted to the dark to the extent that one cannot be put in one's place there' (ibid.). It is suggested that in the process of desubjectification, how the erotic is experienced thus becomes delimited. For example, Graham talks about the first time that he experienced a different way of being sexual:

> It was the first time I experienced it and I just basically went with the flow and it was ... I discovered that there was a guy on one side of me, there was a lady on the other side of me and it was just, it was just everyone, you know, it just happened I suppose. And I think you go with it. So one minute you've got a woman there and she's on top of you and then next, someone's basically got your balls in their mouth, and you don't know whether it's a man or a woman and that's just, that was electric. It's absolutely electric. And then basically, I suppose, having a situation where a few people are, basically have got your cock in their mouth, and I think you know when it's a guy, it's more physical. And there's a lot of women and it was just a lot of kissing and it didn't matter whose nipples, whether it was women or whether it was ... it was just, it was very wet and very .... At one point I had hold of a guy's cock and I had my fingers inside of a woman, and I knew that they were kissing over the top of me and it was just ... and then we ended up the three of us just like wrapped in each other, literally

wrapped in each other. And it was quite fabulous, honestly it was, and I was in there for about an hour and I came out, I was completely drained when I came out, you know.

It appears that Graham is explaining a dark room encounter that operates beyond the normative desires that are embedded in heterosexual masculinity. Instead, intense and fluid identifications and affects constitute a desubjectified being that operates counter-discursively. Graham uses the term 'electric' to capture an experience that appears to exceed popular sexual discourses, suggesting the possibility of an anti-phallocentric erotic current. While it is important not to suggest that there is no gendering and sexualization taking place in the dark room, rather it is almost as if they become points of departure. For example, men's same-sex experiences in the dark room are not configured through identities. Instead, same-sex encounters become a means through which to engage with an alternative, post-masculinity experience that stands outside of gay identifications.

Conclusion

It is important not to simplistically see sex clubs as places that offer men and women empowerment and liberation from existing gender and sexual hierarchies. There is much evidence to suggest that sex club cultures operate through the valorization of particular sexual femininities and masculinities. However, this chapter argues that there are spaces in the sex club that challenge and problematize men's conventional heterosexual masculinities, to the point where it no longer makes sense to perform them. In the process of leaving behind their heterosexual masculinities, men may experience new forms of intimacy. The eroticization embedded in the 'lack' of masculinity points to new circuits of desire that create an anxious and exciting unknowability. Almost thirty years ago, Silverman (1992:37) suggested that men could not tolerate the eroticization of the lack 'without calling into question their identification with a masculine position'. However, rather than resorting to a form of female masochism, it is argued here that the eroticization of lack can fall outside of a conventional binary gendering. The conventions and codified rituals that often scopically enable and reinforce patriarchal power are less available for men (and women) to draw upon to navigate relationships. If the visual operates as a mechanism that facilitates the deployment of cultural narratives of patriarchy, then the dark room disrupts conventional modes of patriarchal power. This is not to say that there could be moments where patriarchal masculinities may indeed reassert themselves because of the lack of social convention. And this is exactly the point. In the dark room, the dynamics of masculinity have to be asserted, have to be reinforced in order to be possible; they are not there by default. As a result, in the dark room, we get fleeting glimpses of a possibility of an alternative, erotic gendered subjectivity that not only problematizes heterosexual masculinities but also has the potential to exceed patriarchal, if not post-patriarchal masculinities.

Not only is there a form of safety in the dark room for the men (and women) who visit it, but also a feeling of safety when theoretically and conceptually making sense of their experiences. In other words, what is the theoretical narrative of masculinity away from the dark room and outside of the heterotopic space of the sex club? In response, patriarchy demands a precarious masculinity, constituted through an ever-present anxious pursuit of assembling a self that is aligned with hegemonic sexual, gendered and cultural imaginaries. Thus, contemporary masculinity has an identificatory architecture that is haunted by its own fragility. Given that precarity constitutes the identificatory architecture of masculinity, we need to think about the spaces that facilitate a stabilizing, consolidating and recuperating masculine status. It is argued that the dark room temporarily disrupts this structure of identification. Therefore, the emergent post-patriarchal masculine subjectivity is not simply a result of non-oppressive men, men's allyship or men's feminist activism; these are incredibly important and valuable interventions that enable the cluttering of patriarchal power. Rather, there will be encounters and moments outside of the darkroom that rupture the conventional architecture of men's identifications and in turn dissipate the articulation of patriarchal power. Such places may not be ones that we might not find through simply looking or hearing, but may, like the dark room, be encounters and moments, that affectively speak to us through touch.

Bibliography

Adler, G. (2019) *Empathy beyond US Borders: The Challenges of Transnational Civic Engagement.* Cambridge: Cambridge University Press.

Bentzen, A. S. and Træen, B. (2014) Swinging in Norway in the Context of Sexual Health. *Sexuality & Culture*, 18(1), 132–48.

Bersani, L. (2002) Sociability and Cruising. *Australian and New Zealand Journal of Art*, 3(1), 11–31.

Bird, S.R. (1996) Welcome to the Men's Club: Homosociality and the Maintenance of Hegemonic Masculinity. *Gender & Society*, 10(2), 120–32.

Branfman, J., Stiritz, S. and Anderson, E. (2018) Relaxing the Straight Male Anus: Decreasing Homohysteria around Anal Eroticism. *Sexualities*, 21(1–2), 109–27.

Braun, V. and Clarke, V. (2006) Using Thematic Analysis in Psychology. *Qualitative Research in Psychology*, 3(2), 77–101.

Brook, H. (2015) Bros before Ho(mo)s: Hollywood Bromance and the Limits of Heterodoxy. *Men and Masculinities*, 18(2), 249–66.

Calogero, R. M. and Tylka, T. L. (2014) Sanctioning Resistance to Sexual Objectification: An Integrative System Justification Perspective. *Journal of Social Issues*, 70(4), 763–78.

Canham, S. L. (2009) The Interaction of Masculinity and Control and Its Impact on the Experience of Suffering for an Older Man. *Journal of Aging Studies*, 23(2), 90–6.

Diefendorf, S. and Bridges, T. (2020) On the Enduring Relationship between Masculinity and Homophobia. *Sexualities*, 23(7), 1264–84.

Fulcher, K., Shumka, L., Roth, E. and Lachowsky, N. (2019) Pleasure, Risk Perception and Consent among Group Sex Party Attendees in a Small Canadian Urban Centre. *Culture, Health & Sexuality*, 21(6), 650–65.

Gove, B. (2000) *Cruising Culture: Promiscuity, Desire and American Gay Literature*. Edinburgh: Edinburgh University Press.

Grazian, D. (2007) The Girl Hunt: Urban Nightlife and the Performance of Masculinity as Collective Activity. *Symbolic Interaction*, 30(2), 221–43.

Green, T. (2020) *Swingers*. Channel 4 Nineteen11.Ltd.

Green, A. I. (2014) The Sexual Fields Framework, in A. I. Green (ed.), *Sexual Fields: Toward a Sociology of Collective Sexual Life*, 25–56. Chicago.

Hamlall, V. (2018) Heterosexual Relationships among Young Black Men in the Construction of Masculinity at a South African University. *Social Dynamics*, 44(2), 306–21.

Hammers, C. (2009) Space, Agency, and the Transfiguring of Lesbian/Queer Desire. *Journal of Homosexuality*, 56(6), 757–85.

Haywood, C. (2018a) *Men, Masculinity and Contemporary Dating*. New York City: Springer.

Haywood, C. (2018b) 'Leaving Masculinity at the Car Door': Dogging, De-Subjectification and the Pursuit of Pleasure. *Sexualities*, 21(4), 587–604.

Haywood, C. (2022) *Sex Clubs: Recreational Sex, Fantasies and Cultures of Desire*. London: Palgrave.

Hess, K. L., Crepaz, N., Rose, C., Purcell, D. and Paz-Bailey, G. (2017) Trends in Sexual Behavior among Men Who Have Sex with Men (MSM) in High-Income Countries, 1990–2013: A Systematic Review. *AIDS and Behavior*, 21(10), 2811–34.

Hollway, W. (1989) *Subjectivity in Method and Psychology*. London: Sage.

Holmes, D., O'Byrne, P. and Murray, S. J. (2017) Faceless Sex, in Holmes, D., Murray, S. J., and Foth, T. (eds.), *Radical Sex between Men: Assembling Desiring-Machines*, 177–90. Oxford: Routledge.

Hoyt, T., Klosterman Rielage, J. and Williams, L. F. (2011) Military Sexual Trauma in Men: A Review of Reported Rates. *Journal of Trauma & Dissociation*, 12(3), 244–60.

Hunter, M. (2010) *Love in the Time of Aids. Inequality, Gender and Rights in South Africa*. Indianapolis: Indiana University Press.

Hyde, A., Drennan, J., Howlett, E. and Brady, D. (2009) Young Men's Vulnerability in Constituting Hegemonic Masculinity in Sexual Relations. *American Journal of Men's Health*, 3(3), 238–51.

Kaplan, D. (2011) Sexual Liberation and the Creative Class in Israel, in S. Seidman, N. Fisher and C. Meeks (eds.), *Introducing the New Sexuality Studies*, 357–63. London: Routledge.

Kaplan, D. (2020) The Atmospheres of Sex Work. *Sexuality and Gender at Home: Experience, Politics, Transgression*, 1, 216.

Knight, K. (2016) '*These Political Games Ruin Our Lives': Indonesia's LGBT Community under Threat*'. Human Rights Watch: New York 10 August. Available at: https://www.hrw.org/report/2016/08/10/these-political-games-ruin-our-lives/indonesias-lgbt-community-under-threat (accessed 16 February 2022).

Montemurro, B. and Riehman-Murphy, C. (2019) Ready and Waiting: Heterosexual Men's Decision-Making Narratives in Initiation of Sexual Intimacy. *Men and Masculinities*, 22(5), 872–92.

Moss, D. (2001) On Hating in the First Person Plural: Thinking Psychoanalytically about Racism, Homophobia, and Misogyny. *Journal of the American Psychoanalytic Association*, 49(4), 1315–34.

Payne, R. (2014) Frictionless Sharing and Digital Promiscuity. *Communication and Critical/Cultural Studies*, 11(2), 85–102.

Pérez, A., Santamaria, E. K. and Operario, D. (2018) A Systematic Review of Behavioral Interventions to Reduce Condomless Sex and Increase HIV Testing for Latino MSM. *Journal of Immigrant and Minority Health*, 20(5), 1261–76.

Reeser, T. and Reeser, T. W. (2017) Theorizing the Masculinity of Affect, in J.M. Armengol, M.B. Vilarrubias, À Carabí and T. Requena (eds.), *Masculinities and Literary Studies: Intersections and New Directions*, (Vol. 22), 109–119. Oxford: Taylor & Francis.

Reynolds, C. (2015) 'I Am Super Straight and I Prefer You Be Too' Constructions of Heterosexual Masculinity in Online Personal Ads for 'Straight' Men Seeking Sex with Men. *Journal of Communication Inquiry*, 39(3), 213–31.

Ricco, J. P. (2002) *The Logic of the Lure*. Chicago: University of Chicago Press.

Richters, J. (2007) Through a Hole in a Wall: Setting and Interaction in Sex-on-Premises Venues. *Sexualities*, 10(3), 275–97.

Scoats, R. (2020) *Understanding Threesomes: Gender, Sex, and Consensual Non-Monogamy*. Oxford: Routledge.

Seabrook, R. C., Ward, L. M. and Giaccardi, S. (2018) Why Is Fraternity Membership a Associated with Sexual Assault? Exploring the Roles of Conformity to Masculine Norms, Pressure to Uphold Masculinity, and Objectification of Women. *Psychology of Men & Masculinity*, 19(1), 3–13.

Silverman, K. (1992) *Male Subjectivity at the Margins*. New York and London: Routledge.

Siisiäinen, L. (2018) *Foucault, Biopolitics and Resistance*. Oxford: Routledge.

Sowell, R. L. (1998) It Isn't Over until It Is Over. *Journal of the Association of Nurses in AIDS Care*, 9(1), 11–14.

Stick, M., and Fetner, T. (2020) Feminist Men and Sexual Behavior: Analyses of Men's Sex with Women. *Men and Masculinities*, 24(5), 780–801.

Sweeney, B. N. (2014) Masculine Status, Sexual Performance, and the Sexual Stigmatization of Women. *Symbolic Interaction*, 37(3), 369–90.

Taylor, D. (2013) Resisting the Subject: A Feminist-Foucauldian Approach to Countering Sexual Violence. *Foucault Studies*, 16, 88–103.

Wagner, B. (2009) Becoming a Sexual Being: Overcoming Constraints on Female Sexuality. *Sexualities*, 12(3), 289–311.

Wolkomir, M. (2020) Swingers and Polyamorists: A Comparative Analysis of Gendered Power Dynamics. *Sexualities*, 23(7), 1060–79.

Wood, N. (2021) Bodies in the Field: Methodological Reflections on Tai Chi and Pregnancy in an Ethnographic Study at a Chinese Community Centre in the North West of England. *Qualitative Research*, 21(5), 736–49.

Worthington, B. (2005) Sex and Shunting: Contrasting Aspects of Serious Leisure within the Tourism Industry. *Tourist Studies*, 5(3), 225–46.

Zaider, T., Manne, S., Nelson, C., Mulhall, J. and Kissane, D. (2012) Loss of Masculine Identity, Marital Affection, and Sexual Bother in Men with Localized Prostate Cancer. *The Journal of Sexual Medicine*, 9(10), 2724–32.

7

Misogyny, fear or boundary maintenance? Responses to brand activism on gender diversity amongst players of Magic: The Gathering

Ceri Oeppen

Introduction

The trading card game Magic: The Gathering is now over twenty-five years old and played by at least thirty-five million people worldwide; in its 'paper' form, and as an e-sport. Most visible players, including the vast majority of competitive pro players, are cisgender men, but the player-base is becoming more diverse, and more women play the game at home with friends or online, even if this is not reflected in attendance at public competitive events (Rosewater 2015).[1] The company that makes Magic, Wizards of the Coast (WotC) has an understandable commercial interest in increasing player diversity, and thus, their market. In recent years, they have made efforts to promote diversity in the lore, characters and artwork of the game, by expressly including autistic, trans, non-binary and non-white[2] characters, whilst also altering the representation of many women characters: a shift from the kinds of gendered tropes often seen in video and fantasy games, e.g. 'the sexy sidekick', 'the harlot' or the 'damsel in distress' (cf. Shaw 2015; Trammell 2018) – to strong practically dressed women, coded as agents rather than subjects. Head Designer at WotC, Mark Rosewater,

---

[1] A precise gender breakdown is not available, at least partly because of the variety of different ways Magic is played. Head Designer of Magic, Mark Rosewater, claims their market research indicates between 25 and 38 pre cent of players are women.

[2] Magic has always included non-white characters, but those characters are increasingly being given more prominent roles. For example, the way the African-American coded Kaya is placed at the forefront of marketing material for the 2021 Magic set release *Kaldheim* (https://youtu.be/DmSpD4VINNs, accessed 25 February 2021).

has described this design choice as a mechanism to enable resonant reactions in a wider customer base (Rosewater 2019a). Concurrently, efforts have been made to include more women and non-binary players in the coverage of competitive play.

Based on participant observation in online and offline Magic-player community discussions and playing spaces between 2016 and 2020, as well as my reading of online texts produced by WotC staff, I discuss some of the effects of these top-down[3] efforts to promote gender diversity.[4] My offline participant observation is necessarily shaped by my experiences as a competitively orientated Magic-player, and as a white cisgender woman, playing primarily in the south-east of the UK, and some events further afield (e.g. in Europe). My online participant observation has also been solely focused on English-medium social media (Twitter, Facebook, Reddit, Twitch and YouTube). While many Magic-players have welcomed WotC's top-down actions on diversity and claim to not care as long as the mechanics of the game remain, I have also observed a discursive backlash (from within and outside the subculture) by those who perceive this as unnecessary 'virtue signalling', or worse, as 'Social Justice Warriors' pushing (gender) politics into 'their' game and 'their' spaces.

While Magic is a social game with its own associated material objects and opportunities for consumption, creating its own 'manufactured subculture' (Dayan 1986), it exists alongside, and interacts with, a range of related online and offline communities. As a result, my analysis will inevitably engage with intersecting areas of academic literature – on gaming more generally, online communities, fandoms or 'geek culture(s)', 'trolling', the 'manosphere' and of course, feminism, masculinities and patriarchal hierarchies. I build on existing work that identifies 'geek masculinities' as an alternative to hegemonic masculinities (Connell 2001; Redman, Mac and Ghaill 1996; N. Taylor and Voorhees 2018), and e-sports as an alternative form of masculine sporting competition (T. L. Taylor 2012). I also draw on literature from marketing about 'brand activism', as well as potential backlash against such efforts, in order to place WotC's actions in a wider consumer capitalism context.

---

[3]	There have also been multiple 'bottom-up' efforts to encourage a broader range of people to play Magic (e.g. the player-led initiatives Planeswalkers for Diversity and The Lady Planeswalker Society) but here my focus is on efforts from WotC in relation to game design and international organized competitive play.

[4]	I focus on women as a minority group of Magic players, because as a woman player, that is the minority experience I am most familiar with. Much of what I say about wider community responses to women players and content creators could potentially be extrapolated to any Magic players who are not cis heterosexual able-bodied white men; likely with more extreme effects when intersectionality is considered.

I start by discussing a subset of the masculinities literature: focusing on 'geek masculinities'. I discuss the cultural significance of Magic and explore the brand activism of WotC in relation to gender diversity and explore some of the community response to those top-down efforts to create cultural change. I conclude by arguing that responses from players to a real (or perceived) increase in gender diversity is a form of 'boundary maintenance' (Graham 2019) or 'territory protection', informed by fear and misogyny (Manne 2017) held by those shaped by a key aspect of geek hegemonic masculinity: a gendered perception of intellectual/technological superiority, juxtaposed with a sense of social marginality and exclusion.

Geek masculinities

There are multiple masculinities, and expressions of masculinity, shaped by issues such as class and culture (Connell 2001). Whilst Connell indicates we should recognize certain masculinities as being hegemonic, she highlights that no particular form of masculinity is intrinsically 'fixed' as hegemonic (or subordinate), but rather should be considered a form of relational identity and thus changeable in relation to cultural norms or contexts. Key to Connell's discussion is how hegemonic masculinity exists in relation to patriarchal hierarchies of male dominance and female subordination; she argues that masculinities that 'protect' (or are assumed to protect) this hierarchy are hegemonic. The maintenance of particular hegemonic masculinities is therefore enacted through interactions with femininity and other forms of masculinity (ibid.; T. L. Taylor 2012).

The concept of relational masculinities and no fixed category of what is hegemonic is important to the case of Magic players (and others commonly labelled 'geeks'), because stereotypically they do not conform to a common image of hegemonic masculinity – often based around strength, competitive sports success and (hetero)sexuality (Redman and Mac an Ghaill 1996; T. L. Taylor 2012; Ward 2018). There is no one definition of geek, but they are often portrayed as being 'bookish' rather than sporty, with intense, niche, interests in media such as computer software, games, comics and films (Lane 2017; Massanari 2017; Salter and Blodgett 2017; Ward 2018). While it is not the case that all geeks are male, 'geek culture' is predominantly masculine (and white) (Lockhart 2015; Salter and Blodgett 2017). As Massanari (2017:332) puts it, 'to discuss geek and nerd culture is to discuss masculinity – in particular, white male masculinity'. She continues by highlighting how geek masculinity exists in relation to hegemonic masculinity, by rejecting some signifiers (sportiness, sexuality) but reifying others (knowledge and intellect) and valuing those over emotional intelligence or social interaction (Massanari 2017; see also Reagle 2016; T. L. Taylor 2012).

While the term 'geek' was once a pejorative label, it has become more of a positive self-identification, partly echoing the growing importance of computers and smart technology expertise in mainstream society (Salter and Blodgett 2017). Clearly, despite the marginality some geeks feel, knowledge and expertise also represent a form of privilege (Mendick and Francis 2012). Nevertheless, for many geeks the idea that they could be seen as relatively privileged 'may create a sense of cognitive dissonance for these individuals, who likely view themselves as perpetual outsiders' (Massanari 2017:332). Arguably, their feeling of marginality may well be related to the differences between geek masculinities and perceived hegemonic masculinity, shaped by school experiences in particular.[5] The overlaps between geek-orientated communities and 'the manosphere' suggest that relative difficulty/ease of social interactions with women might also be a self-perceived distinction between the two (Massanari 2017; Salter and Blodgett 2017).

Examining 'nerd/geek masculinity', Lockhart (2015:22) draws out the juxtaposition between a self (and exterior) perceived intellectual superiority existing alongside a feeling of unfairness that this superiority does not result in greater social or sexual success. She describes geek masculinity as 'a discourse that grows from a perception of sexual and even economic alienation, but also affirms the positive (and often framed as superior) qualities of those who practice it' (ibid.). Lockhart argues that geek masculinity – while expressed differently – shares many similarities with stereotypical hegemonic masculinity, including the reification of knowledge, career success, heterosexuality and male superiority over women; 'nerd hegemonic masculinity is hegemonic masculinity with an inferiority complex' (ibid.:140). As such, and particularly in her discussion of misogyny and transmisogyny in relation to #GamerGate, she makes a convincing case for why wider society should be concerned with the toxic elements of geek masculinity, and the angry (mostly white) young men

---

[5]   The vast majority of English-language literature on geek culture and geek masculinities is written about North American contexts where the high school tropes of 'jock' versus 'geek' have particular implications in terms of perceptions of youth development (Lane 2017), even if the separation is overstated (Muniowski 2018; T. L. Taylor 2012).

who exhibit it (Lockhart 2015). The combination of a sense of victimization combined with privilege has also been cited in discussions of masculinities in the alt-right (Boehme and Scott 2020).

Playing Magic: The Gathering, and its cultural significance

Magic was launched in the USA in 1993 and was initially envisioned as a quick-to-play portable game that would appeal to those who had time between rounds of Dungeons and Dragons at gaming conventions (Chalk 2017). It was the first-to-market of a now well-established sector of the table-top games industry: trading card games. As well as the 'paper' game played face-to-face, there are online versions, *Magic Online* and *Arena*. The material component of Magic is constantly evolving as new 'sets' of cards are released multiple times a year, adding to the card pool available to players as they build their decks. The lore of the game positions the player as a 'Planeswalker', casting spells and engaging in battles while inhabiting fictional 'planes', inspired by science fiction, fantasy and 'other' (i.e. non-American) cultures.

Organized competitions, from tournaments at local games stores, and international 'MagicFests' (large official competitions that operate somewhat like Magic fan conventions), to the professional level, including the international 'pro tour', which has operated in various guises since 1996, are the focus of competitive players. From 2018, alongside the launch of *Arena*, WotC has reinvigorated Magic's profile as an e-sport as well as a card game, and they created a Magic Pro League (MPL) of twenty-four players who received an annual income alongside any prize winnings. Nevertheless, WotC's market research suggests most Magic games are played outside of formal competition settings (Wizards Play Network 2015).

Exact player numbers and company value are not in the public domain, but an estimated 35 million people play worldwide, as well as over 3 million users on *Arena*, predominantly in the USA, Japan and Europe, but also Latin America and the Asia-Pacific region (Forster 2019; Jarvis 2020). In 1999, Hasbro bought WotC for US$325 million (Ewalt 2021) and more recently, an e-sports news website estimated that Magic made Hasbro US$500 million between January and July 2019 (Forster 2019); it is not a small endeavour. Alongside the official WotC products and web resources, Magic has generated a huge variety of associated media, both official and unofficial, creating content in the form of articles, YouTube videos, Twitch streams, and podcasts, as well as a secondary market (on eBay and sites established specifically for buying and selling Magic cards) ranging from 1 cent to just over $500,000 for a mint-condition *Alpha Black Lotus* – a card from the first set (Beer 2021). Alongside these media, there are countless Magic-specific Facebook groups, Discord servers and subreddits.

As with all 'fandoms', insider knowledge, in-jokes, and the distinction between a 'newbie' and expert shape interactions between players. Magic-related considerations such as what level of competition you play at, style of deck you prefer, format you play and whether you 'brew' your own deck list or 'net deck' (use pre-existing lists shared online), all further influence interactions between players including the creation of sub-groups within the wider magic-playing community, implicitly creating (contested) hierarchies, which also relate to the prioritization of knowledge and intellect that forms part of the expression of geek masculinities (Graham 2019; Lockhart 2015; Miltner 2014; Reagle 2016).

Part of Magic's wider cultural significance that may not be immediately apparent is its role in the development of the internet. Launching in 1993, Magic grew as a game and a gaming community alongside the shift from Usenet discussion boards (a precursor to web forums, based on the sharing of messages and files amongst a network) to 'websites' as we recognize them today, and Magic players were integral to that shift. The overlap between Magic players and early adopters of the internet for home use was significant, and internet discussion boards provided an opportunity for geographically dispersed players to find each other and discuss deck choice and strategy, such that in the mid-1990s Magic-related traffic on Usenet was third only to pornography and weather (Chalk 2017). Some of the first html-based websites were developed in response to the limitations of Usenet for sharing Magic strategy and articles. Chalk makes a convincing case for the links between the needs of Magic-playing consumers and the development of several online ideas we now take for granted, such as eBay, bitcoin and even Tinder. Magic is heavily intertwined with online culture, and its lengthy history and status in 'geek culture' means its influence goes beyond just current players and overlaps and ties into the kind of online communities that see newer users as 'newbies' at best, and worse, as 'interlopers or spoilers' of the supposed freedoms of the early days of the internet (see Miltner 2014 for a similar discussion, related to memes).

The art of Magic

Another aspect of Magic's cultural significance is its role in the evolution of 'fantasy' genre art. From the start, unlike contemporaneous fantasy games, WotC used new colour art works for each card, which in early years they bought from local artists (mainly students). Artists received limited art direction but the then WotC vice-president, Lisa Stevens, and art director Jesper Myrfors, did specify no female nudity and no 'scantily clad maidens being rescued by beefcake barbarians' clichés which, according to Chalk (2017:43), demonstrates WotC's hope that the game would be 'female-friendly'. By the early 2000s however, WotC saw a culture shift in terms of both the departure of key women employees like Stevens and the decreasing use of women artists. Some see this as an effect of the commercialism Hasbro brought to WotC, alongside attempts to develop Magic as a competitive 'mind sport' with the development of the international pro tour, which in turn gave it a more 'masculine' image (Chalk 2017; Jameson and Roman 2016). By the mid-2000s, while the WotC art style guide reminded artists of the no nudity rule, and said 'feel free to paint beautiful women, as long as they're shown kicking ass. No damsels in distress. No ridiculously exaggerated breasts', it also said 'Remember, your audience is BOYS 14 and up' (Cavotta 2005). Regarding this, Matt Cavotta, creative lead at WotC, wrote,

> I hope this is not offensive to the female Magic fans out there. Mostly, this is just to give the artists a barometer on what the majority of their audience is like. [...] *we* are definitely sensitive *to* women and how *they* may feel as players and how they are represented on cards.
>
> (Cavotta 2005, my emphasis)

His wording implicitly implies the separation of the 'we' at WotC (the creators who emphasize the male audience) 'to' women. The focus on an audience of 'boys' was reflected in the card art, particularly in relation to key narrative characters. In 2012, Mark Rosewater explained that planeswalkers were 2:1 male to female because 'planeswalkers are designed as player analogues' and the game was predominantly played by men (Rosewater 2012). He continued, 'If the game ever got to a 50/50 male/female mix we'd have a 50/50 mix of male and female planeswalkers'. This is interesting because WotC currently say they have an explicit policy of having an even gender split in card art, which they credit with increasing the number of female players (Rosewater 2019b), illustrating how issues such as gender representation can be instrumentalized in relation to changing times.

WotC's brand activism on gender diversity

In recent years, particularly since public discussions around #GamerGate, Black Lives Matter and #MeToo, WotC have made a concerted effort to (re)adjust their portrayal of gender, sexuality and ethnicity in the aesthetics and narratives of the game (e.g. in card-art, marketing visuals and storyline). This has been particularly apparent in relation to gender, where a design decision was made to have a roughly even split of men and women in card-art, as well as including some non-binary characters (Rosewater 2019b). While this may in part be due to the politics of WotC personnel, they are also a commercial company, and decisions about aesthetic direction must be taken with commercial considerations in mind. For example, some suggest new expansions referencing non-American cultures are timed to attract new geographical audiences (Jameson and Roman 2016).[6] Interpretations suggest that they either want to increase diversity because they are reflecting increasing diversity in their customer base or they want to increase their customer base by appealing to a more diverse range of people – or most likely, a combination of both.

On the official Magic website, Mark Rosewater addresses the issue indirectly while writing about 'resonance' in game design, which he describes as 'when you build a game component on top of information the audience is already familiar with' (Rosewater 2019a). Rosewater suggests that in order to create a positive experience for the player you have to resonate with them by tapping into their emotions and creativity, and by creating familiarity between the in-game world and the real world by including elements that are evocative of the players lives (ibid.). He goes on to say, '[this] is one of the reasons we've made such a push for diversity in Magic because when players see people like themselves in the game, it increases their ability to connect and bond' (ibid.). This is a related – but reverse – reasoning to his 2012 comments about the gender split of planeswalkers as analogous to the player base (see above), suggesting a shift in attitudes towards a model of portraying diversity to encourage diversity, rather than portraying a level of diversity similar to the existing player base.

This makes good commercial sense in relation to attracting new players, which from Hasbro's point of view may be more significant than representing those already committed, and points towards the potential changeability of brand activism, according to commercial priorities. Rosewater (2019a) points

---

[6] For example, the set *Ravnica* having an Eastern European 'flavour', just as WotC started publishing cards in Russian, and *Kaladesh* referencing Indian aesthetics after Hasbro identified India as an emerging market for the company.

out that learning a complex new game is a commitment of time and energy on the part of the player (customer), so it is up to game designers to ensure that those trying a new game have a positive experience and want to keep playing (ibid.); and relatedly, to buy the associated product(s). In another article later the same year, Rosewater writes more explicitly about 'why diversity matters in game design' (Rosewater 2019b). He reiterates the points about the player personally connecting and bonding with the game and highlights how that connection brings comfort too. He writes, 'as a game designer, you want to make sure that every player has the potential to see themselves in your game', and that seeing themselves in the game will increase 'their ability to form emotional bonds which makes them more likely to start playing and more likely to keep playing' (ibid.).

What is particularly interesting about this 'why diversity matters' article (Rosewater 2019b) is its structure. Rosewater makes a general comment about diversity in the leader, but in the main body of the text, the word diversity, as it might be understood by a more general audience – in terms of social identity categorizations – is not mentioned until over 1,000 words in. Before that, Rosewater instead uses the analogy of designing the game for different types of Magic consumer (e.g. those who are more or less competitive, those who play different formats) as a rhetorical device to build the overall message that diversity is good for the game. He then uses a similar analogy-based technique to justify why although some people might fear change, it is actually good for the game; he does this by comparing increased diversity in the game aesthetics and player base to innovative developments in the design of the game itself (e.g. new in-game mechanics). The method of persuasion he uses suggests that he is fully aware that not all readers will be inherently in favour of increased diversity.

Next, I provide further examples of efforts made by WotC to promote visible gender diversity through art and language, and examples of community responses, some of which might explain the carefulness of Rosewater's approach.

'Spike, Tournament Grinder'

In 2017, WotC released a new card called *Spike, Tournament Grinder*. It was the third card produced representing the main player psychographic profiles: Timmy, Johnny and Spike. WotC use the profiles to represent the different types of Magic players: 'Spike is the competitive player (...) to Spike, the thrill of Magic is the adrenalin rush of competition' (Rosewater 2013), while Johnny and Timmy are focused on other aspects of the game. Significantly, the card art for this new card – the first visual representation of competitive 'Spike' – showed a player coded as female. Sporting short, dyed hair, a t-shirt reading 'nope' and a reference to the 'banned and restricted list' in the card text, Spike not only symbolizes competitiveness, but understanding the significance of the card mechanics and aesthetic requires a good deal of insider knowledge, a key component of geek masculinities (Phillips 2018).

The card was an immediate hit with competitive women players, some changed their social media avatars to Spike, and pro-player Emma Handy wore a 'nope' t-shirt on her Twitch stream. As a competitive player myself, local magic-playing friends shared the picture with me, and I even cut my hair like Spike for an international tournament I went to shortly afterwards. Spike also coincided with an obvious effort by WotC to increase the representation of women on competitive event coverage – such as hiring Melissa deTora and Maria Bartholdi as commentators for the Minneapolis Grand Prix in 2017. This was the first time I had seen two women 'in the booth' and it was very important to me as a competitive player to feel this representation.

Spike excited intense discussion, both positive and negative, in Magic's online communities. The representation of agentic women in card art had been discussed before,[7] but it was clear that Spike was particularly dissonant to some, particularly the use of a woman to represent the most competitive psychography. Commentors posted that, if so few competitive players were women, why was Spike female (see Phillips 2018; Stein 2017, for a discussion of how such comments can also be a form of 'dog whistle' recruitment to the alt-right). Spike continues to be a discussion point and is used as an 'in-joke' representing WotC's 'woke' values on subreddits such as /r/FreeMagic (an 'alternative' subreddit created after commentor-banning's on mainstream Magic-community subreddits).

Women 'taking up space' and misogynistic responses

As a player and participant observer, what struck me about the response to Spike was the sheer volume of commentary. I was not surprised, however, as I had witnessed similar before; for example, when women are featured on tournament

---

[7]   For example, the proportion of female to male pirates in the *Ixalan* set. https://www.reddit.com/r/magicTCG/comments/6zsh8b/female_pirates_galore/ (accessed 25 February 2021).

coverage. Because visible women players are such a minority, their presence can be 'a spectacle' in Magic-playing spaces, online and offline (McKinnon-Crowley 2020). If their very presence is 'spectacular', it is not surprising that when Magic content-creators speak specifically to women's experiences of Magic they excite a disproportionate response.

Being competitive – and thus, playing in public competitions – is stereotypically coded as 'masculine', and when the game in question requires in-depth knowledge as well as skill, fits the concept of 'geek masculinities' outlined earlier. As a woman Magic player, I find it extremely frustrating when commenters in Magic-playing communities explain the fewer women than men playing competitive Magic with variations of, 'perhaps, on average, women have different goals than men when it comes to social spaces and competition'.[8] Variations of this argument are often used to justify a refusal to accept that women magic players face significant sexism or misogyny in Magic spaces, as an obstacle to competing even when commenting in response to a woman player writing about how they have faced sexism in Magic-playing spaces (e.g. Miller 2018). Whilst experimental studies do indicate women are less likely to want to enter competitions than men, they also suggest that this is not through an inherent disinterest in competition, but more likely due to issues of self-confidence (Niederle and Vesterlund 2011).

On Twitter, my own efforts to counteract perceptions that women are less competitive by highlighting two successful local women players resulted in responses from misogynist 'sock puppet' accounts who used the very argument I was trying to counter, as well as language that seems straight from an alt-right playbook to accuse WotC (the 'corporate') of becoming 'to PC' [*sic*]. To quote this exchange from 20 November 2017 in full:

> Ceri Taylor (@Ceri_MTG): 'But women just don't want to play competitive magic ... ' Apparently nobody told Harriet and Emma, who top 8'd @DiceSaloon's PPTQ y'day!'

> The Scarab God (@scarab_god): Zero people care. Less than 1 per cent of competitive players are female.

> Lilliana of the Veil (@VeilLiliana): Women are ruining Magic. B/C of the estrogen influence at corporate the cards are becoming to PC [*sic*]. How much

---

[8] A subreddit contributor discussing an article about microaggressions and sexism by Thea Miller (2018).

longer until Liliana Vess is wearing a full on hijab on a card. Women should make their OWN card game and leave the White Males alone.

The premise that women do not want to play Magic competitively because they are not interested in being competitive is a 'strawman argument' that many women players have questioned. But when they do, they are often subject to accusations of not-knowing, and overstating their case, for example, 'Is [sexism] severe enough that it warrants so much drum beating, chest thumping and article after article?'[9] The perception that there is 'article after article' about women in Magic (or, indeed, too many women in Magic art) ties into wider discussions about the visibility of women, physically, and vocally, in public spaces and discussions. Experimental studies show that both men and women overestimate the degree to which women speak in mixed-gender settings (see Cutler and Scott 1990). Studies in courtrooms suggest that women legal professionals are more likely to be interrupted than men, even when factors like speaking length are controlled for (Feldman and Gill 2019), while studies of participants in academic seminars found women presenters were more likely to be asked more questions of a 'hostile' or 'patronising' nature (Dupas et al. 2021) – phenomena which are borne out in my experience of online Magic discussions.

Overestimations and criticisms of the amount of attention given to women by WotC, and hostile responses to successful competitive women (see Estephan 2018), are just some of the misogynistic 'policing' conducted to maintain male dominance of Magic spaces, particularly competitive spaces (Manne 2017). Such actions could be seen as a 'backlash' against women's advancements in representation and competition (Faludi 1992); however, my observations are not fully captured by 'backlash', which implies a reactionary response. While there may be a 'new' response to WotC's renewed brand activism around gender diversity, responses are also representative of, and shaped by, an *ongoing* systemic suppression embedded in modern society (Rowley 2019; Tyler 2020) that maintains the subordination of women to men, through misogyny (Manne 2017).

An important question is 'why?'. Most Magic players do not perceive themselves as sexist (Miller 2018). Instead, a common response to accusations of poor treatment of women players is to blame players' social awkwardness or lack of experience interacting with women, which plays into the image of 'geeks' as socially unsuccessful. That might explain some interpersonal interactions at

---

[9]   Another contributor on the subreddit thread about Thea Miller's article, https://www.reddit.com/r/magicTCG/comments/7vysjj/death_by_a_thousand_paper_cuts/ (accessed 25 February 2021).

tournaments, but it does not explain the strength of feeling represented by the volume of discussion raised by gender-related issues. And it certainly does not explain the more extreme forms of misogyny experienced by prominent women players and content creators via trolling and other forms of harassment (see Estephan 2018).

Another possibility is that WotC's increased representation of women has been picked up by those who perceive a 'culture war' taking place between socially progressive liberals and the libertarian right, who have then stoked the flames of dissatisfaction by infiltrating and 'trolling' Magic-players' discussions. The use of 'sock puppet' accounts and deliberately inflammatory posts do suggest this is part of the picture, as does the overlap between some people and online spaces in Magic-playing communities, and the 'manosphere', #GamerGate and other alt-right networks. Indeed, the recent art direction of WotC has been picked up on by alt-right sites such as *Breitbart.com*, where they have tried to portray a 'rational' concern (see Jones et al. 2020) about 'Social Justice Warriors' who are trying to enforce 'woke politics': 'like Gamergate, it concerns ordinary people who just want to be left alone to enjoy their hobby ... playing games is not a left-wing thing or a right-wing thing but an everybody thing', wrote Delingpole (2017) for **Breitbart.com**. The suggestion of an unwelcome intrusion of politics has been echoed by those who portray themselves as more liberal too, such as the YouTuber, 'Boogie', who tweeted: 'I love this game, I always will. They've made a TON of mistakes over the past few years, one of which is to press a overly progressive narrative on its gamers. I love progression. I lean left. That's fine. But it doesn't benefit the community or the game itself to do this.'[10]

While for feminist social scientists it seems clear that without representation of diverse bodies, then 'the community' will not be an 'everybody thing', that is perhaps less obvious for those not trained to examine their own privilege (especially if they themselves feel marginalized, as geeks). This observation is reinforced by the large number of commenters in online discussions about sexism who claim to have never witnessed sexism themselves while playing Magic. For them, brand activism on gender diversity is either an unnecessary distraction about a non-issue, or, more worryingly, an unwelcome political invasion, into *their* leisure space. **Breitbart.com's** and Boogie's implication that hobbies and politics should be kept separate might well seem rational to many players, and

---

[10] Steven Williams (aka Boogie, a YouTuber with 4.25 million subscribers) in response to an ongoing debate about misogynistic bullying against Magic cosplayer Christine Sprankle in 2017. His involvement in the debate was significant as he is primarily associated with wider-reaching video games, rather than Magic.

the presentation of supposedly rational arguments based on presumed intellect and knowledge has been instrumentalized both as an expression of hegemonic masculinities and as geek masculinities (Jones et al. 2020; Reagle 2016).

Philosopher Kate Manne (2017) posits that the policing of feminine incursions into masculine spaces is key to the logics of misogyny. Arguably, a combination of Manne's understanding of misogyny, combined with Connell's (2001) conception of hegemonic masculinities, while also acknowledging the notion of 'geek masculinities' (Lockhart 2015; Massanari 2017), can go some way to explaining the 'why' of the strength of feeling towards WotC's brand activism on gender diversity; especially when we consider the nature of Magic-players as a long-established 'manufactured subculture' (Dayan 1986), that has grown up alongside the internet.

Using Faludi's (1992) analysis of an all-male military college in South Carolina that was legally obliged to start admitting female cadets, Manne (2017) examines the question of male shame, and its role in reinforcing misogyny. After discussing the way in which feminized traits of giving, caring and admiring are the 'goods and services' expected to be provided by women to men, Manne explains how female incursion into a previously all-male space disrupted this dynamic. The male cadets (and their superiors) were used to working free from a 'female gaze'; cadets did feminine-coded domestic work, they were made vulnerable by training and hazing, they comforted each other when needed, and they made ample use of derogatory sexist terminology – all of this had the potential to appear shameful when seen through (their perception of) a women's viewpoint (Faludi 2019; Manne 2017). Women cadets observing potential weaknesses in their (previously) private masculinized space could remove the rationale for men to assume their position as receivers/takers of feminine admiration and care (Manne 2017).

While military cadets might be an example of traditional hegemonic masculinity, a similar process could be taking place in Magic-playing spaces, with the additional consideration that these predominantly male Magic players have created spaces, linguistically and materially, that reify aspects of geek hegemonic masculinity – the masculine-coded 'goods' of knowledge and expertise. If a woman enters that space to, literally or virtually, 'compete' for those 'goods', then according to Manne (2017), this can ferment misogynist aggression. This might be further complicated by Magic-players' previous experiences of marginalization from other more-hegemonically masculine spaces. Responding to cases of bullying, pro player Brian Braun-Duin tweeted, 'The Magic community is a haven for people who were bullied or excluded from other groups. How can we then turn around and harass or exclude other members of our community the same way many of us once were?'.[11] While Braun-Duin maturely recognizes the risk of repeating previous abuse, not all victims of bullying have reached his point of security and confidence, or his position as a successful pro player, and may feel more threatened by 'newcomers', particularly those (women) who they fear may, literally, 'beat them at their own game' (after Manne 2017) upturning gendered hierarchies.

Conclusion

In recent years, WotC have employed brand activism to increase representation of gender diversity in Magic art, narrative and content creation; these activities may be read as both politically progressive and commercial (trying to appeal to a wider audience of consumers). As Graham (2019) argues in relation to trolling, and Miltner (2014) in reference to memes, some of the community's negative responses to WotC's activities could be considered a form of 'boundary maintenance' between perceived 'newcomers' and 'insiders': a way of maintaining established hierarchies. This boundary maintenance, however, is highly gendered and can be misogynistic. I suggest that a combination of the perception that WotC are 'pushing' an unasked-for socio-political agenda, the potential of newcomers (women) to compete for the masculine-coded 'goods' of knowledge and play-skill, and a fear of feeling 'shame' or 'embarrassment' in front of women, have led to some of the misogynistic responses I outline above (after Manne 2017). For Magic players, as a long-established male-dominated online and offline manufactured subculture, insider-knowledge and experience are reified as indicators of intra-community hierarchical position. I have suggested that these hierarchies suggest an expression of 'geek masculinities' (after Lockhart 2015) within the subculture. Responses to WotC's brand activism illustrate the potential risks of brand activism, especially when related changes threaten to disrupt the gendered community hierarchies of that brand's established market.

For many active in Magic, the opportunity to be part of a competitive community where play-skill and knowledge are respected (a 'geek masculinity') holds the promise of an alternative to stereotypical hegemonic masculinities that prize physical strength and social success. Having established spaces where their own attributes are recognized, changes to the social (and gendered) make-

---

[11] Brian Braun-Duin, Twitter post. 25 November 2017, 04:01 a.m. http://twitter.com/BraunDuinlt.

up of those spaces may be perceived as threatening by some Magic players. Certainly, not all community responses to WotC's actions have been negative, many – myself included – have welcomed the greater diversity, and say it adds to their love of the game, even while recognizing that they still have work to do in this area to avoid diversity 'tokenism'. However, the sheer volume of Magic community discussion and reaction suggests there remains significant tension and uncertainty about this aspect of WotC's design and direction for Magic, and what it means for Magic players going forward. While some tension relates to an understandable cynicism about the combination of commercial and political claims and interests, the visible overlaps, at least linguistically, between responses from a minority of Magic players and texts from 'the manosphere', and other alt-right networks, is a serious cause for concern.

What is also particularly upsetting in an immediate sense, however, for women (and other minority) players, is what negative responses to WotC's brand activism on gender diversity reveal about the underlying structures that shape their opportunities to exist and thrive in this predominantly masculine space. Assumptions about women not wanting to be competitive, the refusal to acknowledge sexism unless directly witnessed, the perception that agentic women are disproportionately visible, are all indicators of underlying assumptions about gendered interests and norms, and who has the right to be active in which spaces. As Manne (2017) and other feminist theorists make abundantly clear, those who attempt to push the boundaries of gendered spaces, and especially those who try to 'compete' with men for space, are often subject to increased risk of misogynistic vitriol and even violence.

Bibliography

Beer, T. (2021) EBay Reports Increase of 4 Million Trading Cards Sold in 2020. *Forbes*, 2 February. Available at: https://www.forbes.com/sites/tommybeer/2021/02/11/ebay-reports-increase-of-4-million-trading-cards-sold-in-2020/ (accessed 18 February 2021).

Boehme, H. M. and Isom Scott, D. A. (2020) Alt-White? A Gendered Look at 'Victim' Ideology and the Alt-Right. *Victims & Offenders*, 15(2), 174–96.

Cavotta, M. (2005) The Magic Style Guide (Part 1). *Savor the Flavor*, 7 September. Available at: https://magic.wizards.com/en/articles/archive/savor-flavor/magic-style-guide-part-1-2005-09-07 (assessed 6 March 2021).

Chalk, T. (2017) *Generation Decks: The Unofficial History of Gaming Phenomenon Magic: The Gathering*. Oxford: Solaris.

Connell, R. W. (2001) The Social Organization of Masculinity, in S. Whitehead and F. Barrett (eds.), *Masculinities Reader*, 30–50. Cambridge: Polity.

Cutler, A. and Scott, D. R. (1990) Speaker Sex and Perceived Apportionment of Talk. *Applied Psycholinguistics*, 11(3), 253–72.

Dayan, D. (1986) Review Essay: Copyrighted Subcultures. *American Journal of Sociology*, 91(5), 1219–28.

Delingpole, J. (2017) Magicgate – the Ugly Story of How Social Justice Warriors Ruined an Innocent Collectible Card Game. *Breitbart*, 20 December. http://archive.fo/3dopy (accessed 24 June 2019).

Dupas, P., Modestino, A. Sasser, Niederle, M., Wolfers, J. and the Seminar Dynamics Collective (2021) 'Gender and the Dynamics of Economics Seminars', National Bureau of Economic Research Working Paper, 28494, Cambridge, MA: NBER.

Estephan, J. (2018) Oh You're the Girl That Won a GP. *Channel Fireball*, 3 August. Available at: https://www.channelfireball.com/articles/oh-youre-the-girl-that-won-a-gp/ (accessed 24 June 2019).

Ewalt, D. M. (2021) Dungeons & Dragons Gets a Bigger Role at Hasbro. *Wall Street Journal*, 25 February. Available at: https://www.wsj.com/articles/dungeons-dragons-gets-a-bigger-role-at-hasbro-11614254403 (accessed 25 February 2021).

Faludi, S. (1992) *Backlash: The Undeclared War against American Women*. New York: Three Rivers Press.

Faludi, S. (2019) *Stiffed: The Roots of Modern Male Rage*. Anniversary Edition. New York: William Morrow & Company.

Feldman, A. and Gill, R. D. (2019) Power Dynamics in Supreme Court Oral Arguments: The Relationship between Gender and Justice-to-Justice Interruptions. *Justice System Journal*, 40(3), 173–95.

Forster, D. (2019) MTG Continues to Make Millions for Hasbro despite MTG Arena Problems. *Dot Esports*, 8 July. Available at: https://dotesports.com/mtg/news/mtg-continues-to-make-millions-for-hasbro (accessed 18 February 2021).

Graham, E. (2019) Boundary Maintenance and the Origins of Trolling. *New Media & Society*, 21(9), 2029–47.

Jameson, A. D. and Roman, J. (2016) If Magic: The Gathering Cares about Women, Why Can't They Hire Any?. *Vice.com*, 18 July. Available at: https://www.vice.com/en/article/4xkk8q/if-magic-the-gathering-cares-about-women-why-cant-they-hire-any (accessed 6 March 2021).

Jarvis, M. (2020) Magic: The Gathering's Commander Format Saw Its Player Count Triple in Two Years, Wizards of the Coast Says. *Dicebreaker*, 18 September. Available at: https://www.dicebreaker.com/games/magic-the-gathering-game/news/mtg-commander-audience-tripled (accessed 18 February 2021).

Jones, C., Trott, V. and Wright, S. (2020) Sluts and Soyboys: MGTOW and the Production of Misogynistic Online Harassment. *New Media & Society*, 22(10), 1903–21.

Lane, K. E. (ed.) (2017) *Age of the Geek: Depictions of Nerds and Geeks in Popular Media*. Berlin: Springer.

Lockhart, E. A. (2015), Nerd/Geek Masculinity: Technocracy, Rationality, and Gender in Nerd Cultures Countermasculine Hegemony, PhD Thesis, Texas A&M University, College Station.

Manne, K. (2017) *Down Girl: The Logic of Misogyny*. Oxford: Oxford University Press.

Massanari, A. (2017) #Gamergate and The Fappening: How Reddit's Algorithm, Governance, and Culture Support Toxic Technocultures. *New Media & Society*, 19(3), 329–46.

McKinnon-Crowley, S. (2020) Fighting Gendered Battles: On Being a Woman in a Contemporary Gaming Community. *Journal of Contemporary Ethnography*, 49(1), 118–42.

Mendick, H. and Francis, B. (2012) Boffin and Geek Identities: Abject or Privileged? *Gender and Education*, 24(1), 15–24.

Miller, T. (2018) Death by a Thousand Paper Cuts. *TCGPlayer.com*, 2 July. http://magic.tcgplayer.com/db/article.asp?ID=14439 (accessed 24 June 2019).

Miltner, K. M. (2014) 'There's No Place for Lulz on LOLCats': The Role of Genre, Gender, and Group Identity in the Interpretation and Enjoyment of an Internet Meme. *First Monday*, 19(8).

Muniowski, Ł. (2018) Geek Is the New Jock: The Relationship between Geek Culture and Sports, in K. E. Lane (ed.), *Age of the Geek: Depictions of Nerds and Geeks in Popular Media*, 129–47. Berlin: Springer.

Niederle, M. and Vesterland, L. (2011) Gender and Competition. *Annual Review of Economics*, 3(1), 601–30.

Phillips, R. (2018) Crisis and Controversy in Magic: The Gathering's Contested Online Spaces. MA diss., University of Cardiff.

Reagle, J. (2016) The Obligation to Know: From FAQ to Feminism 101. *New Media & Society*, 18(5), 691–707.

Redman, P. and Mac An Ghaill, M. (1996) Schooling Sexualities: Heterosexual Masculinities, Schooling, and the Unconscious. *Discourse: Studies in the Cultural Politics of Education*, 17(2), 243–56.

Rosewater, M. (2013) Timmy, Johnny, and Spike. *Making Magic*, 3 December. Available at: https://magic.wizards.com/en/articles/archive/making-magic/timmy-johnny-and-spike-2013-12-03 (accessed 7 March 2021).

Rosewater, M. (2015) Blogatog. *Tumblr*, 15 June. Available at: https://markrosewater.tumblr.com/post/122446948628/38 (accessed 7 March 2021).

Rosewater, M. (2012) Blogatog. *Tumblr*, 17 April. Available at: https://markrosewater.tumblr.com/post/21270120918/re-your-latest-answer-about-female-planeswalkers (accessed 7 March 2021).

Rosewater, M. (2019a) Resonate Spinning. *Making Magic*, 18 March. Available at: https://magic.wizards.com/en/articles/archive/making-magic/resonate-spinning-2019-03-18 (accessed 24 June 2019).

Rosewater, M. (2019b) Why Diversity Matters in Game Design. *Making Magic,* 19 August. Available at: https://magic.wizards.com/en/articles/archive/making-magic/why-diversity-matters-game-design-2019-08-19 (accessed 21 August 2019).

Rowley, M. V. (2019) Anything but Reactionary: Exploring the Mechanics of Backlash. *Signs: Journal of Women in Culture and Society,* 45(2), 278–87.

Salter, A. and Blodgett, B. (2017) *Toxic Geek Masculinity in Media: Sexism, Trolling, and Identity Policing.* New York: Palgrave Macmillan.

Shaw, A. (2015) *Gaming at the Edge: Sexuality and Gender at the Margins of Gamer Culture.* Minneapolis: University of Minnesota Press.

Stein, R. (2017) Thoughts on Spike, Tournament Grinder. *Hipsters of the Coast,* 20 November. Available at: https://www.hipstersofthecoast.com/2017/11/thoughts-spike-tournament-grinder/ (accessed 8 March 2021).

Taylor, N. and Voorhees, G. (2018) *Masculinities in Play.* Berlin: Springer.

Taylor, T.L. (2012), *Raising the Stakes: E-Sports and the Professionalization of Computer Gaming.* Cambridge: MIT press.

Trammell, A. (2018) Militarism and Masculinity in Dungeons and Dragons, in N. Taylor and G. Voorhees (eds), *Masculinities in Play,* 129–47. Berlin: Springer.

Tyler, I. (2020) *Stigma: The Machinery of Inequality.* London: Zed Books.

Ward, M. R. M. (2018) 'I Am Going to Uni!' Working-Class Academic Success, Opportunity and Conflict, in C. Walker and S. Roberts (eds.), *Masculinity, Labour, and Neoliberalism: Working-Class Men in International Perspective,* 125–45. Cham: Springer.

Williams, S. (2018) Twitter post. 27 November, 01:08 am. Available at: http://twitter.com/Boogie2988 (accessed on 23 February 2022).

Wizards Play Network (2015) Why Your FNM Could Be 15 Times Bigger. *Wizards Play Network,* 4 May. Available at: https://wpn.wizards.com/en/article/why-your-fnm-could-be-15-times-bigger (accessed 25 February 2021).

8

It takes a lot of balls to be a lady: Drag queens, masculinity and stigma

Elisa Padilla

Drag queens in academia have often been used as pawns in debates about sex, gender, subversion and feminism. On the one side, they seem to have become somewhat mythological creatures, subversive avatars of queer excellence; on the other, they represent conservative and offensive parodies of womanhood. For queer theory, drag represents a parody of the naturalness of gender, 'a kind of persistent impersonation that passes as the real' (Butler 2006 [1990]:viii). Drag can function as a showcase of the permeability, blurriness and messiness of gendered identities (Halberstam 1998); as a playful inversion of male-female, outside-inside, appearance-reality (Newton 1979:100–1) and as a 'condensation' of some 'emotional and identity linkages' between gay men and women (Moon and Sedgwick 1994:213–14). Conversely, some feminist scholars have described drag, or female impersonation, as a sort of cruel satire akin to blackface, a performance fuelled by misogyny: a 'casual and cynical mockery of women' (Frye 1983:137) that, exercised from a position of power, only reflects male privilege (Williamson 1986). In its most transphobic incarnation of the argument, drag is, alongside 'transsexualism',[1] an exercise of male power that finds 'gender relief, sexual pleasure, and/or stardom and financial profit in this mimicry' (Raymond 1994:xxvii). Yet some contributions have attempted to balance these two positions, recognizing that drag can be as conservative as it might be revolutionary and is often both at the same time (Schacht and Underwood 2004).

Amidst this discussion, this chapter will provide an exploration of drag that revises some of its concepts and terminology. I am less interested in discussing what drag queens look like (the clothes, wigs and make-up) or represent (the

---

[1] This is the term Raymond uses, throughout this chapter I employ trans or transgender.

glamorous and/or comical illusion of femininity). 'Where drag is debated and studied', acknowledge Edward and Farrier, 'it is often done so within terms of drag as parody or drag as queer resistance' (2020:9), in detriment to the study of the communities and context that produce it. Instead, I want to focus on what drag does, as a cultural practice: the way it presents and defines itself, as a form of show-business, an art-form and a profession, and the inner logics and contradictions of this functioning. Choosing to focus my contribution solely on drag queens might seem counterintuitive, given the focus of this volume on masculinities; since, historically, drag kings have received considerably less popular and scholarly attention.[2] However, instead of focusing on the kings' staged gender, I will be focusing on the gender behind the queens' performances: the masculinity that has been repeatedly discussed and flaunted when describing drag in mainstream media appearances. I arrived at the topic of drag queens and masculinities after observing the increasing masculinization of drag queens' public personas and their relentless pursuit of male acting roles in their journey to stardom, as well as the existing tension between queer subcultures and mainstream commercialization. Before the so-called contemporary 'golden age of drag' (Brennan and Gudelunas 2017:1), some famous drag queens established a definition of drag based on the sartorial that positioned itself as solely a job or occupation. Under these identifying characteristics, drag queens could function as representatives of queer culture while also safeguarding their male identity in public. These discursive operations manifest most vividly in the most lucrative and popular iterations of drag. Thus, this chapter will focus on American drag queens Divine and RuPaul, the most famous drag performers of the late twentieth and early twentieth-first century,[3] as case studies, in order to explore the conceptualization of their drag in their engagement with media.

Studying the different roles and achievements of these performers, as well as their press appearances and gender identification, I want to question why these established drag queens, later in their careers, persistently pursued career opportunities to put their drag aside and 'go legit' by playing the man. In doing so, I aim to excavate the nebulous negotiation of gender identity that mainstream drag queening entailed for Divine and RuPaul's. Such negotiation, I

---

[2] 'In all the articles and studies and media exposes on drag queen culture, very little time and energy has been expended on the drag queen's counterpart, the drag king', explores Jack Halberstam in the book Female Masculinity: 'As I have argued throughout this book, the history of public recognition of female masculinity is most frequently characterized by stunning absences' (1998:231).

[3] Upon his death, Divine was coined 'drag queen of the century' (Darrach 1988). RuPaul has similarly being proclaimed 'the most famous drag queen in the world' (The Late Show with Stephen Colbert 2019).

argue, demonstrates that masculinity is still a strong holder of social capital, and that queer stigma and fear of femininity coexist with the glamour, celebrity and acclaim of these two queer performers.

In the first section, I offer some clarification on the concept of drag as queer labour and explore why I believe contemporary definitions of drag need to move beyond the sartorial and approach drag through the lens of queer materialism. The following sections provide a comparative analysis of the professional careers of Divine and RuPaul, studying early talk show interviews when they performed in drag, and later ones where they presented as male, excavating their similarities and differences. Lastly, the chapter concludes by reflecting on drag queens' masculinities and stigma.

'Professional homosexuals': Drag as queer labour

The Oxford Dictionary entry of drag describes it primarily as a question of attire: clothing more conventionally worn by the opposite sex, especially women's clothes worn by a man.[4] The term has an unambiguous connection with dresses, dating back to the nineteenth century, as 'the word derives from "the drag of the dress, as distinct from the non-dragginess of the trouser"' (Partridge in Baker 1968:17). If dresses are understood as female, having a male wearing one is an anomaly, a switch of their natural order: an act of cross-dressing. Yet, when defining the act of cross-dressing one runs into the arbitrariness of gender, for as Marjorie Garber notes in the introduction of *Vested Interests*, throughout global history, men have dressed in dresses and women in pants; blue was associated with girls and pink was a boys' colour (1992:1–2). To complicate matters further, cross-dressing is part of a wider tradition that has undertaken many shapes and meanings – that of the transvestite, or the transgender, or the theatrical crossdresser. 'Whenever and whatever drama began', notes Roger Baker, 'it was automatically the man's business to play the woman' (1968:31): a tradition devoid of queer subtext and controversy. And, for all the gendered cultural meanings associated to clothes, Judith Butler, the theorist of gender performativity, warns that genders are not to be confused with clothes, nor do clothes 'make' gender (Butler 1993:230–1). Moon and Sedgwick (1994) note that crossdressing can be made to pass convincingly or not, represent either

---

[4] 'drag' (2021) *The Oxford English Dictionary*. Available at: https://www.lexico.com/definition/drag (accessed 10 April 2021).

homosexuality or heterosexuality, and be public or private. The focus on clothes is superficial, they argue, because it fails to consider how gender is rooted 'in the body itself: in habitual and largely unconscious physical and psychological attitudes, poses, and styles of bodily relation and response' (ibid.:215). Putting clothes at the forefront of definitions of drag is, therefore, somewhat akin to foreground umbrellas in the study of rain.

If clothes are too mundane to encapsulate the complexities of gender, and crossdressing similarly lacks precision is too vague a term, drag needs to be described as a cultural practice inextricably connected to queerness and spectacle. It has been historically difficult to pinpoint the origin of the term 'drag queen' but the moniker seems to condense theatrical drag, as an act of crossdressing or gender bending, with queen, 'a term of reproach and defamation' that contains 'a willed or hapless effeminacy' (Koestenbaum 1993:108). Queen, argues Koestenbaum, becomes a derogatory term that mocks male effeminacy and 'puts down the queer because it implies that he wants to be a woman and he wants to be a queen and, pathetic soul, he never will attain either incarnation' (ibid.). Drag's connection to queerness and spectacle, henceforth, signals the transformation of a source of stigma into a form of spectacle. Drag historians establish that men dressing up as women, singing and playing female roles in the late nineteenth and early twentieth century, became a spectacle of its own, a type of show that inherited from the music hall, vaudeville, pantomime and cabaret (Ackroyd 1979; Baker 1968; Harris 2005). The development of such spectacles converges with the discursive establishment of homosexuality as a peripheral sexuality. Following Foucault, this means that homosexuality, as a discursive category, displaces the focus from same-sex relations and becomes 'a certain way of inverting the masculine and feminine in oneself [...] a kind of interior androgyny, a hermaphrodism of the soul' (1998:43). The concept of homosexuality as inversion is explicitly present in drag, according to Esther Newton, who traced an ethnographic investigation of the world of female impersonators[5] in the late 1960s in the United States. Drag plays with opposition between 'inner' or 'real' self (subjective self) to the 'outer' self (social self). The oppositional play is twofold: between 'appearance', the female clothes, and

---

[5] 'Female impersonator' was then often preferred to drag queen as it was considered more professional and respectful (Newton 1979). Today, drag queen is the most prominent term. 'I do not impersonate females', RuPaul said, 'how many women do you know who wear seven-inch heels, four-foot wigs, and skintight dresses?' Corso, D. S. (2009) 'Drag Queen Theology', *Huffington Post*. Available at: https://www.huffpost.com/entry/drag-queen-theology_b_175120 (Accessed 31 January 2021).

'reality' or 'essence', the male body, but also between the exterior of the male body and the female sensibility inside:

> At the simplest level, drag signifies that the person wearing it is a homosexual, that he is a male who is behaving in a specifically inappropriate way, that he is a male who places himself as a woman in relation to other men. In this sense it signifies stigma. At the most complex, it is a double inversion that says 'appearance is an illusion.'
>
> (Newton 1979:103)

Newton documents a divide between the 'street fairies' or transvestites, who would be in drag as part of their daily lives, in the streets, stage or the club; and the 'female impersonators': those who aimed to segregate 'the stigma from the personal life by limiting it to the stage context as much as possible' (1979:8). Newton finds simultaneously sentiments of pride and shame in these drag performers, who seem to not be able to get rid of the stigma of dressing as women for a living:

> These men often said that drag is simply a medium or a mask that allows them to perform [...] The stated aspiration of almost all stage impersonators is to 'go legit', that is, to play in movies, television, and on stage or in respectable nightclubs, either in drag or (some say) in men's clothes. Failing this, they would like to see the whole profession 'upgraded', made more legitimate and professional.
>
> (1979:98)

Newton's work situates drag alongside the stigma of effeminacy and queerness, which is particularly relevant to my discussion of drag queens' masculinities and pursuit of male roles. She describes the unstable and precarious drag economy and its relation to gay pride and strategies of assimilation. Embracing this ambivalence between pride and shame, Newton describes how drag 'form(s) an illegitimate junction of the homosexual and show business subcultures: [female impersonators] which can be considered as performing homosexuals or homosexual performers' (1979:7). Nowadays, theorizing drag queens as performing homosexuals/homosexual performers is arguably a simplification of queerness as a mode of cultural production and critique (Meyer 1994). Contemporary understandings of drag position it as 'theatrical gender-bending' (Heller 2020:1), a practice vastly richer and more diverse than gay men dressing and performing as women. Nevertheless, Newton's succinct 'performing homosexuals or homosexual performers' (ibid.) enables a queer cultural materialist framework for the analysis, insofar as it grounds drag praxis in 'deviant' sexuality, while also considering the ways that peripheral sexualities, as Foucault describes them, engage with spectacle, labour, stardom and profit. Newton grounds drag as a practice in the professional world, asserting its place in the cultural field and neoliberal market. Consequently, drag fundamentally exists in relation to queerness and capital.

In attempting to move drag studies beyond the impasse of crossdressing and gender performativity, I choose to focus on drag's ambivalent relation to queerness and capital. I am arguing here for a theoretical push towards the material 'not to reassert the priority of the economic' (Liu 2020:41) but to examine the ways in which gender and sexuality are ingrained in the matrix of power and capital and understand the precarious position of queer subjects under capitalism. Through a queer materialistic analysis, I read drag queens as professional performing subjects whose work is affected by queer labour and the burden of liveness. Matthew Tinkcom discusses queer labour as a force that, following capital mandates to work, produces a particular response: 'camp'. Beyond the initial theoretical enquiries that approached camp as a form of aestheticism, sensibility or taste (Booth 1983; Isherwood 1954; Sontag 1964), Tinkcom proposes to read camp as an artistic response under capitalism, an 'alibi for queer men to labor' (Tinkcom 2002:xvi). Within a system that demands circulation of commodities, exchange-value operations, the sale and purchase of their labour power, queer subjects in cultural production seek to produce work that can potentially advantage them in the economy. Following Bourdieu, capital cannot be defined in purely economic terms. Cultural capital, such as camp, is also a fundamental currency in late capitalism. By exploring the relationship between queerness, labour and capital I am arguing for a definition of drag as a specific cultural praxis produced by queer labour. Because of their subaltern positions, queers that perform suffer what Jose Esteban Muñoz described as 'the burden of liveness' (1999:182), a hegemonic condition by which their only survival strategy is that of entertainment for the elite. Muñoz writes:

> The story of 'otherness' is one tainted by a mandate to 'perform' for the amusement of a dominant power bloc. If there is any acceptable place for queers in the homophobic national imaginary, is certainly onstage – being 'funny' for the straight audience.
>
> (1999:187)

The burden of liveness that exists within queer labour and performance is foundational for my study of the most mainstream iterations of drag. In the next sections, I position the careers of Divine and RuPaul within as examples of queer labour under capitalism. I explore the commodification of their drag identities and male personas. Beyond the subversiveness or gentrification that one might identify in their drag, I argue that the way Divine and RuPaul flaunt their maleness demonstrates the patriarchal accumulation of capital. Others have written about queens' patriarchal appropriation of femininity, describing it as 'real estate' that can bring them status and power (Schacht and Underwood 2004:9) and 'patriarchal dividends' (Berkowitz and Liska Belgrave 2010:162). That is not my focus: I analyse, instead, the ways in which mainstream drag is explicitly presented in American talk shows and the ways in which their male identity is repeatedly flaunted.

Divine and RuPaul have had successful drag careers that have tapped into a lot of different mediums: theatre, film, TV, music, night clubs, festivals and advertising. It would be a book-length feature to study all the different forms their drag has taken throughout the years, and its evolution from the most underground scenes to mainstream respectability. I have chosen to focus, therefore, on a very narrow aspect of their careers: interviews and talk shows appearances in promotion of their work. Talk shows are media events where celebrities negotiate their stardom, providing, with assistance of the host, a narrative in which they wish to be included. In the next section, I analyse and compare two interviews in which the queens appear in drag, promoting their work, followed by a comparative analysis of two later interviews in which they present out of drag, highlighting their male personas.

Tell me what you are

Divine

Divine's drag career cannot be understood without a reference to independent filmmaker John Waters. It was the film *Pink Flamingos* (1972)[6] which propelled these two Baltimoreans to Midnight Movie cult stardom. A carnivalesque show of taste transgression, the film is most infamous because of its ending, in which Divine picks up a dog excrement from the floor and eats it, looking into the camera. Ten years after the release of *Pink Flamingos*, Waters and Divine appear

---

[6]   *Pink Flamingos* (1972) Directed by John Waters. USA: New Line Cinema.

on *Late Night with David Letterman* promoting *Polyester* (2005 [1981]).[7] This media appearance showcases an open bid for legitimation by both director and actor, as they promote a film that is centred in suburbia as a metaphor for the mainstream. Unlike Waters's early films, which were focused on episodes of shock value and depicted the crimes of a group of outsiders, *Polyester* tells the story of a distressed housewife, Francine Fishpawn (played by Divine), with an acute sense of smell, and her struggle to keep a clean and tidy home and a normal family living happily inside: her husband owns a porn cinema, their teenage children are taking drugs and skipping school, her mother steals from her and she is an alcoholic. Divine compared his part in *Polyester* to Jane Crawford's *Mildred Pierce* (1945), where the suffering and pain of the mother-heroine substituted the rage and iciness of their previous roles, transforming their star image with a compelling performance. Such a comparison aligns him with Hollywood stardom, displaying ambition but also legitimizing his craft.

Divine's appearance on Letterman starts with the drag queen live singing the single 'Born to Be Cheap'. She wears a short, skin-tight colourful dress and a white teased wig, and fondles her big body as she sings. The performance is dominated by the raspy voice and the sexual grunts and moans: it signals a vulgar 'unruly femininity' (Rowe 1995) that was cultivated by Waters's films, especially *Female Trouble* (1974).[8] The lyrics – 'as sure as there's trash, I was born to be cheap' – signal towards Waters's bad taste, and the trash cinema tradition.[9] Cheapness, a concept that symbolizes class anxieties towards tawdry femininity, is a feature of Divine's drag, which has been described as a 'combination of abjection and defiance' (Moon and Sedgwick 1994:214).

Immediately after the song, Divine and Waters sit next to Letterman's desk, who introduces Divine with feminine pronouns and then immediately auto-corrects. 'I'm a little flustered', he admits as a comic interjection, although still seeming visibly uncomfortable. 'Let's start with some obvious thing … You are not … tell me what you are.' Laughter erupts. The question is positioned as an invitation to speak but also as a demand, as if to say: explain what is in front of our eyes, make this make sense for us. Why would a man present himself in public as a sexy fat woman? Divine immediately answers 'I was born a male;

---

[7] *Late Night with David Letterman* (1982) March 18. Available at: https://www.youtube.com/watch?v=AIPF8mk1a4Q&t=354s (accessed 1 February 2021). *Polyester* (1981) Directed by John Waters. USA: New Line Cinema.

[8] *Female Trouble* (1974) Directed by John Waters. USA: Dreamland.

[9] Trash is better understood as an 'elastic textual category' (Barefoot 2017:21) that can refer to everything coded as low, underground or marginal – trash aesthetics – or to a particular form of cinematic expression and/or exploitation – the trash label. Waters's cinema, Barefoot summarizes, adopts both.

I still am a male ... these are all added parts that come off ... as my work clothes'. Letterman follows up with the query, 'you are not a transvestite?' to what Divine replies, 'no, I am an actor that specializes in women's parts'. This statement encapsulates how Divine translates to the straight world the gender trouble that his presence causes: summarizing his drag as an acting job, he is limiting its scope, as he has just demonstrated that he is also a musical performer.[10] He is also seeking legitimation, as unlike drag, acting is an understood and respected craft. Last, he is also doing the emotional labour of reassuring Letterman (and, by proxy, the audience) that he was born as male and still is male, and that the makeup, the wigs, and the clothes are artefacts that do not cling to his true male identity.

RuPaul

RuPaul's appearance in the late night The Arsenio Hall Show in 1993 also commences with a musical performance.[11] 'Supermodel (You Better Work)' was RuPaul's debut single and first foray into the mainstream: the song featured in the Billboard Hot 100 and was nominated for the MTV video awards. The song positions RuPaul as a *glamazon,* a term he coined to describe what would be the most successful iteration of his drag: a glamorous supermodel/pop diva. The lyrics of 'Supermodel (You Better Work)' introduce the biography of a fictional supermodel. Calling out the names of the most successful models of the time (Linda Evangelista, Naomi Campbell and Cindy Crawford, amongst others), RuPaul was not only paying homage but infiltrating their exclusive group, positioning himself as an insider. The song's call to 'Work!' alludes to the labour that spectacular hyper-femininity demands. Work also symbolizes 'the queer, racialized performativity of the sashay, the strut, the stroll' that describes Elspeth Brown 'produces an affective excess that, [...] offers possibilities for both capitalist dream worlds and for queer worldmaking' (2019:14). The recurring calls to 'Work!' across RuPaul's career exemplify the taste-shaping operations of his drag, which takes a 'prominent example of drag vernacular' (Hargraves 2011:18) and incorporates it as professional ethos. It is now displayed in neon lights in *RuPaul's Drag Race* workroom.

---

[10] As the documentary *I Am Divine* (2013) explores, Divine also participated in pageants, worked in theatre, did professional appearances in clubs and discos and featured in advertising.

[11] *The Arsenio Hall Show* (1993) Available at: https://www.youtube.com/watch?v=WbINxJJY7u4 (accessed 1 February 2021). *The Arsenio Hall Show* (2014) February 20. Available at: https://www.youtube.com/watch?v=wwkQg9IQFM0&t=176s (accessed 1 February 2021).

The audience on set applauds rabidly, and RuPaul ecstatically thanks them. He immediately establishes a good rapport with Arsenio, as they jokingly plan to play basketball afterwards. The host then addresses the fact that many spectators might be puzzled by what they are seeing on TV and asks RuPaul, 'would you have rather been born a woman?'. Quickly and jokingly, RuPaul responds:

> No, no, no, I am very happy being a big, old, black man. [Laughter erupts] I'm an entertainer, I have done many different personas, but this one, baby, this one clicks. The children respond to me in drag.

RuPaul's answer is doing a similar presentation of his identity to Divine's, while also gaining the sympathy of Arsenio and his audience. He clarifies that he is not a woman and does not wish to become one. He is also covertly positioning his drag as the mask or medium identified by Newton, where drag is simply as a successful strategy which allowed him to perform.

The palpable difference between the Divine/Letterman interview, in 1982, and the RuPaul/Arsenio one in 1993 is that the former is tense and slightly awkward, while the latter pair seem to be much more relaxed and at ease with each other. Both Divine and RuPaul get asked the question of how their families respond to their drag and while both performers attempt to provide a positive answer, Divine admits to having being estranged from his parents for nine years, and reports that they are now 'friends ... long distance'. RuPaul however happily replies that his family loves his act, that he even performed in the last family reunion and then proclaims his now famous catchphrase, 'my show is about loving yourself, because if you don't love yourself, how in the hell are you gonna love somebody else? Can I get an Amen up in here?' These differences are not surprising: they document an increase in queer representation in society, media and culture alongside the advancement in civil rights. The eleven years that go by from Divine/Letterman to RuPaul/Arsenio also document significant governmental changes – from Ronald Reagan to Bill Clinton. However, it is important to also note than Divine's 'loud and vulgar drag' was always much more visibly queer, and threatening, because of its association to Waters's cinema, while RuPaul subscribes to a much more traditional feminine representation. Divine's drag was much more RuPaul displays thinness and success, which is the antipode to Divine's attachments to fatness and cheapness. If television was much more welcoming towards RuPaul than it ever was for Divine, it was not simply so because society was less queerphobic. RuPaul, as well, crafted an image that was much more 'sanitized and desexualized' with a 'strand of integrationist liberal pluralism' (Muñoz 1999:99) and therefore could sell and be commercialized with greater success.

Playing the man

RuPaul

RuPaul's career reached his greatest hit yet with the reality show *RuPaul's Drag Race*, a reality competition television series to search for America Next Drag Superstar. The show is a platform that has been said to represent 'the high watermark of mainstream success for drag culture' (Feldman and Hakim 2020:396) and it has done so by engaging with operations of capital: first, building itself as a media empire that attracts sponsorship and endorsing products, and then, exporting its product in the form of world tours and drag cons. The show has reached an unprecedented level of international success, spurring its own versions in Thailand, Australia, Canada and the UK, while also achieving critical success (19 Primetime Emmy Awards).

'My first guest is an actor, a singer, author, and cultural icon.' In 2014, in promotion of season 6 of *RuPaul's Drag Race* and the album *Born Naked*, RuPaul reunites with Arsenio Hall, this time out of drag, wearing a men's suit. They review a photo of their 1993 interview, and Arsenio enquiries how long does he take to get in full drag, to what RuPaul responds, in a deadpan manner: 'it depends on what the client needs'. When Arsenio asks him how often he gets into drag nowadays, RuPaul quickly chimes back: 'the only time you see me in drag if is I am getting paid. Honey. Work. Hey!' However, he is increasingly getting paid without getting in drag. He is out of drag in his workroom appearances in the show and in other work commitments such as media appearances, drag con inaugurations and awards ceremony. In fact, one of the last times RuPaul publicly appeared in drag and performed outside of his show was November 2013, in the Thanksgiving special *Lady Gaga and the Muppets Holiday Spectacular* (LeBlanc 2021:135).[12] He has also played small male acting roles in TV, in the series *Broad City, Girlboss, Two Broke Girls* and *Frankie and Grace*. And for all the publicity

---

[12] LeBlanc notes this occasion as 'the last time RuPaul ever appeared in drag outside of his own franchise' (2021:135); however, this is not entirely accurate: in the Netflix TV show *AJ and The Queen*, RuPaul starred as drag queen Ruby Red. However, as RuPaul is credited as writer and creator in all 10 episodes, we can conclude that he has not appeared in drag outside of his own media since 2013.

that the reality show does of his records, RuPaul does not play live music, nor does he tour anymore.

In the 2019 Met Gala, that celebrated the opening of the exhibition Camp: Notes on Fashion, RuPaul also appeared out of drag, which provoked some curiosity, to which he simply replied: 'I decided I can do drag not in drag' (Muller 2019).[13] This paradox reveals RuPaul's extremely elastic definition of drag. *RPDR* continually operates under RuPaul's aphorism, 'we are all naked and the rest is drag'. In his first book, RuPaul argues that drag is not a 'some kind of thing or freak with a sex fetish' but a simply a job uniform, much like those sported by Wall Street businessman, cops or nurses (1995:iii). We are all 'metaphorical' drag queens because class stratification means that we are continuously performing our 'gender, race, class, sexual orientation, and so forth' (Schacht and Underwood 2004:13). The problem with this argument is that it simplifies the idea of performativity by not considering the domain of intelligibility (Butler 1993:11–13): the matrix by which some lives are considered abject. Most importantly, Butler's theory of gender performativity includes the idea of citationality. Citations only work when they 'fit within boundaries of the norms they cite' (Gerstner and Staiger 2003:51). When RuPaul writes 'no one ever thinks twice about the priest in his robe or the Supreme Court justice in his gown' (1995: iii), he is failing to notice (or, at least, pretending to) the power structures that deem what he calls 'executive drag', i.e. wearing a business suit, as a mandate of labour and class stratification. Executive realness, as portrayed in the documentary *Paris is Burning* (1992), is a category in the ballroom scene, one that subaltern subjects make theirs by performing opulence. Their transformation, argues Schacht, 'throws into question some of our society's most fundamental, albeit socially constructed, values and corresponding realities' (2000:150) since executive realness showcases how situational, and malleable, identity can be. RuPaul, however, is arguing that real executives, and not just executive realness, are drag. If everything is drag, there is no subalternity. When RuPaul claims that drag for him is simply work-clothes, a uniform, he is presenting his performance in the most non-threatening terms imaginable, dissipating its queer meaning to contain the stigma.

There is another fascinating contradiction at the heart of the 'everything is drag' statement. RuPaul's seemingly elastic understanding of drag and identity was revealed to have some very real material limits: the casting of transgender

[13] Muller, M. G. (2019) 'RuPaul Explains Why He Didn't Wear Drag to the 2019 Met Gala'. In: *W Magazine | Women's Fashion & Celebrity News*. Available at: https://www.wmagazine.com/story/rupaul-met-gala-2019-no-drag-mean/ (accessed 1 February 2021).

performers in RPDR. In an interview with *The Guardian*, RuPaul admitted that he would 'probably' not accept transgender women in the show. 'It takes on a different thing; it changes the whole concept of what we're doing'. He also argued:

> Drag loses its sense of danger and its sense of irony once it's not men doing it, because at its core it's a social statement and a big f-you to male-dominated culture. So, for men to do it, it's really punk rock, because it's a real rejection of masculinity.
>
> (Aitkenhead 2018)[14]

With the interview, RuPaul acknowledges who stands outside the boundaries in the so-called golden age of drag: trans performers, drag kings, bioqueens or AFAB queens.[15] Paradoxically, by presenting drag as an artform that rejects a patriarchal culture, he is simultaneously arguing that drag could only be dangerous, ironic and subversive if it was done by men. Coming back to Newton's notion of the performer homosexual/homosexual performer, this is not simply a simplification, but a discursive formulation that seeks to disavow drag outside of the cis-male homosexual formulation.

Divine

Months before his death, Divine went to *The Late Show*, guest-hosted by actor Shawn Thompson, to promote his work on *Hairspray* (1988),[16] which would become Waters's most lucrative film, where he played the female character Edna Turnblad and the male character Alvin Hodgepile. Divine wears a black suit, with a blue jumper underneath, short hair and a diamond earring. Thompson's first comments are upon male appearance and ask Divine if he gets recognized out of drag.

> Well, more and more now that I'm doing more shows like this … and people see me as my version of a man [Laughter] … So, when they see me out of my version as a woman they know who it is [Laughter] It's difficult for me!

[14] Aitkenhead, D. (2018) 'RuPaul: "Drag Is a Big F-You to Male-Dominated Culture"'. In: *The Guardian*. Available at: http://www.theguardian.com/tv-and-radio/2018/mar/03/rupaul-drag-race-big-f-you-to-male-dominated-culture (accessed 1 February 2021).
[15] AFAB queens are performers assigned female at birth that perform as queens. This term has gained importance over bioqueens, which reinforces a binary association between biology and gender and has been acknowledged as 'inadequate' and 'potentially contentious' (Farrier 2019:103).
[16] *Hairspray* (1988) Directed by John Waters. USA: New Line Cinema. *The Late Show* (1988) Available at: https://www.youtube.com/watch?v=cLZ5Eh8JCQw (accessed 1 February 2021).*The Late Show with Stephen Colbert* (2019) Rupaul Charles: Who Was 'Pure Camp' at Met Gala? In: YouTube. Available at: https://www.youtube.com/watch?v=crB3jHCs1gg (accessed 1 February 2021).

This interview hints at some of the gender trouble around drag. Divine reportedly hated his birth name, Glenn Milstead, and changed his passport to Divine (Waters 2005:142). However, as his appearance out of drag in The Late Show attests, during the last years of his career there seemed to be an explicit will to reaffirm his male persona as an actor. In his manager's book, there is a chapter aptly titled 'Divi Goes Legit', where the manager explains how, when he was offered a male role in the film *Trouble in Mind* (1985), he:

> Would have let Divi do it for nothing. It was such a wonderful opportunity for him. [...] He was ready to prove to his public what he had believed for so long– that the dress wasn't an essential prop in order to hire Divine.

(1993:179)

The manager then retells a story from the set, where actor Kriss Kristofferson congratulated Divine on his acting and really being 'one of the guys', a moment that he reports as 'the most satisfying moment in Divine's career and one of which he, justifiably, boasted to all who would listen' (1993:183). The affective response that Divine and his manager produced towards a small token of acceptance by a male star is significant, because it exemplifies how, to them, to be respected in the business is akin to be treated as men, to abandon the stigma of the dress. Jay's book constructs a narrative by which, despite all of the successes Divine had, the mainstream strategy never fully succeeded for 'Divine was still considered to be a freak, a crossdresser, a transvestite-in short, and actor who had to wear dresses to get a job' (Jay 1993:5).

Drag is, I have argued, a cultural praxis that involves labour, capital and revenue. As such, it is also subjected to the rules of the market and the neoliberal social order. Drag might be a lucrative income-earning activity but its benefits are capped: at some point, drag prevents the performer from steadily progressing in mainstream show-business. The burden of liveness, argues Muñoz, puts the queer performer in a subaltern position where their otherness is exploited and commodified. Divine's career could not follow the mainstream path he and his manager envision, playing the man, because drag sticks to the body of the performer, and the capital operations by which drags succeeds cannot be undone by the simple removal of the dress. The stigma of drag, explores Esther Newton, 'lies in being less than a man and in doing something that is unnatural (wrong) for a man to do' (1979:108). Despite all of Divine's utterances that he was a male, in a patriarchal world that reviles femininity, he was still branded a subaltern subject.

Divine's maleness, disavowing gender trouble, effeminacy and transness, is a repeated citation in his biographies (Jay 1993; Schwarz 2013; Sherman 2019:60–2). Nevertheless, upon reading Divine's iconic queer stardom, Moon and Sedgwick questioned, 'doesn't it devalue a creativity as deep as the bones and musculature, imperfectly delible as lipstick, and as painful as 300 pounds in high heels to define it in the inconsequential terms of the free market in genders and identities?' (1994:220). Questioning the need to situate Divine's stardom in closed categories of identity, what Moon and Sedgwick seem to suggest is that such enquiries undo the queer labour in Divine's drag. If, following Sedgwick, queerness represents 'an open mesh of possibilities, gaps, overlaps, dissonances and resonances, lapses and excesses of meaning' that occurred when 'the constituent elements of anyone's gender, of anyone's sexuality aren't made (or *can't be* made) to signify monolithically' (1994:7), there is a palpable contradiction in the need to circumscribed drag with a fixed meaning. The boundaries Divine attempted to put on his drag therefore run alongside the queer excesses of meaning his drag embodied. Because of its origins within Waters's trash cinema, Divine's stardom is historically linked to bad taste, perversion (Studlar 1989), social negativity (Breckon 2013), imperfection (Schoonover 2010), effeminacy and fatness (Moon and Sedgwick 1994) and gender trouble (Butler 2006). Yet precisely because of its embrace of alterity, Divine also hailed social recognition and success, mobilizing his body, as Moon and Sedgwick note, in order to mobilize 'across chasms dividing classes, styles, and the ontological levels of privacy, cult-hood, fictional character, celebrity, and, of course, godhead' (1994:220). Divine's celebrity stands today as an interesting incongruity insofar as one attempts to reconcile the mythical stature of this figure, a herald of queer anger and defiance, with a man that simply wanted to be respected as 'one of the guys'. Such incongruity is an aftermath to the patriarchal distribution of the social order, where masculinity is, still, a strong holder of social power asserted through the marginalization of queerness.

Queer subjects, as Divine and RuPaul, work simultaneously according to the mandates of capital to produce profit under the burden of liveness, where their drag is commodified as a spectacle to be consumed by the elites. In order to thrive in a heterosexist world, they need to provide a non-threatening and monolithic understanding of drag and identity which clashes against the queer refusal to conform or signify, to use Sedgwick's concept, in a definite sense. These interviews, in which drag queens encounter mainstream television networks, showcase discursive negotiations that attempt to pinpoint a definition of drag that disavows what is excessive and unclear. This is the fundamental contradiction: these two mainstream performers pursue a legitimization of their work that attempts to distance itself from the stigma of the dress. However, queerness, as the resignification of a slur, cannot disavow itself from stigma without completely undoing itself.

Conclusions

The existing tension between queer cultural praxis, subcultures and success under capitalism is reflected in recent contributions to drag studies. Edward and Farrier establish that mainstream drag obscures the anarchic creativity and disruption one can find in grass-root activism and underground performances (2020:3–4), while Crookston acknowledges the perils of 'adapting a queer art form for mass cultural consumption' (2021:3). The hegemony of drag queens over other types of drag, argues Meredith Heller, has limited drag discourse and foreclosed 'the spreadability of queer acts' (2020:31). The prevalence of drag queens in the mainstream has surely obscured queerer underground expressions. However, dismissing mainstream drag risks failing the opportunity to understand its success. Raising the operations of identity, celebrity and status behind queer performances under capital might be 'messy', to use the term Edward and Farrier employ (2020:6) but I believe is a fundamental task.

In the complex business of situating drag in relation to queer culture, TV, masculinity and capitalism, it is necessary to tackle the mainstreaming question and avoid a simplistic 'yay or nay binary' interpretation. Recent contributions note how the focus on gender theory has obscured a much-needed analysis of drag praxis (Edward and Farrier 2020:9). At the beginning of the chapter, I argued that academia has often used drag queens as pawns. Academic discussions have used drag as a shorthand to write about sex, gender, feminism or appropriation. Those debates displace the focus from the drag praxis, and when producing a theoretical assessment on what drag is, or stands for, they inevitably flatten all differences. There has been a tendency to mobilize drag to argue for or against gender performativity and feminine appropriation, queer subversion or commercialization. This chapter has moved beyond those parameters towards the discursive contradictions in Divine and RuPaul's drag, where their queer icons status coexists with certain operations that uphold masculinity and reflect the stigma of effeminacy.

In this chapter, I have summarized the different roles that drag queens have played in gender theory across different disciplines and explored why the study of the most mainstream iterations of drag provide useful case studies of masculinity. In the section 'Professional homosexual: Drag as queer labour' I launched a definition of drag that switches the focus from the sartorial and focuses instead on queer labour, addressing drag as a cultural materialist practice. I defended the idea that drag is a performance by which queer men work within and against the system of accumulation.

In 'Tell me what you are', I analysed and compared a David Letterman/ Divine and Arsenio Hall/RuPaul's talk show interviews in which the drag queens performed one of their singles. I established the similar ways in which they explained their identity and their job and the radical aesthetic differences in their drag. In the section 'Playing the man', I studied the contradictions at play in RuPaul and Divine's ongoing negotiations of gender and drag. While RuPaul has cultivated his drag to great success, he has been relentlessly pursuing opportunities to be as much out of drag as possible. His repeated statement that 'You are Born Naked and the Rest is Drag' disguises hierarchies of power in the social order, and disavows queer meaning. Divine's male presentation during the last years of his career showcased a strong will to quit drag and prove himself as a legitimate actor. The difficulties he experienced in this regard demonstrate the burden of liveness by which the queer subjects can only safely exist by performing to entertain the elites and the contradictory state of queerness as a form of pride but also shame and abjection. Divine and RuPaul commodify their queerness for mass consumption as a form of survival. Under the burden of liveness, they are propelled to make a spectacle of their queerness. That queerness, however, is always accompanied by stigma. By positioning their drag as non-threatening in talk shows, circumscribing drag to clothes, and flaunting their masculinity, they attempt to limit this stigma with little success.

My study of drag queens' media appearances concludes that mainstream drag, in the American context, has been forced to constantly define, re-articulate and make sense of itself. In order to flourish under capitalism, drag queens have flaunted their maleness outside of the performance, reinscribing femininity into a corner, pretending is all an act, that drag queening is simply a job. Within the patriarchal order in which femininity is devalued, embodying the feminine is a source of stigma. If mainstream drag appears contradictory it is because it attempts to simultaneously display and contain queerness: such are the contradictions of working under capital.

Bibliography

Ackroyd, P. (1979) *Dressing Up, Transvestism and Drag: The History of an Obsession*. London: Thames and Hudson.

Aitkenhead, D. (2018) RuPaul: Drag Is a Big F-you to Male-dominated Culture. *The Guardian*, 3 March, 18. Available at: https://www.theguardian.com/tv-and-radio/2018/mar/03/rupaul-drag-race-big-f-you-to-male-dominated-culture (accessed 12 June 2022).

Baker, R. (1968) *Drag: A History of Female Impersonation on Stage*. Washington Square, NY: New York University Press.

Barefoot, G. (2017) *Trash Cinema: The Lure of the Low*. New York and Chichester: Columbia University Press.

Berkowitz, D. and Liska Belgrave, L. (2010) 'She Works Hard for the Money': Drag Queens and the Management of Their Contradictory Status of Celebrity and Marginality. *Journal of Contemporary Ethnography*, 39(2), 159–86.

Bernard, J. (1993) *Not Simply Divine: Beneath the Make-Up, above the Heels and behind the Scenes with a Cult Superstar*. New York: Simon & Schuster.

Bernard, J. (1994) *Not Simply Divine*. New York: Touchstone.

Booth, M. (1983) *Camp*. London, New York and Melbourne: Quartet Books.

Breckon, A. (2013) The Erotic Politics of Disgust: *Pink Flamingos* as Queer Political Cinema. *Screen*, 54(4), 514–33.

Brennan, N. and Gudelunas, D. (2017) *RuPaul's Drag Race and the Shifting Visibility of Drag Culture*. New York: Palgrave Macmillan.

Brown, E. H. (2019) *Work! A Queer History of Modeling*. Durham: Duke University Press.

Butler, J. (1993) *Bodies that Matter: On the Discursive Limits of 'Sex'*. New York: Routledge.

Butler, J. (2006 [1990]) *Gender Trouble: Feminism and the Subversion of Identity*. New York and London: Routledge.

Crawford, J. (1945) *Mildred Pierce [Film]*. United States: Warner Bros.

Crookston, C. (ed) (2021) *The Cultural Impact of RuPaul's Drag Race: Why Are We All Gagging?*. Bristol and Chicago: Intellect Books.

Darrach, B. (1988) Death Comes to a Quiet Man Who Made Drag Queen History as Divine. *People*, 21 March. Available at: https://people.com/archive/death-comes-to-a-quiet-man-who-made-drag-queen-history-as-divine-vol-29-no-11/ (accessed 31 January 2021).

Edward, M. and Farrier, S. (Eds.) (2020) *Contemporary Drag Practices and Performers*. London and New York: Methuen Drama.

Farrier, S. (2019) Theatre, Queer, in Arondekar, A. and Chiang, H. (eds.), *Global Encyclopaedia of Lesbian, Gay, Bisexual, Transgender, and Queer (LGBTQ) History*, 1573–1580. Michigan: C. Scribner's and Sons.

Feldman, Z. and Hakim, J. (2020) From *Paris Is Burning* to #dragrace: Social Media and the Celebrification of Drag Culture. *Celebrity Studies*, 11(4), 386–401.

Foucault, M. (1998) *History of Sexuality, Volume 1: An Introduction*. Translated by Robert Hurley. New York: Vintage Books.

Frye, M. (1983) *The Politics of Reality: Essays in Feminist Theory*. Trumansburg, NY: Crossing Press.

Garber, M. (1992) *Vested Interests: Cross-Dressing and Cultural Anxiety*. New York and London: Routledge.

Gerstner, D. A. and Staiger, J. (2003) *Authorship and Film*. New York: Routledge.

Halberstam, J. (1998) *Female masculinity*. Durham: Duke University Press.

Hargraves, H. "'You better Work': The Commodification of HIV in RuPaul's Drag Race." *Spectator*, 31(2) (Fall 2011), 24–34.

Harris, D. (2005) *Diary of a Drag Queen*. New York: Carroll & Graf Publishers.

Heller, M. (2020) *Queering Drag: Redefining the Discourse of Gender-Bending*. Bloomington, IN: Indiana University Press.

Isherwood, C. (1954) *The World in the Evening*. London: Methuen.

Koestenbaum, W. (1993) *The Queen's Throat: Opera, Homosexuality, and the Mystery of Desire*. New York: Poseidon Press.

LeBlanc (2021) RuPaul's Franchise: Moving toward a Political Economy of Drag Queening, in C. Crookston (ed.), *The Cultural Impact of RuPaul's Drag Race: Why Are We All Gagging?*, 131–55. Bristol and Chicago: Intellect Books.

Liu, P. (2020) Queer Theory and the Specter of Materialism. *Social Text*, 38(4), 25–47.

Livingston, J., Labeija, P., Pendavis, K., Pendavis, F., Corey, D., Xtravaganza, V. and Ninja W. (1992) *Orion Home Video (Firm)*. Paris is burning. United States: Fox Lorber Home Video.

Meyer, M. (1994) Introduction: Reclaiming the Discourse of Camp, in M. Meyer (ed.), *The Politics and Poetics of Camp*, 1–19. New York, NY: Routledge.

Moon, M. and Sedgwick, E. K. (1994) Divinity: A Dossier, a Performance, a Little Understood Emotion, in Sedgwick, E. K. (ed.), *Tendencies*, 213–57. Durham and London: Duke University Press.

Muller, M. G. (2019) RuPaul Explains Why He Didn't Wear Drag to the 2019 Met Gala. *W Magazine | Women's Fashion & Celebrity News*. Available at: https://www.wmagazine.com/story/rupaul-met-gala-2019-no-drag-mean/ (accessed 1 February 2021).

Muñoz, J. E. (1999) *Disidentifications: Queers of Color and the Performance of Politics*. Minneapolis and London: University of Minnesota Press.

Newton, E. (1979) *Mother Camp: Female Impersonators in America*. Chicago: University of Chicago Press.

Newton, E. (1999 [1972]) Role Models, in F. Cleto ed., *Camp: Queer Aesthetics and the Performing Subject, a Reader*, 96–116. Edinburgh: Edinburgh University Press.

Raymond, J. (1994) The Politics of Transgender. *Feminism and Psychology*, 4(4), 628–33.

Rowe, K. (1995) *The Unruly Woman: Gender and the Genres of Laughter*. Austin: University of Texas Press.

Rudolph, A. (1985) *Trouble in Mind [Film]*. United States: Pfeiffer/Blocker Production and Embassy Home Entertainment.

RuPaul (1995) *Lettin It All Hang Out: An Autobiography*. New York: Hyperion.

Schacht, S. (2000). Paris is Burning: How Society's Stratification Systems Make Drag Queens of Us All in *Race, Gender & Class*, 7(1), 147–66.

Schacht, S. and Underwood, L. (2004) *The Drag Queen Anthology: The Absolutely Fabulous but Flawlessly Customary World of Female Impersonators*. New York and London: Routledge.

Schoonover, K. (2010) Divine: Towards an 'Imperfect' Stardom, in Morrison, J. (ed.), *Hollywood Reborn: Movie Stars of the 1970s*, 158–81. Piscataway, NJ: Rutgers University Press.

Schwarz, J. (2013) *I Am Divine [Documentary]*. United States: Automat Pictures, Making it Big.

Sedgwick, E. K (1994) *Tendencies*. Durham and London: Duke University Press.

Sherman, D. (2019) *FAQ John Waters: All That Is Left To Know about the Provocateur of Bad Taste*. Guilford, CT: Applause Theatre Books.

Sontag, S. (1964) Notes on 'Camp'. *Partisan Review*, 31(4), 535–30.

Studlar, G. (1989) Midnight S/Excess: Cult Configurations of 'Femininity' and the Perverse. *Journal of Popular Film and Television*, 17(1), 2–14.

Tinkcom, M. (2002) *Working Like a Homosexual: Camp, Capital, Cinema*. Durham and London: Duke University Press.

Waters, J. (1972) *Pink Flamingos [Film]*. United States: Dreamland.

Waters, J. (1974) *Female Trouble [Film]*. United States: Dreamland.

Waters, J. (2005 [1981]) *Shock Value: A Tasteful Book about Bad Taste*. New York: Thunder's Mouth Press.

Williamson, J. (1986) *Consuming Passions: The Dynamics of Popular Culture*. New York: Marion Boyars.

Yudelman, J. (2017) The 'RuPaulitics' of Subjectivation in RuPaul's Drag Race, in Brennan, N. and Gudelunas, D. (eds.), *RuPaul's Drag Race and the Shifting Visibility of Drag Culture*, 15–28. New York: Palgrave Macmillan.

Part Three

Bodies and Minds

9

Sobriety, service and selfhood: Moral-existential reconfiguration of masculinity in alcoholics anonymous in a large English city

Lucy Clarke

Alcoholic Anonymous (AA) is a transnational fellowship of self-diagnosed[1] alcoholics who hold regular meetings in order to recover. It has its roots in 1930s Ohio, America, where it emerged from the Oxford Group, an upper-class Evangelical Christian organization who stressed the importance of confession, restitution and 'taking stock of oneself' (Kurtz 1979:17). AA's founder, Bill Wilson, attended the Oxford Group meetings and found that some of the mechanisms were helpful for avoiding alcohol. Wilson, and a few others, began to encourage people to join in order to recover from alcoholism. These people (mostly men) formed a sub-sect which eventually split from the Oxford Group in 1937 (Kurtz 1979:27). It was at this point that the infamous central text, named 'Alcoholics Anonymous', was written (the 'Big Book' to members) and AA's twelve-step programme was formed. The twelve steps have since been utilized in fellowships spawned from AA, including Narcotics Anonymous (NA), Overeaters Anonymous (OA), Gambling Anonymous (GA), Co-dependents Anonymous (CoDA) and Emotions Anonymous (EA).

This chapter will explore a range of the practices and concepts that have developed in AA. I argue that through everyday practices that members of AA carry out, and through the discourse they engage in, they come to inhabit a different way of being which interrupts particular elements of gendered practice. This way of being, I suggest, works through the symbol of 'sobriety', a term with a specific technical usage in AA. Sobriety is understood to be both abstinence from alcohol and a particular mode of existence. Members describe sobriety as

---

[1] Also often medically diagnosed.

a 'spiritual' state, which in the AA context tends to refer to a deep sense of well-being, of richness, rather than necessarily in reference to the metaphysical (see also Dossett 2017).

Most members carry out AA's twelve-step programme[2] with the support of a sponsor (a member of AA who has been 'sober' for a significant amount of time). The steps are thought to be 'spiritual [not] religious' (Alcoholics Anonymous 2021a) and encourage members to develop a sense of a Higher Power 'of [their] own understanding' (Alcoholics Anonymous 2001:85). Many of my informants chose their Higher Power to be other people, others told me their Higher Power was a Christian God, the universe, or AA itself. Members stress that it is important that a person's Higher Power is 'greater than [themselves]'.

Scholars of masculinity have articulated how men, through involvement in twelve-step programmes, can come to inhabit forms of masculinity which are inclusive of what are often traditionally seen as 'feminized' qualities such as empathy, humility, vulnerability and mutual care, while relinquishing what, outside of AA, have been seen as 'masculine' ideals such as control, self-will and autonomy. I explore this work in my second section, then build on it by engaging with how broader frameworks in the twelve-step practice and discourse open up opportunities for these alternative masculinities to unfold (Dwyer 2014; Gueta et al. 2019; Irvine and Klocke 2001).

I am guided in my analysis by post-structural feminist theory, according to which, notions of gender are interwoven into the social matrix through which a person comes into being. Through living in a society, we develop particular capacities for understanding, feeling and experiencing. Gender norms operate through us – they are maintained through the ways that we find ourselves responding to the world, the things we desire, what feels natural to us and what feels distant (Butler 2011; Gatens 2003; Mahmood 2005). As Judith Butler puts it: 'gendering is, among other things, the differentiating relations by which the speaking subject comes into being' (Butler 2011:XVI). There is no existence prior to, or outside of, societal narratives, including gendered relations. Individuals do not pre-exist their social contexts but are formed through them.

This raises interesting questions regarding masculinities in twelve-step movements. If we think of gendered identities as bound up with the social matrix through which we are formed, what is it about the 'social matrix' of twelve-step movements which allows for masculinity to be reproduced in different ways?

---

[2] For the twelve steps, please see: "http://www.alcoholics-anonymous.org.uk/"www.alcoholics-anonymous.org.uk

This chapter concerns how twelve-step discourse and practice imbues members with different experiential capacities (that is, new ways of thinking, feeling and experiencing) which manifest in the state of sobriety. These capacities make possible these new forms of masculinity which have been identified in the literature. What I am suggesting is that AA rearticulates being and morality in a way which provides the groundwork for different kinds of masculinity (and different kinds of subjectivities in general) to unfold. It disrupts the existential co-ordinates of the member, the means through which they understand themselves and their relationship with the world, and in doing so it also undercuts the logic of certain kinds of gendered binaries which permeate the West. I posit that this happens because, when a member engages with AA's practice and discourse, their pre-objective assumptions regarding the human subject shifts and changes. Post-structuralist feminists argue that the conception of the human subject which we have developed in the West, and through which many of us in the West come to understand ourselves, is based on a reification of what are seen as masculinized capacities, priorities and experiences. As Gatens writes 'Man is the model – and it is his body which is taken for the human body, his reason which is taken for human reason, his morality which is formalized into a system of ethics' (2003:24). This masculinized self (which is also white, middle class and heteronormative) is the selfhood against which other subjectivities are understood. This 'metaphysical basis' (Gatens 2003:VII) is interwoven with how we understand selfhood, existence and morality. This is, in part, what works to erase and undermine the experiences of women and others who don't embody this form of personhood (see also Lloyd 2004).

The masculinist concept of self which I am referring to understands the individual as able to transcend bodily ways of being in order to reach a higher, universal, objective, truth. Knowledge is gained through denying the body and the intersubjective world in favour of universal truth, which can be accessed through a person's internal rationality. This understanding of self can be traced back to the post-enlightenment period, in particular back to Kant. Reliance on others, in the Kantian analysis, is a sign of moral immaturity, and a mature person (assumed to be male) should be able to access universal truths independent of those around them (Lloyd 2004).

Feminist scholars have argued that this prevailing conception of self-privileges the masculine. Abstract thought is associated with masculinity, whilst emotionally engaged, bodily ways of being are denigrated and associated with the non-masculine. An epistemology which has this notion of disembodied rationality (coded as masculine) at the heart of its conception of self, frames people who are considered to be non-masculine as incomplete, inferior and as reliant on masculine others (Butler 1990:16; Gatens 2003; Norman 2011; Weber 2013). Post-structural feminist thought posits that gendered identity is one register through which the 'I' is produced (and is reproduced), but this register works within, and is supported by, broader shared conceptions of morality, self and the human subject. That is, our notions of being and morality are grounded in Kantian assumptions about the human subject, which are inherently masculinist.

My suggestion is that the discourse and practices that AA members engage in rupture this rationalist model of the self. I argue that, in recovery, members develop a new common-sense understanding of the human subject, they start to work from different kinds of existential coordinates. Once these foundations of self are reconfigured, new capacities for being can be opened up, and different kinds of personhood, including new forms of gendered identities, can emerge. A new understanding of themselves as men comes only because of a new understanding of morality, self and existence. After laying out my methods, I will explore how scholars have demonstrated that masculinity shifts through involvement in AA. I will then elucidate, in the following two sections, on the ways that AA discourse and practice interrupts this post-enlightenment understanding of self, through interrupting the presumptive world of the member.

Methods

I carried out four months of fieldwork in Birmingham, a large city in the UK, much of which consisted of meeting with AA members (individually and in groups) in public spaces. I also went to AA conferences and was invited to attend one secular meeting, which I went to several times. I explained to my interlocutors that I was an anthropologist carrying out research on AA, and gained consent for working with them before speaking to them. Prior to this research period, I supported someone to attend an AA meeting regularly for over a year. I won't refer directly to this period, but it has informed my general understanding of AA.

I met with around twenty-five members altogether, most of whom were white men aged between forty and seventy. This is particularly important for this work, given that the disembodied subject has been characterized as male and white. Alongside my fieldwork, I use secondary ethnographic literature from both AA and other twelve-step movements. Although there are some differences across twelve-step movements, the core concepts and ideologies are relevant to my purposes. I have also used AA literature, as well as testimonies and life stories written by AA members.

Masculinity and twelve-step programmes

As I have outlined above, research has identified that involvement with twelve-step programmes can facilitate a change in how men identify themselves. In this section, I will draw out the ways in which disembodied masculinity plays out in these texts. By disembodied masculinity, I mean the iteration of masculinity which characterises men as able to distance themselves from their emotions, experiences and desires, to exist as something other than bodily beings (Lloyd 2004; Norman 2011; Weber 2013). I will explain how anthropologists have shown that twelve-step masculinity is at odds with disembodied masculinity. Finally, I will look at how I hope to push the understanding of twelve-step masculinity further.

Gueta, Gamliel and Ronel articulate how the men that they worked with in Narcotics Anonymous (NA) in an Israeli prison experienced conflict between their masculinity and the ideals and practices inherent in NA. One example was the practice of sharing. Sharing is a central aspect of twelve-step practice and refers to talking about one's experiences, emotions and everyday thoughts. Gueta et al.'s paper quotes one informant expressing this aversion to sharing:

> I was afraid to share. I did not know what the reaction would be, how they would see me or what they would think of me, how they would take it.
>
> (2019:10)

They also note how the men identified feelings of shame associated with outward displays of emotion, such as crying:

> The [life story] sharing, … [I asked myself]: are you going to cry? It's not masculine; it's inappropriate.
>
> (ibid.:10)

Over time, these men began to feel that they were able to share, they even felt the desire to do so. Gueta et al. (2019) explore how new forms of masculinity were negotiated by men in order to accommodate and facilitate this change.

For instance, they note that 'expressions of vulnerability were reinterpreted as strength and courage, leading to agency rather than weakness' (ibid.:12). Their informants said things such as 'weakness actually solves more problems' (ibid.:11), which reframed expressing vulnerabilities as being a pragmatic act.

Dwyer (2014), similarly, notes how men he worked in Ireland with found it difficult to share their life stories. One informant said:

> Before I'd never reveal feelings or vulnerabilities, for me to go into a meeting and reveal how I might be struggling in front of thirty people when I couldn't tell my mates of twenty years, now that's big change, I would've seen that stuff as being weak and girly.
>
> (188)

Dwyer's informants expressed that, previous to AA, 'an element of fear was attached to ownership of gentler traits such as emotional expression' (190). Once in AA, his informants went through a 'transition from hegemonic norms to a more open and spiritual masculine identity' (187). He stresses the importance of the 'collective culture of recovery' (192) which 'produc[es] a less rigid and restrictive environment' (192). Dwyer writes that, through recovery, his informants were 'striv[ing] for new ways of being against years of masculine socialisation' (191).

Disembodied masculine identity runs through the ways in which the men in these ethnographies express themselves when they first join twelve-step movements. They have a sense that their emotions and subjective experiences should be superseded by (and subordinate to) a controlled, rational self. It is a struggle for these men to reveal themselves as being grounded in bodily ways of being and engaged with the affective dimension of their experience. As members become involved with AA discourse and practice, they loosen their grasp on disembodied masculinity and find sharing less conflicting.

Irvine and Klocke's paper (2001) explores the changes that their informants experienced in Co-Dependents Anonymous (CoDA).[3] They explain how the structure of the meetings impacted upon the identity of the men they worked with. In meetings, attendees are encouraged to avoid 'cross talk', meaning they cannot respond explicitly to what someone else has said. This, they write, is 'distinctly at odds with the characteristic ways in which men are socialized to communicate' (38). They articulate how these men 'were struck by how much

---

[3] CoDA describes itself as a fellowship 'whose common purpose is to develop healthy relationships' (Co-dependents Anonymous UK 2021).

having to listen without voicing their opinions changed them' (38). One of their informants said 'now, I listen to other people share about their lives, and I think to myself, "Maybe they know something I don't". Let's pay attention here' (39). Some realized that 'manhood limits the range of emotion they may feel and express' (41).

These scholars have articulated how the imperative to know best, to be a person who is able to supersede the body and reach truth – is challenged through twelve-step practice. This work has demonstrated how men's conception of what it means to be a man comes into conflict with the ideas in twelve-step movements. It articulates how they dealt with this conflict by rejecting some elements of their concept of masculinity, while redefining and broadening others. Through twelve-step movements, they come to inhabit new forms of masculine identity which are more inclusive of the ideals of twelve-step philosophy, such as empathy, finitude, humbleness and emotional expression.

I want to push this work further by, firstly, emphasizing that gendered identities are lived and experienced. The work on twelve-step masculinity, while it has explained how gendered narratives shift and change, has not yet adequately explored the experiential quality of this process, how it is viscerally felt and lived. Irvine and Klocke (2001) write that CoDA allows men to 'consider what being a man means to them and reject much of their traditional behaviour in favour of more egalitarian options' (42). I am suggesting that their new subjectivity is a result of a new experiential state that they find themselves in, rather than the result of a conscious decision.

This framing derives from the post-structural feminist insight that different kinds of gendered identities require different kinds of experiential capacities, which emerge out of different kinds of practices and discursive frameworks. As Moira Gatens puts it, 'our embodied history cannot be thrown off as if it were a coat' through 'a pure act of will'. That is, we cannot start to exist as something other than what we have been constituted to be, except by being reconstituted through new frameworks, which evolve out of old ones. I argue that these men in AA do not only develop a new masculine identity, but also a new existential position in the world, which frames and intertwines with their masculinity.

Secondly, connected with this, I frame masculinity as something which emerges out of, and is a facet of, a shared conceptual universe. Gendering is one element of the social matrix through which the 'I' comes to exist, and through which the 'I' is reproduced. Masculinity does not exist independently of other frameworks but is reliant on them and intertwined with them. Twelve-step masculinity is not a process whereby men simply learn to develop capacities already largely embodied by women. Rather, it is one manifestation of a shift in their assumptive world, an assumptive world inhabited by people throughout the West (although it is of course experienced and articulated in a variety of different intersections of gender, race, disability and geography). As a result of the social web of meaning which permeates twelve-step discourse and practice, men in twelve-step movements experience a radical (if sometimes gradual) shift in their perceptive universe, which interrupts particular understandings of self and the human subject upon which particular forms of masculinity rely.

The disembodied masculinity which runs through the literature I have cited is reliant on particular existential coordinates. Specifically, it relies upon the Kantian divide between the experiencing, affective self and objective, universal knowledge, as well as the understanding that the experiencing self should be superseded. I am arguing that these new masculinities are made possible through a reworking, and an interrupting, of these post-enlightenment concepts, which uphold traditional forms of masculinity.

Cultivating sobriety

Sobriety in AA is characterized as both abstinence from drinking, and also a particular way of being. Members report that in sobriety they feel calmer, even serene. They accept things more easily and connect more with others. I often heard people say that they found it easier to be humble and to 'go with the flow', to have a 'zest for life' – they report that they are more accepting of themselves and others. These qualities are at the core of twelve-step philosophy, and are the notions which, according to the work on twelve-step masculinity, challenge dominant forms of masculinity. What I want to emphasize in this section is that these qualities, in AA, are bound up with the spiritual state of sobriety, and, as such, they are cultivated and experienced.

The serenity of sobriety is pitted against a past of drinking alcoholism in the narratives told by AA members. Often these stories would describe one's actions in the past, and impose current judgments on them, much like Joel does in the following passage:

> once I had come home from the pub and I was telling my wife what an awful wife she was, no wonder I drank. All of this stupid stuff. And I remember that my daughter came down the stairs and said 'don't you speak to my mum like that!' Now a child should never have to say that to a parent. That's not right.

In judging his past actions, Joel establishes a clear break between the drinking self of the past and the sober self of the present. This is characteristic of twelve-step story structure which says, in the words of one of Dwyer's informants 'that was then, this is now' (Dwyer 2014:187; see also Cain 1991).

My informants described their emotional experiences with this same break. Their life as a drinking alcoholic came across as full of turmoil, anxiety and loneliness – most described suicidal thoughts and feeling disconnected with the rest of the world. Several said that they had had a 'hole in the soul' and had tried to 'grasp' on to things to fill this hole but could never quite succeed. By contrast, life in sobriety is one of connection with other people, of being 'align[ed] with reality'.

However, while drinking alcoholism[4] is firmly in the past, it is also, in another sense, ever-present in their life. The majority of people in AA consider themselves to be eternally alcoholics, and, as such, compulsive drinking continues to hang as a possibility. For instance, Richard characterized sobriety as 'the ability to cope with whatever is happening', but when I noted that this was a very useful skill to have, he laughed and said: 'Well I don't have it all the time. But I usually pull myself back because it's too dangerous for someone like me to go the other way.' He hadn't achieved sobriety as such, rather that it was something he had to 'pull' himself back into. In their everyday lives, my informants were 'pulling' themselves back to sobriety through doing things which are thought to be good for it. Sobriety is, by its nature, ever incomplete – something to be maintained and tended to rather than singularly achieved.

This state of incompleteness, of limitation, is integrated into the AA understanding of self. It is a prevailing theme of Ernest Kurtz's (1979) history of AA, and was something which was repeatedly voiced by my informants – there was an understanding that they are not whole without other people. As my informant Nigel said 'we are all just parts of a greater whole', while Joel told me that 'We need each other, as people we need each other'. In this sense, AA rearticulates the self as in a continual state of becoming.

This manifests in alternative forms of masculinity because it undercuts the existential bases of traditional masculinity. An understanding of a self which is constantly worked on, which is incomplete, disavows the distinction between the complete masculine subject (who is able to overcome the subjective self) and the incomplete feminine one (who is of the body, and so is not a whole human subject).[5] If the human subject is fundamentally incomplete, then the

---

[4]   As opposed to the sober alcoholism of the present.
[5]   Also see Gatens (2003:XI).

masculinist concept of the complete, independent, subject with access to divine reason is no longer a realistic understanding of self. In this way, AA discourse around sobriety reconfigures pre-objective conceptions of the nature of the human subject.

Further, for members of AA, the tenets encompassed by sobriety are not simply qualities which make up a particular ideal of manhood (or of personhood in general), but rather are a manifestation of a particular way of experiencing things. Humbleness, openness to others and compassion are experiential qualities which are cultivated over time through AA practice. One member articulated sobriety as 'like your hair growing'. There is a sense that it infuses into a person's life without them noticing at first. As they 'work the programme' the member starts to experience themselves differently, and as a result, they inhabit a different kind of subjectivity, which manifests in new forms of masculinity.

AA and morality

This section builds on the conceptions of masculinity outlined above through exploring how members conceptualize moral action in a way which undermines the dichotomy between rationality and embodiment. I suggest that the AA view on morality (by which I mean how we understand right and wrong) and moral action (by which I mean how we act upon this understanding – or don't) challenges the Kantian split between subjective experience and absolute moral truth. The moral good, in the Kantian frame of thought, is to be reached through internalized objective reason irrespective of the body, cast as absolute and non-negotiable duty. As Lloyd (2004) writes, through this perspective 'reason of itself yields moral principles universally valid regardless of contingent empirical inclinations, passions or interests' (68).

This sense of morality is commensurate with disembodied masculinity – requiring the subordination of the embodied subject and its needs to a brittle regime of rationality. As such, in this section I will explain how members of AA develop a different relationship with morality than that of denying the body to reach moral truths. I argue that they come to understand their experiences and emotions as bound up with their moral action. Moral action becomes affective, and the person becomes aware of how it intimately affects their experience.

Service

Service in AA means doing things which are thought to help others. Often this is through assisting the running of the fellowship, but can refer to non-AA activities. Service can manifest as making tea and coffee at a meeting, sponsoring other members, helping a neighbour, volunteering at an AA event – the list goes on.

Helping people is thought to be good for sobriety – the beneficiary of the kind act is also the person performing it. This was reflected in how people spoke about moral action. Members would say 'it's for me' when carrying out service, and often I would hear insights such as 'selflessness is actually quite selfish'. One informant I had met at a café insisted on paying the bill, saying 'No really, I hate to be all AA about it, but it is for me'. This was a joking acknowledgement of the tendency in AA to frame moral action as a part of recovery.

In this way, as Gabriella Swora (2001) has noted, AA prescribes social and moral action to treat thoughts and emotions. She uses the following quote to demonstrate how service is the cure for self-pity:

> we don't give the new guy the coffee commitment because, you're new, you're the loser, you do the grunt job. It's exactly the opposite. We give the big gifts to the newcomers so that you get to [...] experience some of the remarkable spiritual principles that are afoot in these rooms [...] [You] know what happens when you make the coffee? You're being of service. You have to think of them, an' their coffee for four hours every Friday night. [...] You're gonna be of service you're gonna get out of self ... When you come back to you, you'll come back with a new perspective, an' it's gonna be different, you're gonna grow. An' you're gonna feel better.
>
> (Swora 2001:17)

As Swora suggests, this member demonstrates that service is both a social and moral action, and a treatment for alcoholism. Making coffee, he explains, helps the newcomer to 'grow' and gain a 'new perspective' – helping others positively affects the new member's emotional state and making coffee for them contributes to his sobriety. Service helps them to 'get out of themselves' and links the needs of others to their own subjective experience. As such, continually carrying out service is thought of as being good for sobriety, as being a part of 'working the programme'. Each time the member is helping someone else, they are helping themselves to steer clear from 'alcoholic thinking' and stay sober for another day.

Members help other people to affect their experience of things, how they think and feel. As Thom said 'altruistic acts are very important for sobriety'.

Conversely, repeatedly being dishonest or unkind is considered harmful to sobriety, something best depicted in a conversation I had with Graham during my fieldwork. He told a story about someone who had revealed to him that she was committing a minor fraud. She came back to him, worried that she had told him too much and that he might tell the police. He repeated his response to me:

> I said 'You don't have to worry about me going to the police and reporting you, that's not something I'm going to do, it isn't something you have to worry about, I also am not going to tell you not to do it, that's not what I'm here for, only you can decide that. But if you ask me if I think it's dishonest and will jeopardize your sobriety? Then I'll say yes, yes I do.

Performing a 'dishonest' act and continuing to do so is a danger to the person's sobriety. Dishonesty, Graham stresses, is something which affects one's sobriety and so should be avoided. His concern is for its harm to the sobriety of the member and the ever-present threat of drinking alcoholism.

Through this notion that moral action is either good or bad for sobriety, members come to understand it as intimately connected to their way of being. Whether they are honest or dishonest, whether they help others or harm others, whether they choose to carry out service or they neglect to, has an effect on whether they have the kind of thoughts, feelings and experiences of sobriety, or whether they have those which lead to drinking alcoholism.

Bringing morality into connection with bodily experience ruptures the assumptive world upon which particular forms of masculinity rely. In the AA frame of thought, moral action is not something which is carried out in *spite* of one's inclinations, experiences and emotions (as in the Kantian model) it is something which *directly affects* these things. In this way, AA members come to understand moral action as intertwined with their bodily and emotional state – the human subject becomes fundamentally affective. Moral choices are thought to have an impact on our inclinations and emotions, our experience of things, our ongoing affective state. Disembodied masculinity, which relies upon the subordination of the experiencing self in favour of rationality, cannot be upheld once there is a connection drawn between morality and subjective experience.

The sense of moral action as affective has been woven into AA discourse since its beginning. Bill Wilson, speaking at Yale, told a story of how he had failed to help other alcoholics at the start. At first, he said, following an experience he called a 'hot flash', he felt 'God had selected [him] [...] to dry up all the drunks in the world'. He tried to help people to 'dry up' for six months, but with no results. He took some time to reflect and realized that, although he had not gotten anyone else sober, he had kept sober himself. He tried again, but, he said 'No longer was I preaching from any moral hilltop [...] No, this time I was looking for another alcoholic because I felt that I needed him twice as much as he needed me' (Taves 2016:93).

Wilson explains how he came to understand that he needed to support other alcoholics in their sobriety in order to maintain his own. He moved from thinking of himself as benevolently attending to the needs of others out of duty to a sense of mutual need. He was not helping others to impart wisdom from his successful recovery, rather he was helping others to help his continual recovery – to 'pull' himself back to sobriety. Wilson also demonstrates here another element of AA discourse which is connected to the 'it's for me' attitude towards moral action. That is, through casting 'preaching' as the unhelpful antithesis to mutual need, he shows an aversion to individual claims of moral authority. First, he was prideful and understood himself as on a 'moral hilltop', helping others out of duty to God, then he was humble and understood himself as in need of other people. The member helps other people in order to help themselves and work on their sobriety, as opposed to because they have reached the 'moral hilltop' of Kantian transcendentalism.[6]

This self-conscious aversion to claims of moral authority was evident in my fieldwork – for instance when Nigel joked with Bruce that he had a list of every favour he had ever done for him and would be tallying up the scores. In mocking this kind of moral bookkeeping, where debts and favours are added up over time, where the individual assesses the good and bad deeds of others, Nigel was mocking the tendency to make morally authoritative judgements, or, as AA members often said, to 'take myself too seriously'.[7]

The 'it's for me' attitude in AA does two, intertwined, things. First, it allows the member to understand themselves as affected by moral action, each moral act in the world is thought to affect their sobriety – their emotionality, their experience and, ultimately, their ability to stay away from booze. Second, it challenges the notion of individual, objective, moral judgements, and in doing so undermines the idea of accessing moral truths through a solely internal rationality. If I carry out kind deeds to help myself, I am not making claims about

---

[6]   Ann Taves (2016:113) has explored the history of mutuality in AA.

[7]   This contrast is also present in the quote from Graham above; 'I'm [...] not going to tell you not to do it, that's not what I'm here for'.

a moral truth which everyone should follow.[8] In undermining these concepts, it also negates the concept of the disembodied masculine subject, whose validity relies on them. The member no longer strives for disembodiment because he understands the self to be fundamentally affective, it is no longer something he considers to be within human capability. I find Vena Das's notion of 'ordinary ethics' (2010) useful to elucidate this further. Ordinary ethics refers to the diverse ways in which people 'engage in the life of another' (376). Das argues that anthropologists have placed emphasis on 'understanding [...] morality as the capacity to form *moral judgments* in which the crucial requirement is that we should be able to take an abstract, non-subjective vantage position from which we can orient our-selves to the world' (377). She argues that, while people do make these kinds of judgements, morality cannot be reduced only to this. Through analysing the elopement of a young couple, a Hindu man and a Muslim woman, she demonstrates how the 'imperative to be attentive to the suffering of another' (377) informs the ethical standpoint of the couple and everyone around them. They do not abandon moral norms, but rather they adjust their position in relation to them, finding ways to adapt them to the situation, or inhabiting them in new ways.

Through integrating moral action with self-care, the member is developing the propensity to engage with 'ordinary ethics'. This framing of morality directs the member's attention away from the notion of objective, moral judgements, and towards the experiencing, affective, self. It opens up the capacity to integrate the experiencing self into moral action. Each time the member helps someone else, they learn to 'get out of self' and experience themselves-in-relation as they engage in other people's lives. In doing this, they are viscerally engaging with that which they understand as being beyond their boundaries of self, which in turn, actually breaks down and reconfigures those boundaries over time.

My informants reported that, as time goes on, they find that they are more comfortable with themselves as moral beings. Thom, for example, described developing the ability to 'be spontaneously kind' after some time in sobriety, and Richard said 'I don't feel right if I'm not honest with somebody in a situation'. Through sobriety they have been able to access a bodily kind of ethics, one which is 'just there', in their perception. Ethics, rather than being a set of abstract principles which individuals choose to live by or not, become something lived and experienced.

---

[8] This follows with the AA attitude to abstinence from alcohol. The member can maintain their abstinence through AA, but abstinence is not an objective moral good in and of itself.

Of course, members do make moral judgements. It is understood that some actions help other people and some don't. However, what I'm pointing to here is how this framing of moral action brings the affective self into contact with such judgements, and in doing so opens up new experiential capacities – including the capacity to understand that these judgements are not necessarily 'right' in a transcendentalist sense. In carrying out service, members are not attempting to transcend the self, but rather they are integrating the affective self into their understanding of morality. Rather than trying to follow the moral good out of duty, they are working to develop the capacity to 'engage with the life of another' (Das 2010). This capacity is then integrated into their masculine identities in the ways that we have seen; a shift from a disembodied masculinity which strives to reject the experiencing self, to an understanding of oneself as affected by one's action in the world, as being fundamentally and inescapably affective.

Conclusion

Throughout this chapter I have shown how, whilst men do develop and inhabit different kinds of masculinities as they engage with AA, these masculinities emerge out of broader frameworks which disrupt post-enlightenment conceptions of selfhood, morality, existence and the human subject. This manifests in the experience of sobriety. Members find that 'working the programme' affects how they think and feel, how they respond to things, even their sense of who they are.

Through continually working on their sobriety, continually striving, they understand the self as fundamentally incomplete, which relieves them of masculine ideals of completeness. Through the notion of 'it's for me' morality, they bring their understanding of morality from a focus on masculinized notions of abstract thought towards being grounded in the intersubjective and the ordinary. They start to feel more connected with the world around them, more 'in reality'. This experience manifests in forms of masculinity which are inclusive of empathy, humbleness and expressions of vulnerability. As the assumptive world which underpins disembodied masculinity starts to unravel, so too does disembodied masculinity itself.

I have shown through this chapter how twelve-step discourse can disrupt particular elements of patriarchy. This is not to say that it creates a space which is free of the influence of patriarchy, nor that it serves as a model for a feminist reconstruction of our system of ethics. I simply wish to demonstrate how different forms of masculinity can emerge out of different kinds of frameworks. Through analysing the ways that patriarchy is undermined – even imperfectly – in diverse, and sometimes surprising, settings, we can broaden our understanding of the mechanisms of gendered power structures. To do this we need to look beyond the gendered narratives themselves and try to understand the bases from which such narratives are operating.

Bibliography

Butler, J. (1990) *Gender Trouble*. London and New York: Routledge.

Butler, J (2011) *Bodies That Matter: On the Discursive Limits of 'Sex'*. London and New York: Routledge.

Cain, C. (1991) Personal Stories: Identity Acquisition and Self-Understanding in Alcoholics Anonymous. *Ethos*, 19, 210–53.

Co-Dependents Anonymous UK (2021) New to CoDA. [online] Available at: https://codauk.org/new-to-coda/ (accessed 2 October. 2021).

Das, V. (2010) Engaging the Life of the Other: Love and Everyday Life, in Michael Lambek (ed.), *Ordinary Ethics: Anthropology, Language, and Action*, 376–99. USA: Fordham University.

Dossett, W. (2017) Reflections on the Language of Salvation in Twelve-Step Recovery, in Hannah Bacon, Wendy Dossett and Steve Knowles (eds.), *Alternative Salvations: Engaging the Sacred and the Secular*, 21–31. UK: Bloomsbury.

Dwyer, D. (2014) The Lived Experiences of Men in 12-Step Recovery against a Backdrop of Hegemonic Masculinity. *Irish Probation Journal*, 11, 177–95.

Gatens, M. (2003) *Imaginary Bodies: Ethics, Power, and Corporeality*. London: Routledge.

Gueta, K., Gamliel, S. and Ronel, N. (2019) 'Weak Is the New Strong': Gendered Meanings of Recovery from Substance Abuse among Male Prisoners Participating in Narcotic Anonymous Meetings. *Men and Masculinities*, 24(1), 104–26.

Irvine, L and Klocke, B. (2001) Redefining Men: Alternative Masculinities in a Twelve-Step Programme. *Men and Masculinities*, 4(1), 27–48.

Kurtz, E. (1979) *Not-God: A History of Alcoholics Anonymous*. Hazelden, MN: Educational Services.

Kurtz, E. (1982) Why AA Works: The Intellectual Significance of Alcoholics Anonymous. *Journal of Studies on Alcohol*, 43, 38–80.

Lloyd, G. (2004) *The Man of Reason: 'Male' and 'Female' in Western Philosophy*. E-library, Taylor and Frances.

Mahmood, S. (2005) *Politics of Piety: The Islamic Revival and the Feminist Subject*. Princeton and Oxford: Princeton University Press.

Norman, M. E. (2011) Embodying the Double-Bind of Masculinity: Young Men and Discourses of Normalcy, Health, Heterosexuality, and Individualism, in Tristan Bridges, Kristen Barber, and JosephD. Nelson (eds.), *Men and Masculinities*, 14 No.4. 430–49. USA, Canada: Sage.

Swora, M.G. (2001) Personhood and Disease in Alcoholics Anonymous: A Perspective from the Anthropology of Religious Healing, in Simon Dein (ed.), *Mental Health, Religion & Culture*, 4 1,1–21. UK: Routledge.

Taves, A. (2016) *Revelatory Events: Three Case Studies of the Emergence of New Spiritual Paths*. Princeton and Oxford: Princeton University Press.

Weber, B.R. (2013) Masculinity, American Modernity, and Body Modification: A Feminist Reading of American Eunuchs. *Signs*, 38(3), 671–94.

AA-References

AlcoholicsAnonymous (2001) *Alcoholics Anonymous: This Is the Fourth Edition of the Big Book, the Basic Text for Alcoholics Anonymous*. New York, USA: Alcoholics Anonymous World Services.

Alcoholics Anonymous (2021a) Frequently Asked Questions. *Alcoholics Anonymous Great Britain*, Available at: https://www.alcoholics-anonymous.org.uk/Professionals/Frequently-asked-Questions (accessed 30 July 2021).

Alcoholics Anonymous (2021b) About Alcoholism. *Alcoholics Anonymous Great Britain*, Available at: https://www.alcoholics-anonymous.org.uk/About-AA/Newcomers/About-Alcoholism accessed 30 July 2021).

10

Unheard voices, untold stories; men with disabilities – The invisible victims of patriarchy, a study of Kolkata, Bengal, India

Debarati Chakraborty

Introduction

People with disabilities are discriminated against on various grounds, but their experiences of gender and sexuality are seldom discussed within academia. Furthermore, the experience of inequality is not confined to public spaces on the grounds of employment and education, but is also common in the private space of the home. The control of women and younger men in India remains in the hands of men who generally control the economy of the household along with land or commercial capital (Kandiyoti 1988:282). Hence, the domestic sphere remains one of the most prevalent areas for the exercise of patriarchal power. This experience of patriarchal domination is compounded given the already marginalized status of disabled people around the world. As Murdick et al. note:

> Disability has been present in all societies in the world throughout history. In spite of the long history and the universality of disability, almost without exception, people with disabilities have been discriminated against; with that discrimination ranging from minor embarrassment and inconvenience to relegation to a life of limited experience and reduced social opportunity and civil rights.
>
> (Murdick et al. 2004:31)

The study of how men are affected by and relate to each-other in a patriarchal society is studied far less than it is in relation to women. In India patriarchy is represented through the concentration of power and control in the hands of

This study is a part of the author's unpublished doctoral thesis.

men, by which they dominate women and other men in both public and private spaces. In the family in particular, women are controlled by male members of the household, while in public spaces women are controlled by collective groups of men as well as those in governments, corporations and other organizations (Dasgupta and Gokulsing 2013:7).

The emergence of neoliberal capitalism has further strengthened patriarchy as an institution through the gendered specialization of work, inequality though markets and commodity consumption (Collins and Rothe 2017; Hartman 1976:137). With this rise of consumerism, lives began to be driven by the needs of the market – conceptions of work and profitability emphasize specific forms of 'normality' (fair, young and able-bodied etc.) as an ideal. Failure to achieve these norms readily becomes identified with inferiority or 'otherness' (Clapton and Fitzgerald 1997:1–2). Appreciating these dynamics around bodily norms is a key part of understanding the oppression and marginalization that disabled people face (Abberley 1987:7). Thus, through close attention to the everyday experiences of disabled peoples it becomes possible to gain insight into these various forms of oppression and their intersection with gender (ibid. 9). In more theoretical terms, Clapton and Fitzgerald assess how both bodily difference and Otherness are incorporated into social structures through the strategic exclusion or inclusion of particular bodies in particular ways, leading to the systemic marginalization of disabled bodies (1997:1). The relationship between the 'norm' and the 'Other' in the context of disabled bodies parallels de Beauvoir's (1956) analysis of gender; like women are a secondary term to men, same way disabled bodies are seen to be inferior to the able-bodied. In and across both instances, structurally privileged bodies and genders are afforded status to their respective 'Other'. Disabled women are placed in a doubly discriminated position (Ghai 2002; Meer 2015; Moin 2009; Vansteenwegen 2003), while disabled men are placed in a strange, contradictory slot where their male privilege is in tension with the marginalization afforded by their disability. The analysis of this tension forms a key part of this chapter.

Literature review

Patriarchy is a complex system of beliefs and practices, legitimizing the oppression of women and their domination by men (Walby 1989). Yet despite this, it has profound effects on men which can easily remain invisible due to their gender and the positions of power they typically hold within society, the workplace and the patriarchal family. This is not to say that the effects between men and women are of comparable degree, but rather that it is easier to miss the impact on men in general. For men with disabilities, the experience of patriarchy is especially complex, layered and often overlooked in much of masculinity studies literature. The invisibility of male privilege as the normative, unmarked term sits at odds with the 'Othering' invisibility of disabled bodies un-useful to the market logics of neoliberal capitalism. As with much work carried out at the intersection of ableism and masculinity (Connell 1991; Saczkowski 2011) an emphasis is placed on how disability may impact men's social, cultural and economic position, which in turn may affect the construction of gender identities, sexualities and other relationships in their day-to-day lives. For example, Gerschick and Miller (1995) carried out a landmark study on disability and masculinity in which participants noted a sense of exclusion from many spheres of life, the most notable being decision-making. For their participants, this manifested as less confidence, feelings of disempowerment and being unable to make the informed choices due to lack of access to information. A particularly key challenge that many of my own participants noted was a lack of access to sexual health information and stigma related to sexuality. A key limitation on Gerschick and Miller's work was the absence of how gender and power impact disabled men through patriarchy, contributing to their marginalization in and outside the home. This limitation is true in a range of other studies on disability and gender, which have focused specifically either on either marginalization of disabled women (Ghai 2002; Meer 2015; Moin 2009; Vansteenwegen 2003), or disability as a whole but without a focus on gender (Manoj 2018; Retznik et al. 2017).

The above demonstrates that the intersection between masculinity and disability is complex, producing a complicated relationship between marginalization and privilege for disabled men. A way to explore this tension is via Connell's famous concept of Hegemonic masculinity, which explains how women and 'lesser' forms of men not only takes place but is socially legitimized by patriarchy (Connell 2005). She further uses the term 'gender order' to articulate the existence of and multiple masculinities, femininities and the hierarchical relationship between them. These are accompanied by societal and institutional relationships (such as law, politics and the family) in the form of a complimentary 'gender regime'. The differences in power relations exist at the micro and macro level, with the latter influencing the former and vice versa. Importantly, Hearn (2004:50) identifies power itself is often equated with masculinity, being arguably the most important aspect of gender. This analysis highlights that disabled masculinities exist in a gender order, within a neoliberal, capitalist gender regime that devalues non-profitable bodies against the backdrop of a traditionalist Indian patriarchy.

Hegemonic masculinity and patriarchy are, in this sense, deeply linked. Any non-conformity, particularly with regard to gender, is seen as a threat to hegemonic masculinity (Cheng 1999). Deviation from normative gender performances that do not conform to the hegemonic ideal may be seen as not 'normal' and can have wider implications for everyday life. How is it, then, that these types of gender performance and embodiment are integrated (or fail to integrate) into patriarchal systems? How do disabled bodies enact masculinity? This chapter will explore these questions and the construction of masculinity amongst disabled men in Kolkata, highlighting their experience of marginalization in their everyday lives, negotiation with patriarchy and degree of disability.

People with disabilities are often grouped together regardless of their experiences of gender, sexuality and even abuse. Moreover, disability is often approached from a perspective of rehabilitation services rather than from a purely academic perspective (Reddy 2011:299). This medicalized, service-oriented understanding of disability can blunt the nuanced understanding of more multiple oppressions, intersections (particularly with gender and caste) and other pluralities that characterize the experience of disability in India (Ghai 2002:51–2). Margaret Mead (1978) stated that the progress of a society is measured by how it treats women and the disabled; as such, the importance of developing a nuanced, academically independent discipline of disability studies cannot be overstated for the well-being of Indian society.

Another barrier to accessing the position of disabled men in is the traditional, patriarchal notion of masculinity which is still largely prevalent in India. Some studies in Indian context threw light on gender and disability aspect (Ghosh 2010; Mehrotra 2013; Mehrotra and Vaidya 2008). Ghosh (2010) put forward the issue of femininity and disability in Bengal, whereas Mehrotra (2018, 2013) threw light on the issue of manhood and disability in northern India. A great deal of pressure remains on men to move out of their homes for work and becomes independent, regardless of their disability status. Yet disability impacts their position in the labour market, the outcomes of which is mostly related to unemployment (Jones and Sloane 2006), with levels of unemployment being significantly higher than those of employed men (Uppal 2005). Men and women's distinctive roles in the workforce and productivity often affect their economic independence and sense of empowerment (Hatt 1997). Even once employed, there also instances of harassment and bullying in the workplace that prevent disabled men working in a positive environment. Apart from discrimination in the workplace through neglect, bullying and harassment, the stigma around disability prevents men applying for various jobs (Salin 2021; Vickers 2009). The type of work, skills and training may also pose a challenge to disabled men; for example, physically demanding labour may prevent their entry in the labour market.

The experiences of subjugation become intense, not only in the home, but also in public spaces such as the workplace, colleges and universities. From a Marxist point of view, disability is the outcome of society's economic condition (cited in Thomas 2006:179). This means the consequences of disability become more evident in social life for men who are not working or are unemployed. By not being financially productive, their position is diminished. With the global dynamics of capitalist and hierarchical gender relationships, the complex capitalist patriarchy has changed the material character and meaning of disability (Connell 2011:1371). During the twentieth century, the overseas colonial systems ended and opened to a competing global corporate economy, with integrated international markets and massive flows of capital (ibid.:1374–5). At the cultural level, the capitalist order draws a boundary between two categories of bodies: those which generate profit, and those which do not. Disabled falls under the second. Another important part of colonized societies was the transformation of gender order where the workforces became segregated by gender (ibid.: 1376). Thus, the gender order has been absorbed into a global economy and a modernized patriarchy has become 'internationally hegemonic' (ibid.).

In the Western context, a landmark study by Gerschick and Miller (1994, 1995) constructed a framework through which masculinity is enacted out through dominant patterns: reformulation, reliance and rejection, by men with physical disabilities. The research questioned the creation, maintenance and recreation of gender identity through conforming to a particular ideology of masculinity, either believing in the dominant traits or refusing it and reconstructing an alternative idea (Gergen et al. 1996:456). Shuttleworth has also engaged in research with regards to how disabled men moved beyond the definition of hegemonic masculinity in interpersonal spaces especially during sexual intimacy, using bodies differently during sexual acts claiming them as assets (2004).

In the Indian context, however, the ideals of masculinity and femininity are often deeply rooted in Hindu texts (Osella and Osella 2006:1). Masculinity in Bengal, which is the focus of this chapter, was constructed on the basis of colonizer and the colonized; where the former is referred to as 'manly' where the latter is 'effeminate' (Sinha 2017). The patriarchal culture in East India, especially in Bengal, is different from other parts of country as the rejection and ostracization of other forms of masculinities are not rampant, though hegemonic masculinity is practiced through institutional spaces.

Methodology and limitations

This study was carried out in Kolkata, Bengal, amongst twenty male identifying participants aged between twenty and thirty-five. All have mainly locomotor disabilities since birth. The participants are from middle-class backgrounds, and all use either a wheelchair or crutches. Out of twenty participants twelve are students, two are working, and the rest are unemployed graduates.

The data was collected using snowball sampling where a set of respondents were contacted through the first set of respondents. The mode of interview was done through semi-structured interviews and the responses were recorded. Most of the responses were collected through in-depth face-to-face interviews and observing the participants closely. The interviews were conducted with the participants' consent and according to their availability. Pseudonyms were used, meaning none of the participants' real names are mentioned in the study.

Face-to-face in-depth interviews were done on campus, or cafés, according to participants' preference. The main limitation of this study was the gender barrier. As a female researcher, they hesitated to open up about certain sensitive issues at the start of the research, but later on came be able to express opinions about their marginalized way of living, concepts of being a man and their vulnerabilities. The topic of discussion was new to them, as they never had the opportunity to talk about matters of discrimination, neglect and abuse. In the beginning none of them acknowledged any kind of challenges, or the subordination they faced, but increasingly they opened up over time.

Objectives

Against this background the objectives of the study are as follows:

1. To explore the invisible power conflict in private spaces among disabled men.

2. To understand the significance of patriarchy and how the participants negotiate it in their lives.
3. To understand how risk interacts with disability in everyday life.

Invisible power dynamics in private and public spaces

In a patriarchal society like India, the home is a crucial space for understanding power dynamics; emotional and physical violence is mediated through discriminatory practices, abuse, harassment and neglect (Geetha 2002). This is particularly complex in Indian homes, which act as a seat of patriarchal values and bear the additional influence of kinship and caste systems (ibid.). Considering that sixteen of my twenty participants said they had stayed indoors since childhood, this suggests the domestic situation is a key dynamic to be considered in understanding the experience of disabled men. The exploitation of gendered power dynamics occurs from an early age and if a child is disabled this discrimination becomes more prominent (Gupta 1987; Jangir and Azeez 2017; Kohli 2017). Participants who were financially better-off were only privileged in terms of caregiving and having twenty-four-hour care, other than this, all of them acquiesced to feeling that they embody a subordinated position in the house.

Due to my interlocutors' non-participation or restrictions in outdoor activities (especially sports) they were rarely, if ever, exposed to male peers. Despite this they related to specific types of masculine image through social media, the internet and television; whilst not isolated from masculine ideals, their participation in them remains different to many of their able-bodied peers. Their isolation from an early age has affected the ways in which they have taken up various behaviours considered normal for young boys that represent masculinity, including risky pursuits like bike racing, drinking and body building. A majority of respondents claim they are considered to be non-competitors or outside the realm of competition entirely. As Rishav, twenty-seven, says:

> I don't feel any pressure like my other non-disabled friends, neither in studies nor for career since I have no competition and no comparison, I am happy. I guess disability has made my tasks easier and I don't feel bad about it. I see my younger brother who is always pressurized or faces criticism or comparison from family members who have high expectations for him, but not me.

Their socialization patterns have been different with little and no pressure to perform from within the family. Despite this, the adherence to various gendered norms still remains prominent; the home always creates a hierarchy, and inequality between them and other male members of the family. As will be outlined in the upcoming accounts, the participants felt comfortable sharing spaces with mother or sister in family but refrain from sharing spaces with other female members (for example sister in law, aunts) of the house in order to not to appear 'feminine'. Barun, thirty, who wants to enrol in a PhD programme, mentions:

> In Bengali households boys are not conditioned into very tough masculine roles, as men here are often seen as soft and less tough than men from other communities, therefore I did not face a very tough time from my peers who are also Bengalis, as they could understand my needs and never made me feel unimportant or secondary in that way, but I faced constraints from home at times, nonetheless the pressure on me was always less as compared to other non-disabled friends of mine ... My father always said that I have a lack, a problem which can only be compensated with a good job and income, so a lot of pressure was on me.

Restrictions in the home

Participants felt that the restrictions on moving out of the home gradually became a means of control by the other members of the family who took decisions on their behalf. A few complained about receiving too much attention from parents and other family members which was embarrassing for them. Even when they are in their thirties, this attention and over-protectiveness remained, which is quite stigmatizing for their age and image. Sarat, twenty-eight, speaks of how he is still being accompanied to a friend's house:

> Someone from my family will accompany me to college and even friend's house, I feel very embarrassed, A boy of my age still accompanied by someone is shameful. I have a disability so may be this is a reason my friends don't bully me. There is an instance when I was travelling with a friend who is a girl at night, and her parents were reluctant about her safety since she has to drop me first and then reach home alone. Such thoughts are not good for my image.

Surveillance and restrictions from family members are more or less common amongst my interlocutors, which have severely affected their confidence and self-esteem. They are taken for granted as having no agency, lacking autonomy, and are controlled in the name of care and love. As Piyush, twenty-nine, says: 'My disability has posed more restrictions for me, I have accepted it. I have been given extra attention and things are done for my wellbeing only.' Although three of my participants are working and even financially secure, their opinions or say in matters of household decisions are not considered by the family members. However, in families where the father is absent, especially where households are run by mothers, the men show significantly more levels of confidence. As Bijoy, twenty-one, explains:

> My mother always encouraged me to do what I wanted, I am very close to my mother and sisters, I am never ashamed of doing household chores with my mother and at the same time went out to financially support my family. I never felt I am dependent on someone, they have respected all my decisions and gave me an important position in the house, equivalent to my father … I do not know how it would have been if I had a non-disabled brother instead of sisters.

Another hurdle comes when choosing a profession or career path. For example, none of my participants took up engineering as for many engineering is supposed to be a male dominated stream but it would be considered risky owing to the involvement of heavy machinery. Yet at the beginning of my interviews, none of my participants acknowledged the challenges of being a disabled man or expose their more vulnerable selves. Men and issues of empowerment or vulnerability are less discussed than they are as issues which affect women (Chandra 2007; Duflo 2012; Hill 2003; Ibrahim et al. 2007). Despite the challenges that their physical disability presents them, the majority of interviewees did not feel or accept the state of being completely disempowered, but instead mention being 'partially empowered'. The ambivalence between patriarchally endowed masculine agency and disabled marginality is particularly apparent in the examples given above. Most denied being totally helpless in matters related to asserting their authority, but also could not relate to a dominant role played in any sphere of their lives – be it professional or domestic. Space remains a barrier not just in terms of pure physical accessibility, but also in defining zones for exercising autonomy and wider physical or personal needs.

Patriarchy and its meanings: Complying with masculine norms

The everyday experience of domestic space also shapes the meaning of patriarchy in the lives of those in this study. Patriarchy for most was related to compliance with gender norms and preserving masculinity through involvement in financial decision-making or activities which carry some form of risk. Risk could be subjective and varied with the experiences of the individual, defined by social and cultural factors like group membership i.e. how particular groups perceive risk, for example men, and how risk could become a part of hegemonic practice (Lupton 1999:27–9). Two of my participants mentioned that they try to comply with masculine norms through seeking involvement in certain risky pursuits. Sambhu, twenty-six, remembers one incident where he took the risk of riding a bike for a few miles in a busy road which his parents are unaware of:

> I once rode a bike of my friend, he was insisting me to take his bike and he sat behind me, that experience was heaven, like taking the charge of the bike, but at the same time I was scared if I lose my balance what will happen.

Sambhu also feels that as a man, he needs to take certain risks in life, that without pain or risk there is nothing to be gained. Rakesh, thirty, mentions: 'My father says that even though you have a disability you are a boy, you have to learn work and go outside, if you would have been a girl then things would have been different.' The participants mentioned that they try to participate in most of the duties assigned to them in the home mostly by their fathers and but in spite of that a kind of insecurity prevails in relation to their position within family. All of my participants spoke of their interest in getting involved in work outside of the home instead of tasks allotted to them within it and a few even explained how they would maintain a distance from household chores, as adherence to these tasks would diminish their social status even more.

Despite their complex relationship with it, some participants supported patriarchy as an institution which justified men's authority as supreme. In doing so they feel they may get certain benefits like being accepted as an authority in the family, or in order to receive status in the workplace. Anup, third-two, stated that 'there is a tendency of isolating us, not to take our views [seriously], see us as secondary or inferior, people have already pre-assumed I am good for nothing'. Rahul, twenty-nine, explains that:

There are subtle ways of domination which I realized in the course of this interview. No one will show you that they are discriminating against you but will practice this by intentionally or unintentionally making you feel unwanted, This makes me feel I am unfit for any job especially any responsible task, people may think twice before giving it to me.

Rishav, twenty-seven, says:

If given an opportunity I too like to see people below me, I too want to make decisions for someone else. Power is essential, you need to have a certain amount of power be it financial or by the virtue of being a man, but you should possess it.

Interestingly, throughout the interviews, such sentiments of support for patriarchal values were evident even though my disabled participants do not get the same benefits from them as other able-bodied men. While Kolkata, Bengal, represents a patriarchal culture, the participants mentioned that they do not feel very isolated for not complying to patriarchal norms or ridiculed for being a disabled man when compared to friends from other regions of India. As Niraj, twenty-four, elaborates:

I have seen my non-Bengali friends hailing from other parts of the country believe in strong patriarchal ideologies and also are very conscious about their masculine image, but my Bengali male peers(my close friends) do not follow such standards of patriarchy or masculinity, neither [do] they pressurize others to follow that way, nor [do] they bully so much, yes but verbal taunting is there, like cracking sexual jokes after me, giving me names, but they have not isolated me out of the group due to my disability.

Patriarchy and its meaning are shaped by participants' everyday experiences. For my participants, it is understood as the rule of powerful men in society, except for a few who see it not just as the rule of men but by anyone powerful. 'Patriarchy is seen as a system of powerful made to rule the weak', says Piyush, twenty-seven. Though none of the participants saw how patriarchy and disability are related, they nevertheless agreed that patriarchy does have an effect on their everyday lives and individuality. Tuhin, thirty, said:

Patriarchy may define my roles as a man; it always gives power to men who could follow the rules of patriarchy, and if one is not powerful, he will be controlled by others, though it does not affect me directly, but it is my disability or the norms of patriarchy and practices that has side-lined me more.

Twenty-nine-year-old Ashok mentions: 'Patriarchy is inevitable, this is how it has been created, we need to follow it, I don't think patriarchy has diminished my status because of my disability.' He also adds 'This is true that I don't have the same position as other men of my age.'

There is a close association between heterosexuality and able-bodiedness in patriarchal culture, as both reflect what is seen as a complete whole being. Thus, McRuer (2006) used the term 'heteronormative epiphanies' where able-bodied and heteronormative persons experience a sense of completeness, while disabled and queer people are seen 'deviant' or not normal (cited in Cheng 1999:117). While masculinity is represented by able-bodied, hegemonic masculinity as an ideology can also be practised by anyone. My participants, while remaining at or near the bottom of the power hierarchy, still follow and practice hegemonic masculinity to secure their position in the wider social group. This could be in their peer group, family or in a relationship. Rudra, twenty-eight, mentions:

> I often used to tease my sister, and tried to dominate her as I don't feel [like] being the submissive one always; she is the only one who listens to me and respects my views.

Sumit, twenty-seven, also says:

> There is a pleasure of having power in [my] hands, if I ever get a chance maybe I too would like people to be below me whom I can control, or rather guide, as I guide my fellow peer who is completely blind, my position is at least better than his.

Connell viewed hegemonic masculinity as not being practised by all men but only by a few (2005). Outside the home, in spaces like colleges and workplace a few respondents mentioned that they have tried taking up certain self-defined 'risky' behaviours to display 'hegemonic' or patriarchally expected masculine characteristics and secure their place in within their social circle. These include riding a bike, going to the gym and engaging in fights with other men. As Rahul, twenty-nine, mentions, 'You have to take risk and feel pain at one point of life or other or else you won't be looked upon'.

Agha (2015) conducted a study among women in Sindh, Pakistan, and describes how women navigate patriarchal expectations to improve their power and self-esteem by being a 'good mother'. Within a given gender order, various roles can therefore be used to negotiate status within the constraints of patriarchal control and surveillance from within a structural position of disadvantage.

Kandiyoti examined how women bargain within patriarchy in the household by utilizing different strategies to optimize their life options with passive or active resistance in the face of oppression (1988:274). There strategies were also pursued by my participants to assure their position within the household. For example, most have tried to associate with more important people like their brother or fathers, or take responsibility for important financial decisions. In trying to project a responsible image, they hoped to be considered an important member of the house in spite of the fact they need assistance and care in many other spheres. The participants try to retain an image as other male members have like 'responsible', 'smart', 'efficient' and 'authoritative'. In order to maintain this they try to be more strict or even control younger women members of house (mostly sisters/mothers) and this becomes prominent in the absence of any older or able-bodied men in the house. And indeed, some have successfully used these strategies in order to gain better standing within the household gender order.

Ultimately, the most important thing for participants who are currently employed is to contribute financially to the household. Those who are students try to compensate in other ways, like being the tech-savvy person in the house, where all members are dependent on them for any online task like paying bills or purchasing goods. 'I am very good at technical stuff, know computers and mobiles well, so my sister, parents all come to me for help, even my other relatives', boasts 23-year-old Indra. In this way, some disabled men particularly in the Indian scenario find different ways to establish themselves within the domestic gender order despite the various challenges they face in doing so.

Risk as a part of Image: Risk and disability

Disability is frequently seen as a barrier to participation in patriarchally inflected modes of masculinity. While there is typically some gap between able-bodied men and a masculine ideal that requires risk-taking behaviour to try and attain, the degree of risk is heightened in particularly complex ways for disabled men. In particular, disability itself is not only an accentuator of risk experienced by men-in-general via the pursuit of patriarchal status, but a risk in itself. As Ram, twenty-four, stated: 'disability itself is a risk, I have to take care of everything, therefore experiencing the risk every day, I can't move beyond it.' Thus, the meaning of risk for the majority of my participants is bound up in a double overcoming; the overcoming of risk to demonstrate patriarchally accepted virtue and the mitigation of risk present in the disability itself. As Sourav, twenty-six, also puts it:

> Staying away from any kind of assistance like assistive equipment or crutches, glasses is risky for me, but I have done without them in order to produce an attractive image, as without the crutches I look more attractive.

Working without assistive devices even for a short span of time is potentially dangerous. Therefore, risk is present not just in grand, status-seeking performance of gender for disabled men, but in mastering very small, simple tasks. Risk is thus perennially present in everyday tasks, requiring keeping their disability in mind while doing something 'unexceptional' which could potentially injure them. All of my participants felt that risk is a part of everyday activities in this way. For example, Pijush, twenty-two, says: 'Masculine identity or manliness is to do something risky in life, what is a life without any risk? I feel each and every individual should take risk in order to achieve something better.' Abhishek, says: 'I don't think masculinity has anything to do with risk, but men are always made to do riskier stuff than women.'

As Butler (2011) highlights, performing is an important aspect of gender, with identities being constituted through performances. From gender role-based performance to sexual performance, risk exists everywhere. Risk is not just physical but also emotional, as Monish, who has sixty percent locomotor disability, says:

> I like to play sports, but due to my impairment, I can't often, but still once I took part in college sports and made a half century, all my friends applauded me for the effort, but later on I could not move for a week, heavily hurting my spine, so this amount of risk and pain is needed for a man.

Jeet, twenty-three, does not use a wheelchair or crutches but has dysfunctional motor functions. He also adds, 'My posture is a bit odd, made me look bad, and un-smart, but there is no way to cover it'. Similarly, Abhi, same age as Jeet, says:

> When I first got enrolled into college, I wanted to have a smart image, if you have a disability you are not smart, so [I] tried to avoid crutches when in canteen. I used to stand for hours without them, keeping my back at the wall, but after one or two days it was impossible for me to stand even with the crutches. I took this pain but later on realized it was of no use, it gave me more trouble.

Whereas Nilanjan, twenty, states:

> I cannot indulge in any fitness routine. Once I thought of visiting the gym, but hesitated as to how would people react, and what will I do by making a good body, my disability will still be there?

All of my participants have little confidence when it comes to presentation and grooming, agreeing that disability has an impact on their body image. The main fear lies in rejection, not only for romantic partnerships, but also for friendships. Some used social networking sites to reformulate their image and all felt that social networking is a platform where they could hide their disability, although none of them have tried to hide themselves or make a new identity for their social media profiles. Most of the participants rely on a 'tough voice' as an important aspect of expressing masculinity online, there are instances where a few of them have preferred online conversations or phone calls over face-to-face interaction. Thus, risk is a dynamic in the negotiation of masculinities by Indian men. In one sense, there is either the 'double overcoming' of their disabled status and striving for recognition against hegemonic ideals of masculinity, or the usage of digital technologies to mediate their social interactions in a way that de-emphasizes the anxieties they face in forming social or romantic bonds.

Mapping sexual awareness: Risk and violence

Disability poses a range of practical, social and emotional challenges for disabled people of all genders in the area of sexual and reproductive health. This includes general sexual and emotional well-being such as the ability to confidently explore sexual orientation or form a healthy and satisfying sexual relationship. It also encompasses challenges in accessing services or information around sexual and reproductive health, such as STI prevention or education, family planning and abortion. Esmail et al. (2010) explain how predominant heteronormative ideas around sex and its relationship to able bodies a major contributing factor towards the stigma are attached to disability and sexuality. In the case of my male participants, this sense of stigma instilled negative sexual self-image, reduced confidence and as self-esteem. Low self-confidence, the need to navigate a complex and often social environment with a lack of information on how to do so leaves many disabled people in a remarkably challenging social position. My participants felt that they had not just a lack of information, but most importantly, they did not have access to spaces where they could safely express their emotions on the topic. In particular, participants expressed uneasiness around accessing information on contraception or sexually transmitted diseases, a main reason being that they did not know whom to approach.

Alongside issues with access to general information on sexual health, my participants also reported not having access to information specifically focused on disabled men. As Suvro mentions: 'There are workshops on sexuality and reproductive health for disabled women but not for us, then if we have a problem where do we go?' A lack of proper guidance on general sexual health and hygiene, challenges with peer-group socialization, personal experiences of sexual development, as well as specific information about HIV, pregnancy, family planning and menstruation has made the situation worse among disabled people generally in India (Cole 1993:190), with men facing their own particular challenges. One of my participants noted: 'When I first discussed about these things I was in college, my friend gave me a pornography video and said I will learn, but that did not suffice my actual concern.' Among the participants, six acknowledged having partners, where four are heterosexual and two are homosexual. According to them, a major risk was in pursuing sexual activity without information on sexual health and hygiene, especially when the partner is disabled too since the partner is also less likely to have access to said information. Dibakar, twenty-five, says, 'I once had an infection in my private part, but don't know whom and how to approach as we are not informed when infections are related to sexual health.'

Disabled people (and disabled men in particular) are also at an elevated risk of sexual violence, exploitation or abuse (Calderbank 2000). The issue is compounded by the fact that the sexual abuse of men in general is an issue seldom discussed. Disability once again doubles the vulnerability for my participants when they tried to talk about incidents of abuse. Anup, twenty-six, told of a sexual assault in the hands of a relative, 'My uncle used to hit my private part whenever I could not follow maths.' Such incidents never come up and remain buried throughout their lives. Participants also felt that there could be incidents of abuse, especially when they are in new or unknown places.

The structure of their domestic situation already outlined prevents additional complications for disabled men and the development of their sexuality. Samar, twenty-eight, says: 'Anyone accessing my room without my permission, this hampers my privacy.' In adolescence where a child learns to discover his/her sexual body, disabled children may not have the opportunity to explore these due both a lack of privacy and an overdependence on family and care givers.

Limited access to the outside world due to movement restrictions and a limited peer group may mean that they have fewer opportunities to learn appropriate behaviours (or unlearn inappropriate ones), resulting limited knowledge and communication about sex education and sexual behaviour (Cole 1993:192).

Cumulatively, my participants suffered from low self-confidence, a sense of bodily stigma in a complex domestic and social environment. There was a hesitancy in attempting to access information about sex, as a lack of certainty about what was available and a sense that what they were aware of failed to explicitly cater to their needs as disabled men. The impact of patriarchal masculinity on disabled bodies throughout several domains has been explored throughout this chapter, but is particularly complex and sensitive in considering sex and sexuality. My participants have always felt anxious and ashamed about discussing about their body, but especially in relation to sexuality. The sense of isolation and stigma is felt particularly strongly by both disabled men and women; not because of their disabilities, but rather how patriarchy has not normalized them.

Conclusion

This study aims to highlight the perception of disabled men about their masculinities and sexualities in a patriarchal society. The way they perceive patriarchy also has an effect on how they relate to their gender. Both private and public spaces remain a barrier not just in terms of mobility but also in terms how unequal power relationships play out in both.

The first two sections in this chapter dealt with the complexities of domestic power relations. Invisible discrimination existed in subtle modes of dominance, neglect and feelings of being unable to exercise agency were common, also affecting the ability to make their own decisions. These experiences sat in tension with their patriarchally inflected understandings of gender roles; that men were expected to leave the home and become independent, authoritative heads of their own families was in direct contrast to their experience of care. The subtle conflict between disability and masculinity is rooted in patriarchal understandings of gender. My participants attempting to negotiate their place in the domestic hierarchy through a range of strategies, such as claiming competence in specifically 'male' domains such as technology or finance, or by attempting to establish power over younger and/or female family members. They sought to carry out tasks effectively; participating in all male-centric work, proving themselves to be the 'kayaker chele' and man of the household. The majority felt this could improve their status, but at the same time they believed patriarchy has diminished their status, as disability impacts their performance as a 'man'. Negotiating the tension between patriarchy and disability in domestic spaces is therefore a key aspect of my participants' experience of masculinity.

The last sections deal with risk, sexuality and disability. The meaning of risk for the majority of participants is to challenge their disability and perform in order to be accepted in patriarchal society. Risk is of various kinds in their lives. Disability itself is a risk, as they have to be cautious about their body all the time – making them think twice before indulging in any risky pursuits. A few mentioned being involved in the kind of activities which require strength, but the consequences were not pleasant. They either injured themselves or were unable to finish the task. Risk is also present in things as simple as trying a new hairstyle or new look. While this might be seen as true for most men, my participants expressed anxiety even about trying to project themselves as having style or being smart at all – fearing they might not be accepted or would be ridiculed. Another form of risk lies in uniformed decisions. Lack of access to information on reproductive health may result in increased risk of sexually transmitted diseases and infection, particularly between disabled couples, whereas the stigma surrounding disability poses a barrier to finding information in the first place. Sexual abuse is another neglected area among disabled men. Incidents of sexual misconduct were seldom discussed and often remained buried in their memories. The general stigma attached to male sexual abuse was compounded by their disability. Being a man with a disability means having a constant fear of disapproval from peers, family and work colleagues. They feared that if their stories of abuse come into the light, they would experience further ridicule and rejection. As well as the lingering emotional and persona impact, they were concerned that this would further push them towards the bottom of the social hierarchy.

The dilemmas men with disabilities face in struggling with masculinity or work to create an alternative identity, has been documented (Gerschick and Miler 1994, 1995). However, many studies have failed to notice how invisible power struggles in domestic spaces have affected their sense of empowerment and perceptions of masculinity. The well-being of disabled men is at stake, yet their voices and stories are rarely heard owing to the marginalization of disability and its complex relationship with gender underpinned by patriarchy.

Bibliography

Abberley, P. (1987) The Concept of Oppression and the Development of a Social Theory of Disability. *Disability, Handicap & Society*, 2(1), 5–19.

Agha, N. (2015) *Women Bargaining with Patriarchy in Rural Pakistan: A Case Study of Khairpur, Sindh*. Leeds, Sheffield and York: WhiteRose eTheses Online.

De Beauvoir, S. (1956) *The Second Sex*. London: Jonathan Cape.

Bogdan, R. and Taylor, S. (1987) Toward a Sociology of Acceptance: The Other Side of the Study of Deviance. *Social Policy*, 18(2), 34–9.

Butler, J. (2011) *Bodies That Matter: On the Discursive Limits of Sex*. London and New York: Taylor & Francis.

Calderbank, R. (2000) Abuse and Disabled People: Vulnerability or Social Indifference? *Disability & Society*, 15(3), 521–34.

Chandra, R. (2007) Women Empowerment in India-Milestones & Challenges. *PACS Programme Conference, 'What it takes to Eradicate Poverty'*, New Delhi, India.

Cheng, C. (1999) Marginalized Masculinities and Hegemonic Masculinity: An Introduction. *The Journal of Men's Studies*, 7(3), 295–315.

Clapton, J., and Fitzgerald, J. (1997) The History of Disability: A History of 'Otherness'. *New Renaissance Magazine*, 7(1), 1–3.

Cole, S. S. and Cole, T. M. (1993) Sexuality, Disability, and Reproductive Issues through the Lifespan. *Sexuality and Disability*, 11(3), 189–205.

Collins, V. E. and Rothe, D. L. (2017) The Consumption of Patriarchy: Commodification to Facilitation and Reification. *Contemporary Justice Review*, 20(2), 161–74.

Connell, R. (2011) Southern Bodies and Disability: Re-Thinking Concepts. *Third World Quarterly*, 32(8), 1369–81.

Connell, R. W. (1991) Live Fast and Die Young: The Construction of Masculinity among Young Working-Class Men on the Margin of the Labour Market. *The Australian and New Zealand Journal of Sociology*, 27(2), 141–71.

Connell, R. W. (2005) *Masculinities*. Polity.

Connell, R. W. (2013) *Gender and Power: Society, the Person and Sexual Politics*.

Dasgupta, R. K. and Gokulsing, K. M. (2013) Introduction: Perceptions of Masculinity and Challenges to the Indian Male, in Dasgupta, R. K. and Gokulsing, K.M. (eds.), *Masculinity and Its Challenges in India: Essays on Changing Perceptions*, 5–25. Jefferson, USA: McFarland & Co Inc.

Duflo, E. (2012) Women Empowerment and Economic Development. *Journal of Economic Literature*, 50(4), 1051–79.

Ellis, K. (2012) Because of rather than in spite of: 'Friday Night Lights' Important Cultural Work of Intersecting Disability and Masculinity. *Interactive Media E-Journal*, 8.

Esmail, S., Darry, K., Walter, A. and Knupp, H. (2010) Attitudes and Perceptions towards Disability and Sexuality. *Disability and Rehabilitation*, 32(14), 1148–55.

Geetha, V. (2002) *Gender*. Calcutta: Stree.

Gergen, M. M. and Davis, S. N. (1996) *Toward a New Psychology of Gender: A Reader*. Routledge.

Gerschick, T. J. and Miller, A. S. (1994) Gender Identities at the Crossroads of Masculinity and Physical Disability. *Masculinities*, 2(1), 34–55.

Gerschick, T. J. and Miller, A. S. (1995) *Coming to Terms: Masculinity and Physical Disability*. Sage Publications.

Ghai, A. (2002) Disabled Women: An Excluded Agenda of Indian Feminism. *Hypatia*, 17(3), 49–66.

Ghosh, N. (2010) Embodied Experiences: Being Female and Disabled. *Economic and Political Weekly*, 45(17), 58–63.

Gupta, M. D. (1987) Selective Discrimination against Female Children in Rural Punjab, India. *Population and Development Review*, 77–100.

Hartmann, H. (1976) Capitalism, Patriarchy, and Job Segregation by Sex. *Signs: Journal of Women in Culture and Society*, 1(3, Part 2), 137–69.

Hatt, S. (1997) *Gender, Work and Labour Markets*. Basingstoke: Macmillan Press.

Hearn, J. (2004) From Hegemonic Masculinity to the Hegemony of Men. *Feminist Theory*, 5(1), 49–72.

Hill, M. (2003) Development as Empowerment. *Feminist Economics*, 9(2–3), 117–35.

Ibrahim, S. and Alkire, S. (2007) Agency and Empowerment: A Proposal for Internationally Comparable Indicators. *Oxford Development Studies*, 35(4), 379–403.

Jangir, H. and Azeez, A. (2017) Parental Attitudes and Children's Perception on Gender Discrimination: Evidences from Rural Rajasthan. *Indian Journal of Sustainable Development*, 3(1), 29–36.

Jones, M. K., Latreille, P. L. and Sloane, P. J. (2006) Disability, Gender, and the British Labour Market. *Oxford Economic Papers*, 58(3), 407–49.

Kandiyoti, D. (1988) Bargaining with Patriarchy. *Gender and Society*, 2(3), 274–90.

Kohli, S. (2017) Gender Inequality in India. *International Journal of Humanities & Social Science Studies*, 3(4), 178–85.

Lindemann, K. and Cherney, J. L. (2008) Communicating in and through 'Murderball': Masculinity and Disability in Wheelchair Rugby. *Western Journal of Communication*, 72(2), 107–25.

Lupton, D. (1999) Risk. Routledge. *New York*.

Manoj, M. P. and Suja, M. K. (2018) Correction to: Sexuality and Reproductive Health in Young People with Disability: A Systematic Review of Issues and Challenges. *Sexuality and Disability*, 36(2), 207–16.

McRuer, R. (2006) *Crip Theory: Cultural Signs of Queerness and Disability*. (Vol. 9). New York: NYU press.

Mead, M. (1978) *Culture and Commitment: The New Relationships between the Generations in the 1970s, Rev*. Garden City, New York: Anchor Press/Doubleday.

Meer, T. and Combrinck, H. (2015) Invisible Intersections: Understanding the Complex Stigmatisation of Women with Intellectual Disabilities in Their Vulnerability to Gender-Based Violence. *Agenda*, 29(2), 14–23.

Mehrotra, N. (2013) Disability, Gender and Caste Intersections in Indian Economy, in Barnartt, S. and Altman, B. (eds.), *Disability and Intersecting Statuses*, 295–324. Bingley, UK: Emerald Group Publishing Ltd.

Mehrotra, N. and Vaidya, S. (2008) Exploring Constructs of Intellectual Disability and Personhood in Haryana and Delhi. *Indian Journal of Gender Studies*, 15(2), 317–40.

Moin, V., Duvdevany, I. and Mazor, D. (2009) Sexual Identity, Body Image and Life Satisfaction among Women with and without Physical Disability. *Sexuality and Disability*, 27(2), 83–95.

Murdick, N., Shore, P., Gartin, B. and Chittooran, M. M. (2004) Cross-Cultural Comparison of the Concept of 'Otherness' and Its Impact on Persons with Disabilities. *Education and Training in Developmental Disabilities*, 39(4), 310–16.

Osella, C. and Osella, F. (2006) *Men and Masculinities in South India*. London: Anthem Press.

Reddy, C. R. (2011) From Impairment to Disability and beyond: Critical Explorations in Disability Studies. *Sociological Bulletin*, 60(2), 287–306.

Richardson, D. (2000) *Rethinking Sexuality*. London: Sage.

Retznik, L., Wienholz, S., Seidel, A., Pantenburg, B., Conrad, I., Michel, M. and Riedel-Heller, S. G. (2017) Relationship Status: Single? Young Adults with Visual, Hearing, or Physical Disability and Their Experiences with Partnership and Sexuality. *Sexuality and Disability*, 35(4), 415–32.

Salin, D. (2021) Workpalce Bullying and Gender: An Overview of Empirical Findings in D'Cruz, P., Noronha, E., Caponnechia, C., Escartin, J., Salin, D., and Tuckey, M. (eds.), *Dignity and Inclusion At Work*, 331–61. Singapore: Springer Singapore.

Saczkowski, T. (2011) *Narratives of Violence: The Relationship of Masculinity and Ableism*. York University: (Doctoral dissertation).

Shuttleworth, R. P. (2004) Disabled Masculinity, in Smith, B. and Hutchison, B. (eds.), *Gendering disability*, 166–78. Piscataway: Rutgers University Press.

Sinha, M. (2017) *Colonial Masculinity: The 'Manly Englishman' and the 'Effeminate Bengali' in the Late Nineteenth Century*. Manchester: Manchester University Press.

Thomas, C. (2006) Disability and Gender: Reflections on Theory and Research. *Scandinavian Journal of Disability Research*, 8(2–3), 177–85.

Uppal, S. (2005) Disability, Workplace Characteristics and Job Satisfaction. *International Journal of Manpower*, 26(4), 336–49.

Vansteenwegen, A., Jans, I. and Revell, A. T. (2003) Sexual Experience of Women with a Physical Disability: A Comparative Study. *Sexuality and Disability*, 21(4), 283–90.

Vickers, M. H. (2009) Bullying, Disability and Work: A Case Study of Workplace Bullying. *Qualitative Research in Organizations and Management: An International Journal*, 4(3), 255–72.

Walby, S. (1989) Theorising Patriarchy. *Sociology*, 23(2), 213–34.

11

An interview with Ed Fornieles

Ed Fornieles, Amir Massoumian and Dan Nightingale

The editors of the volume became aware of Ed's work in the lead-up to the SOAS conference that was the genesis of this book, in particular his latest film 'Cel'. Ed Fornieles is a London-based artist who specializes in integrating various mediums including film, social media, sculpture, installation and performance. His work Cel explores the dark undercurrents of the alt-right along with the ways in which forms of hypermasculinity are idealized within its ideological framework. We invited Ed to screen the film and participate in a panel discussion about its contents alongside Annie Kelley, one of our other contributors to this volume whose ethnographic work focused on the online 'Manosphere'.

Through Cel, Fornieles aims to provide a greater understanding of the affective elements embedded in radicalization, along with suggestions on how to dismantle their prevalence. The project is divided into two sections:

1. A seventy-two-hour immersive role-play performance in which participants embody the simulation of an extremist online community.
2. The documentation of the experience through auto-ethnographic methods.

The intention of the work was for participants to immerse themselves in a real-life model of far-right forums and channels. This was done through immersive role-play performance, also known as 'live action role-play' (LARP), designed to develop a set of rigid tasks while allowing participants to improvise the alt-right space as a particular character. Throughout the performance, CCTV and body cameras were used to record the participants' words and actions.

The second half of the Cel was the debriefing process, in which participants came together to outline what they had experienced in the seventy-two-hour simulation in which they were immersed as their specific character interacting with rules taken from far-right forums. This immersion allowed for in-depth analysis of their own experiences in the world of alt-right extremism.

In order to share these insights, we decided to interview Fornieles about his experiences of creating Cel and his reflections of being a character in the simulation. The following is a transcript of the interview, which focuses on themes of the body, power, masculinity and patriarchy.

> Dan: Could you summarize a bit about your work, your story, and particularly what led up to you making Cel?
>
> Ed: I think there are various reasons as to why I ended up producing Cel, both on a personal and political level. On a personal level, I suppose I was noticing things in my own life, in which, it was like a moment of crisis. I had been in a chain of relationships, and I found the ways in which I was behaving within those was causing distress both to myself and to the person that I was in relationships with. I was disassociating, and found it very hard to feel anything. I felt disconnected from my body and I ultimately found that my reaction to that situation was to retreat into myself. I was not being present, and in that state, when you don't really experience reality fully, you're sort of a 'half being' almost … not to be too dramatic about it.
>
> That crisis led me to therapy, and then to me being on my own for a long time, and to try to reflect into why I was feeling and behaving that way … and to just question life a little bit. I think a lot of people come to therapy within those moments in their lives.
>
> This then sort of dovetails at a point in time, which is about 2016/17, where you have the rise of people like Jordan Peterson, where you have an online male movement that is highlighting and stressing a crisis of masculinity and male identity in general, and coming up with a bunch of solutions around that. These all happen to be very much geared towards knuckling down or doubling down on a sort of 'trad' or traditional mode of masculinity. I had the feeling that this was sort of a terrible cul-de-sac for those people, and just seeing how it is riffing with certain political populist movements on the right wing, and that they were sort of coalescing in this quite extreme way.
>
> So that's the sort of the context by which I came to Cel.
>
> Cel itself was an immersive role-play that went on for over 72 hours, involving 10 participants, all of them male characters, but not all of them being male. So we had two women, one was an artist and a dominatrix, and she brought a lot of her knowhow into the project. Another one was Nina Runa Essendrop, who helped a lot on both the design and developed the whole project with me.

The other participants were a mix between young gamers who understood the culture that we were dealing with, which was the context of a hypothetical radicalized sort of 4chan gamer group.[1] Then you had actors; people from the Live Action Role-Play (LARP) community, specifically the Nordic LARP community, who understood this sort of setup. You also had the leader, Alex, who is a fascinating character. I recruited him from an acting website, but his main job is to make men more confident, or businessman more confident, I should say. So he teaches men how to walk into a room to sort of make sure that they take up space, and to be successful in social and work environments. Having him on board was really amazing. I remember during the auditions, he was terrifyingly captivating. I would emphasize the word 'terrifying' … he just really pushes all of his energy into whoever he's talking to. His journey was interesting because of that, perhaps, and where he got to by the end of the project.

You then had me as the architect, I felt a responsibility to obviously participate, but not only to participate, but participate as the lowest ranking element of the role-play, which in LARP is called 'playing the bottom'. That means that you always put yourself in the trickiest and hardest situations.

The context for Cel is based around radicalized gamer groups. There was and there still is a trend of people from these online gaming communities, that frequent places like as 4Chan or Reddit, meeting up and going through a programme of self betterment by which they try to become physically stronger. Through this they unify as a group, and often have pernicious aims or targets in the real world. They don't always enact them, but when they do, it has sometimes resulted in murder or suicide. In any case, in the first half of this hypothetical scenario, we had a bunch of rules that we created for the environment. The most fundamental rule or protocol was that you should always have somebody lower than yourself. So the group starts off organized within a hierarchical structure with a leader, two enforcers, and then the rest are sort of added subjects who want to go on this programme of self-betterment.

They're all trying to physically improve themselves, so the first part of this, which took a day and a half or two, was spent on an exercising programme. This was done so they become exhausted, which is something we actually took from how cults are run, because it makes people more

---

[1] 4chan is an internet imageboard with a rather controversial and mixed history, but rooted in being a forum for discussion of Japanese anime and manga. Despite the more controversial boards /b/ (random content; essentially porn and memes) and /pol/ (political discussion; largely fascism, alt right populism and anti-semitism although a spectrum of views do admittedly exist). There are over two-dozen other special interest boards from paranormal activity, books, fitness and table-top roleplaying. Each represents a relatively distinct microculture separate from the toxic anarchy of /b/ and /pol/. We would recommend Dale Beran's *It Came from Something Awful* for a good overview.

open and pliable to ideological indoctrination. At that point, anyone could try to push themselves up or down the hierarchy.

Then came another set of rules. These would involve starting fights or the act of symbolically demeaning other people. This could result in a show of support, which then led to alliances being made. So for instance, if there was some antagonism between two characters, other members could physically show support for one of the sides by mimicking them behind their back or physically supporting them in some way. In one case, this escalated into a point where I was waterboarded, and I had my head shaved, and although I'm very aware that I'm in this hypothetical construction, it definitely touched me in a quite a deep way.

Dan: Getting an insight into your thinking and how it's designed is really fascinating. I particularly like that you took some of your architectural decisions from how cults operate. It reminds me of particular strains of gamer masculinity as well. Did you take any inspiration from the GamerGate[2] situation at all?

Ed: The elements of the physical space are not something that really exists. It was set in the 'leaders apartment', although one could imagine gamers congregating in a physical space like that. But the space itself was sort of the allure and the imagery of those online spaces. It's interesting, we use improvisational logic to = enact or inhabit that space … but the gamers are experts at improvisation. So if you look at those online forums and environments, what happens is that somebody makes a proposition which either gets taken up, or rejected by the group. If it gets taken up by the group, it gets expanded on and developed. So an example of this is the development of any meme like Pepe,[3] or a mischievous God called KEK gets created on 4chan and the parameters of what KEK is, how it operates, what its history is, and all of a sudden an allure gets created. Something that tracks back to the mischievous Gods of Egypt, and tries to pinpoint wherever it is still in existence in our contemporary world. So they're [4Chan users] very open to this kind of game like playfulness.

---

[2]   This refers to a significant online event in backlash by the online Gamer community. Whilst it was claimed as 'concerns about ethics in videogame journalism', it manifested as misogynistic, violent outrage targeted at women online. For a sense of this in wider terms, see Ceri Oeppen's and Annie Kelly's chapters in this volume. For a wider overview, see: https://www.vox.com/culture/2020/1/20/20808875/gamergate-lessons-cultural-impact-changes-harassment-laws

[3]   Pepe the frog can be thought of as an unofficial mascot of 4Chan, or at least a semi-recognizable public face. He ends up widely deployed in a range of memes, although there have always been far right and NeoNazi posters on the board, with the rise of Trumpism and QAnon conspiracy movements has become increasingly associated with new alt-right and populist politics. Whilst his usage in pathos-inspiring 'Greentext' stories is relatively apolitical, his association with the overwhelmingly toxic elements of 4Chan.

This is coupled with a kind of aggressive ironic toxicity in which is trying to constantly undermine positions or reduce them down to an ironically detached point of view. Saying that, there is a supportive element, like if you go to those boards [4chan], you see people who are, like, 'I feel depressed and suicidal'. First of all, you don't know if that statement is correct or not, or if it's real or fiction, but the responses will inhabit both those positions. They will view it as fiction sometimes and they'll be like 'go on, kill yourself' and then another response will be supportive and be like 'it's okay, I felt like this before, what's going on your life, talk to me about your relationship to your parents' and some of them will offer genuine support. So those spaces also become very attractive on that level. Even though I got waterboarded and had my head shaved, I had a sense of place within the structure within Cel. That sense of place was very, very attractive ... I had a structure to work within.

Maybe I should talk about safety for a second ... so safety was another really important aspect. This could sound like a crazy psychological experiment, a bit like the prisoner experiment[4] or something like that. But it does come from a very different place, it comes from Nordic LARP. Within that they've been doing this for, I suppose, about thirty years or so now. I mean, maybe you could argue before the advent of role playing games, like Dungeons and Dragons, that kind of has its roots within that. In any case, they developed a mechanism for exploring deep psychological and personal subjectivities and have created a bunch of protocols around that. The premise of Cel was to create this patriarchal 'you should always have someone lower than you' environment. So that's the structural decision which is emblematic of, I think, a bunch of relationships I've had in my life, and as I said, this gamer environment, but the underlying structure is a Nordic One. I think that is what makes it the antithesis of that structure as it requires intense amounts of trust, and willingness to be vulnerable in other people. It requires huge levels of support.

So over two weeks beforehand we mapped out what people's levels were, and how far people were willing to go, what people were not willing to do. We tested things. There were points where you could melt wax on people, and so we tested people's experience of having wax melted on them and whether or not they were okay with that. We had a safety system for all this. If someone says BREAK, it means that the action slows down to the point where it might stop. So that just says 'I felt uncomfortable with what is going

---

[4] In reference to Milgram's famous Stanford Prison experiment, the question was whether a person would administer an electric shock to an innocent bystander if ordered to do so by a perceived authority figure.

on, I don't want to stop completely, but I would like things to sort of calm down'. That was used only once. And then we have CUT, where everything stops immediately and we check in with somebody. Then we have things like a non-game space, so people can go and rest for a moment. We also had a debrief, which is very important. So people check in in the mornings, and at the end of the work. They get to communicate their experience, both as a character, and as a participant, and say, how it's going, how they're feeling about things, how it's affecting them, and what they might need. We had a buddy network afterwards. So a few months afterwards, people could contact each other, and support each other and just check in with how they were feeling about the whole thing.

Dan: You said you had a professional dominatrix as part of the team. I recognize there must have been a lot things around kind of consent and debriefing. Did the dominatrix help design those safety measures?

Ed: Yeah, Penny was fantastic. She brought one 'demonic' aspect to the game, that was a role play called tickle or punch. It's where she would pin you down, or someone would pin someone down and begin tickling them, and then you say 'tickle or punch', you have an option. After a while you can't take it anymore because it's too much, so you say 'punch, punch punch', at which point she starts punching in the ribs. And then you're like, 'Okay, stop! stop! tickle! tickle!' So you just go from one hell to the other. And I think this is very common in the dominatrix scene ... and so that was a mechanicism? She was also an amateur wrestler as well. So her capacity to win during the fights was quite high.

I should also quickly say that this stuff that we're talking about the 'you should always have someone lower than yourself' is only the first stage. There was a symbolic murder-suicide in the middle, which transitions into the second stage, which was looking at how these structures might be dismantled. So the hierarchy was removed instantly after the death, although it kind of kept playing itself out a little bit.

We took a lot of exercises from *Inner Circle*, which is a group that works in prisons with men, and tries to create spaces in which people can be vulnerable and open up about their experiences of how they got there, where the walls of the prison yard are removed for a moment. And it also brings in people who are not prisoners into the prison space, as documentation for the work that goes into it.

In any case, we used the exercises that they use, such 'beige tunnels' where people can physically insert themselves focusing on something that has been psychologically traumatic for them in the past. That's another thing I should mention as well, like, the whole point of this is that it's not about theoretical abstraction, that I understand there's this problem with masculinity and I can theorize that like, society needs to change. It's simply to say, this exists within all of us, or within us that's participating in it, and we need to physically address that within ourselves. Unless we understand or perform it through that way, we will never internalize a lesson or change or mutate, or never really confront it. I think that's important. Also to say that, while it may be about this Incel group or this gamer group, it really is a general structural problem for men. This patriarchal mode of thinking in which the need to dominate is constantly kind of a shadow to their sense of self.

Amir: After Cel, did you receive any messages from people? And if you did, what kind of messages were they?

Ed: Well, there's a mix from the people who participated, and their own experiences, but also my own. So for instance, I couldn't cry before … and now I'm actually able to. I feel much more in touch with my body and my emotional state, I feel much more able to be sensitive, and I feel much more present. It was not just down to that performance, but It that was a big turning point for me. And thankfully it's been very heart-warming to heard similar experiences from the people who participated.

The public response has been mixed. I think it's very hard to if you look at intersectional politics, it's very hard to ask people to emphasize the masculine position, because there's a fear I think that it comes at the cost of other positions.

So that's been tricky. There was one thing written about it which basically said 'they don't have the energy or want to consider the male position because they're concentrating on a feminist project'. And I think for me that's a really tricky thing to confront, or deal with. I mean, these theoretical things that underscore this come from, you know, second and third wave feminism. And predominantly, you know, the book *The Will to Change* by bell hooks is something that really influenced me and changed my life which then subsequently led to the theoretical basis that this work was based on.

Amir: Regarding the changes that you said you and a lot of the other participants experienced, do you feel like these sorts of events or projects have the potential to be utilized within therapeutic spaces to allow for a reconnection towards emotion and body?

Ed: I think that all these experiences force kind of growing … whatever that might be. But in answer to your question, yes, because a lot of the mechanics that were taken or used within Cel were based on therapeutic practices. They were from the LARP community which has a history of confronting this kind of stuff, we also had a Gestalt therapist on the project.

Gestalt therapy focuses and uses the body a lot. It's this sort of developmental psycho-analytical practice with physical aspects. And actually, I've just got a book on my table at the moment which is *The Body Keeps the Score*, which is also another really important text that talks about trauma's effect on the body and how the body can be used within various different therapeutic practices to relieve the effects of trauma.

Amir: How much of the conversation in Cel was just freestyle? How much of it was scripted?

Ed: None of it was scripted, the only thing that was definitive was the shooting. And the rest of it was just tools and mechanisms that people could pick up as and when they wanted.

Amir: So in the end scene, for example, where you had, I forgot his name, but he's weeping. Everyone's kind of coming around him and saying 'I'm sorry'. That just happened organically?

Ed: Yes. I mean, it was very intense. Actually, that participant had something quite bad happened to him just before. I think that was a chance for him to go' there' with us. It's hard, like, I watched and edited Cel for fifteen months. I was just trapped in my bedroom editing that film. I still cry when I watch some reactions.

Amir: Wow, that's really powerful. I did not know … I thought that at least some elements were scripted.

Ed: Yeah and that organic feeling is another thing to represent. So the way that was filmed is you have eight CCTV cameras and ten body cameras in the installation. And so normally, like, I have my experience and I know there are other experiences out there that I can't really make sense of because I wasn't there at the time. And so there was an attempt to deal with the responsibility of what it is to represent other people's positions within that or subjective experiences within these environments. And it's fascinating to go back and realize that all these intimate little moments are constantly happening all around me that I was completely unaware of.

Amir: You talk about the body cams along with CCTV. Did the concept of being observed at all times play a factor in in the performance? Or were you so immersed in the actual role that those kind of things went into the periphery?

Ed: That's a great question. I think that there's two things with that, I think it touches on the fundamental mechanism of how the whole thing works. You move from immersion to reflection. During the immersion, you are the 'thing'; you're moving without thinking. You're just responding to the stimuli around you that are almost exhausted. Then you enter into reflection, and that's when you become aware … so you touch your body camera, you realize the CCTV is there, and you enter the debrief and reflecting on the experiences. Then there's this in-between/limbo zone as well, where all of the body cameras have lasers on them. We use the lasers quite often as a device for either messing with people like shining them in their eyes, so they can make eye contact with you, or as showing support for somebody. You don't realize it, but because all the bodies are turned towards one person, you would suddenly become aware that the focus of attention in the room was all on one person. So yes, there is this movement between emotion and reflection, which I think is really important. And I think that's probably important in therapy as well.

Amir: You mentioned about therapy, psychoanalysis and a lot of the processes that went into this. I was wondering, are there any artistic influences that you had other artists or films that inspired this work?

Ed: I really love the works of people like Mike Kennedy, and other people who use performance art, but they're much more connected to the symbolic. Someone who really influenced me is Joshua Oppenheimer, who did the film *The Act of Killing in 2012*. So one of the editors that worked on this project was an editor on *The Act of Killing*. That work, to me, is the most one of most profound films that's ever been made that looked at the Indonesian genocide and connected it to masculinities. Within that the winners are present, and they're in society, and they're going about their day and consider themselves and what they did as a virtuous act. He allows them to perform themselves in front of camera, and then he also gets them to re-enact these traumatic and horrific things they did to other people within a 'gendered' context. One of the guys chooses to make a film noir scene to act out a murder that he committed with his friends at the time. It's just beautiful and melts the construction between real and fantasy, or says that 'real' isn't this fake objective interviews you do with somebody? It can express itself in other ways.

Amir: And I'm guessing a lot of violence as well?

Ed: Yeah, I mean, it's theatrical violence of the millions of people that were killed by gangs that were kind of given the nod by the Indonesian government who, in turn, were given the nod by the American government. Horrific violence, but within the film, you don't see that, you just have descriptions of it, and you have these performative re-enactments of it.

Dan: It's always really interesting to hear about the differences levels of process that goes into making art. There's always been this really close and tense relationship between art, philosophy, and anthropology … and it always amazes me just how much twentieth-century philosophers that I'm very fond of ended up talking about art, which has left me asking 'but why, what's the relationship?' Hearing you talk about Cel and those crossovers makes more sense with regards to those connections. I'm also curious about how you conceptualize masculinity. In more theoretical terms, you talked about it in terms of quite structural stuff. I tend to take an anti-essentialist view of that kind of thing, but I think conservatives tend to route it to biology. Historically, it was more attached to metaphysics, going back to the biblical stuff – man was created in God's image where the body belongs to the divine. I wondered what conceptual framework you operated in when you thought about what gender is, how it inheres through bodies and how it can be changed through praxis, or just what that vein of thought was for you?

Ed: Yeah, I totally agree. So the way that I see it is that often in the right [wing], you have this essentialist point of view, and you even see that within gaming communities, there's often allusions to evolutionary theory. Whereas I think that if you look at role-play, as an ideological alternative, it emphasizes plasticity constantly. It says, you know, reality is just bad by design and it could be formulated another way. Then you go in to your sandbox, and then you try to enact it. There are also theories within LARP called bleed. You have 'bleed in' where your characters might start affecting you even after LARP has finished. You might find yourself inhabiting the world differently. I definitely had that after Cel where I had a shaved head, and people got out my way. I was definitely read as a skinhead which was kind of interesting for me. I learned something from that. Then you have 'bleed out', when your own character starts affecting your constructed character. That's inevitable, and that always happens to some degree. And then you have 'memetic bleed'. That's something I'm quite interested in. That's when something that is workshopped within the constructed environment, might ideologically start bleeding out or a group of people might start trying to develop a new convention by which they begin living their lives. I'm interested in this plasticity, and that masculinity isn't one thing. That's why I think in your conference, the use of the plural of masculinity is super important. Thinking that it's this singular thing is probably inaccurate, and very damaging.

Dan: Yeah, and that singularity invites violence is sort of my perspective on it. This one standard, that becomes a big stick that you can beat people with. And there's this interplay between necessity and contingency, which things are fixed and which things can stay the same, and then what does it mean if those things can change. Because constructivism is that nothing is real, right? But we know that our bodies exist, and you talked about the transformation of your body through the process of having done Cel and this kind of bleeding out that came, not even from this internal reconfiguration, but the body as a site of the reconfiguration of masculinity, giving yourself these new semiotic properties that might not reflect an internal change, but kind of the way that your body signalled a certain kind of masculinity after that experiment shows that there is this radically transformability.

I find this kind of extant masculinity that exists 'out there' in the world that people can look at as a text via the body or clothing or even artefacts quite interesting. Things like a sword or a gun that tell this story of violence and threat that I think carries a kind of semiotic weight that gets associated typically with masculine things. I think that I'm becoming quite anti constructivist, but also you don't want to collapse into being a naive essentialist. I think the fluidity and plurality that you've demonstrated, just makes me think, well, what is gender? I know it's not a small question but, I'd be curious if you have any thoughts in terms of the interplay between plasticity, necessity, contingency, gendered bodies, how do you think about masculinity on that basis?

Ed: Well it's hard as well, because masculinity is a historic construct. I think for thousands of years, there's been a certain kind of masculinity demanded of the communities that have brought us to this point, at least within England in the West. To dismantle, change or mutate it, has the same linearity to how it was created. It's generational, and it's going to be very difficult to do. I would argue that every being, every human being, at least, regardless of the agenda, needs to be felt and to be heard. They need emotional and physical contact and support from their caregivers at an early stage. I think that if they get that stuff, then often they're much better in terms of being empathetic, and to go out into the world and be playful. If they are deprived of those things, often it results in hardening or a disassociation or the avoidant or the anxious attachment style. Thinking about all those themes is perhaps quite interesting. What is the pipeline of most people who are born gender: male? And how do they get to where they need to be going? I mean, it's weird because you know, kids don't do what you tell them to do. They do what you do. I think that we're mirroring machines. Often as a child, I remember mirroring my father, and often that was a more closed off kind of way of inhabiting a space than my sisters and my mother.

Dan: I'd really like to hear your thoughts on what your experience of feminism been? What was your first engagement with it?

Ed: I grew up in a very female household. Feminist ideas were always present, but I got into Betty Friedan later in my life. She talks a lot about violence being an inability to communicate something in language. And I was very interested in that idea of, lack of language, and what the effect of that is, and I think that, to me, again, pointed to the male condition quite a lot. But then

I went through a hideous breakup and I realized some ways that I had been living my life were not working. So during that time, me and the person that I was breaking up with, read bell hooks' *All about Love*. What's interesting about that book is it talks about defining things like what love is, and she points to it as an action. It's not, you know, this romantic idea that you can, you know, is in your head, it's how you perform yourself, and what the material reality of that is. I think that then also led me to go to *The Will to Change*. I suppose that's been my gateway into feminism. And yes, I would consider myself feminist. But I'm also aware that as I was saying before that the one thing that unites the right, with all these movements, is a hatred of feminism. And I think that's really interesting. And again, I'd point like, needing to develop a pathway through which men can come to different conclusions.

Dan: What do you think is blocking that pathway? Does that blockage relate to this kind of uniting opposition to feminism? What is it about feminism that is provoking such a strong response from so many of these groups of men that seem to feel very alienated and threatened by It?

Ed: I think that there's a sense of loss that potentially is connected to this, that a lot of men feel that their sense of place in the world has been on their minds. It has been on the mind economically, this reality would probably never exist or existed for a few people in the 1950s has always been pointed back to as the male provider, the person who's in charge of their own destiny. So there's this instability structurally. It's kind of delusional anyway. Then you have the feminist discourse, which, from the outside often appears to define itself in a general opposition to most 'normal' things so that the two positions very naturally will defend themselves against each other. The conflict is kind of almost inevitable.

That's why again, Cel was interested in coming through masculinity, rather than critiquing it externally, showing that change needs to somehow well up from within. I think that there are very simple experiences in your life, where you're like, 'oh yeah!' being connected to my body and being more connected to the people around me feels better, you know? But also, we haven't really mentioned how good masculine environments can feel. I find myself attracted to them still, and I have all male groups of friends and I can indulge in certain male ways of being which are great. Even if they have a toxic element to them, too. I know there's a difference between performing in those spaces, knowing and performing in those spaces as if they just simply are reality. I think that's also an important distinction.

Dan: I'd be interested to hear your thoughts about the relationship between masculinity and the body, and in particular, the embodied experience side of Cel because of the extreme things that you went through.

Ed: In terms of my experience, so a lot of people within Cel, I think found themselves going back to a time at school, for instance, and I failed to perform myself at school completely. I found myself retreating into myself in exactly the same way, pretty much as back then. And I remember being about fourteen, and I peed myself in the PE changing rooms. It was the most horrific experience. And after that, I've really survived. I felt good, I felt so good, I figured out that if I shut off my feelings, I feel like I can get by, I don't need to care about what anyone else thinks it's really, it's great. And what you don't realise, especially the age of 14, that has long lasting consequences. So I found myself doing the same thing when I was pinned down and shaved at one point. And although obviously, I can talk to you now about how it was a construction, but it felt very real at the time, and I found myself retreating, descending into myself descending into myself. And then to animate your body through the stuff that came afterwards. I had been experiencing this cathartic release, because I think what happens often is that you spend a huge amount of energy maintaining this equilibrium, but you don't realize your body is asserting itself constantly. Repression takes a lot of energy. And so although it is also energetic, it takes a lot of energy to create that release. It's also great relief, like I think that, you know, you can look at stress and the contributing factors that the people who exist in that way are much more prone to disease, much more prone to get sick and to time young, and spends another perhaps interesting aspect to toxic masculinity.

12

The cultural work of hormones: The story of David and testosterone

Lauren Redfern

Introduction

This chapter explores the context of the European Menopause and Andropause Society (EMAS) conference. It draws upon observational data collected as part of a wider doctoral ethnographic study exploring the use of synthetic testosterone among those experiencing menopausal symptoms. Beyond the ExpoCenter in Berlin, where the majority of the observational data in this chapter is drawn from, ethnographic research has taken place in a UK-based private practice clinic, where the daily routines of healthcare professionals and patients coming into contact with testosterone have been observed.

Underpinning my research is the understanding that categories such as sex and gender are important structural forces that serve a vital function in maintaining social order (e.g. Epstein 2009). As such, the idea that certain hormones belong to particular bodies is thought to reflect a craving for ordered physiology, and the desire for our bodily forms to communicate particular sentiments. The transgression of 'body boundaries' (such as bodies that contradict gendered norms, or hormones in the 'wrong' bodies) is observed as threatening our social order precisely due to it's ability to upset normative ideologies – a powerful disruptive capability that makes following the use of hormones not only intriguing but vitally important in querying latent assumptions. Explorations within this chapter query how testosterone is involved in 'making' bodies and selves, simply through its presence and absence. Fundamentally, it highlights how testosterone's location at the intersection of scientific, commercial and moral-normative discourses communicates particular narratives on masculinities and patriarchal power.

Terminology

For the purpose of this chapter, I have adopted use of the descriptors 'men' and 'women' and 'male' and 'female' as opposed to gender neutral and inclusive terminology such as 'person experiencing menopausal or andropausal symptoms' (as is proffered in this introduction). The rationale for this decision is two-fold. Firstly, it adopts the language that participants themselves used to self-identify during observations, namely – 'men' and 'women'. Secondly, it provides greater linguistic ease to discuss conditions that are typically gendered and largely associated with cisgender persons (cis meaning to identify as the sex one was assigned at birth).

It is important to reference however that the use of this terminology is complex, and that gender identity is not by definition, a precursor to a medical state such as menopause. Indeed, those that identify as men or non-binary may still go through perimenopause and menopause as they may identity as a gender incongruous to the sex they were assigned at birth.

With this in mind, it is important to proceed with a reading that accounts for the level of inflexibility within scientific terminology and medical discourse. To do so, accounts for the complexities facing individuals that identify as a gender that defers from the sex they were assigned at birth when having to navigate medical environments that are profoundly gendered. As this chapter will illustrate, normative gendered ideologies are deeply embedded within the scientific landscape and not only communicate patriarchal oppression, but troubling inflexibility and inaccessibility for those that identify beyond a cisgender state.

For further information regarding the power of language and its ability to shape our perceptions of other people, reference to the PFLAG's glossary of terms is helpful to review (PFLAG 2021).

Andropause's big debut

The expansive Dublin lecture theatre seats between 2,000 and 3,000 people. It is situated (rather confusingly given the name) at the heart of the ExpoCenter in Berlin, Germany, which in May 2019 had just played host to the 12th European Congress on Menopause and Andropause (EMAS). After three days of lectures, seminars, lunch symposiums, TV interviews and professional networking, the final talks of the conference are underway. An optimistic estimate would put the remaining number of attendees at around 150 – a significant decline from the humming throng of bodies that had previously filled the Dublin lecture theatre with ease in the days prior. The absence in attendance is noticeable, and the speakers acknowledge it. They make jokes, drawing reference to the intensity of the material covered over the preceding days. Calling upon a conflict metaphor, the first speaker brands the small collective audience that remain in attendance the 'surviving few'; those brave enough to have faced abnormal uterine bleeding, myoma, vulvovaginal cosmetic surgery and uterine and rectal prolapse, only to return from the intellectual trenches ready for more.

Though menopause and andropause have both been scheduled as topical 'headliners' for the EMAS conference, the subject of andropause has yet to feature. This being the case, it is interesting to observe the dwindling number of attendees that remain that final Friday afternoon. Why, given the fact that andropause has yet to make its debut, have so many opted *not* to attend these talks?

Possible clarification of the 'why' is offered when reflecting upon the conversations that had taken place between myself and practitioners at the conference in the preceding days. The topic of andropause had within these discussions been treated with a level of clinical scepticism. A position, that seemingly stemmed from the knowledge that unlike menopause, which occurs in all women as a result of decreasing hormone levels 'functional hypogonadism' or andropause (a consequence of low testosterone) is thought realistically to only affect a small proportion of men (around 2–5 per cent of the population (Singh 2013)). Practitioners elaborated, explaining that despite this, a demand for a diagnosis of andropause was becoming increasingly prevalent amongst older men. They highlighted how growing demand for testosterone replacement therapy (TRT) could be observed. Fundamentally in these conversations, the increasing use of TRT among older men was positioned by practitioners as not only unnecessary, but problematic.

The concept of andropause was foregrounded in these conversations as arguably undermining the menopausal state as experienced by women, given the disparity in rates of occurrence. The politics of the condition were noted to point towards a wider trend towards false equivalence too often seen in issues – particularly those of gender. Underpinning these conversations was an important observation – though andropause may provide a seductive structural opposite – a gender binary to menopause through which we may find an appeasing medical 'yin and yang'; it ultimately detracts attention away from the experiences of women afflicted by menopausal symptoms.

While by its very name, andropause would imply itself as something coterminous, equal and opposite to the menopause, it's occurrence (the 2–5 per cent statistic) allows us to recognize why it is not and moreover, why it may garner clinical scepticism within the field. Given this, the decision to provide half a day of allotted speaking time to andropause was not only framed within conversations with practitioners as problematically patriarchal, but disproportionately generous. Thus, on that final day, when andropause waited in the wings to make its big debut, the dwindling attendance and sceptical glances made a little more sense. Regardless of the audience's rather lacklustre energy however, as the first of three lectures gets underway andropause is still termed the 'meatiest' of subject matters by the afternoons first speaker and an ardent push to academically 'amp up' the crowd and excite 'team andropause' is made.

Ideal bodies

Each lecture that afternoon focuses on the treatment of hypogonadal men and in particular the diagnosis of 'functional hypogonadism'. In multiple iterations, the speakers explain that hypogonadal conditions vary, highlighting that different types present themselves at different stages of life. The speakers take time to outline how, whilst conditions such as Klinefelter syndrome (where an extra X chromosome is present in boys/men) are diagnosable as present from birth, 'functional hypogonadism' afflicts individuals at a later stage of life, with most diagnoses occurring in 'older men'. The speakers elaborate that prior to a diagnosis of functional hypogonadism, hormonal secretion and gonadal activity for these individuals may have been 'normal', or at least not a cause for concern. The onset of the condition, however, indicates a diminished production of sex hormones which continues to occur with ageing.

Care is taken to outline that the percentage of men suffering from functional hypogonadism, or 'low testosterone' is likely small (an estimation of 2–5 per cent of the population is reiterated). Elaborating on this point, speakers highlight that clinicians should take care to ensure that testosterone treatment is truly necessary, before prescribing testosterone to a patient (Singh 2013).

The question of *why* TRT has become such a sought-after treatment among older men, despite the statistically low percentages suffering from functional hypogonadism, is inadvertently addressed shortly after this point is made. As the next speaker cues up their slides heads snap up. This speaker begins their lecture by outlining the actions in the body that are attributable to testosterone. Using the image of Michelangelo's David for reference, they attach arrows to relevant parts of the sculpture (or man's body) that are likely to be affected by testosterone.

On the speaker's slide, the description of the actions of testosterone includes the brain, with the slide detailing that testosterone is likely to help with concentration and possibly memory; libido, explaining that testosterone increases sex drive; hair, noting that testosterone stimulates growth on the face, chest, genital area and underarms; voice, specifying testosterone as responsible for the deepening of the voice after puberty; muscles, noting that testosterone is accountable for increasing lean muscle mass; fat in the body, emphasizing the association between low testosterone and excess body fat; organs, outlining that testosterone triggers the normal development of male sex organs; and bone health, highlighting that testosterone can help to increase bone density and growth.

On the next slide, the speaker has placed two images side by side. One is of the original sculpture of David. The other is of a photoshopped version of the statue, designed to highlight how testosterone deficiency may affect David (the prototypical man). The most noticeable change in the image is a significant increase in mass. In the edited image, David holds the same pose, but his body has been manipulated and distorted. He now has wider legs, a large stomach that protrudes over his genitals, and his previously distinct pectoral muscles are less defined, as are the muscles on his arms and upper body. Lighting in the images also differs. While a softer red hue surrounds the original David, drawing the eye line to muscular definition, colder green and yellow shades act as the backdrop to the edited David, highlighting shadows where larger parts of the body jut and swell.

The contrast between these two Davids is ultimately attributed to one thing – the presence, or lack there of, of testosterone. Akin to the conversations that took place with practitioners, the speaker had outlined the clinical picture. They too suggested the 2–5 per cent estimate. Yet they opt to show this image. Why? For all intents and purposes the speaker is utilizing (whether intentionally or not) one of the most iconic and celebrated examples of Renaissance sculpture as a 'before and after' body transformation advert. In the case of David however, it appears that instead of a detox tea, he has testosterone to thank for his 'buff bod'. The seductive lure of testosterone – and its use and abuse – suddenly becomes clearer. One's conformity to an ideal-typical body is no longer necessarily a personal or moral failing, but within the medicalized discourse of sickness and cure, a very solvable problem. If gender is at least in part socially constructed and biologically plastic, then testosterone can be considered as represented in this rendering, an ambitious constructor.

Testosterone as king maker

The existence of an *idealized* male body as a reference point (as is shown in the speakers slide) opens avenues to enquire about the relationship between bodies, science and testosterone. The speakers *particular* choice of reference is interesting; Michaelangelo's David is the ultimate European idealization of the masculine body, demonstrated by its high status in the world of art. The sculpture is admired around the world for its proportioned beauty; a manifestation of accumulated changes of heroic form and significance (Starn 1986). Ultimately, if hegemonic masculinity was to be abstracted, a concrete (or at least marble) form of it is seen on the speakers slide.

The ideal body – Davidian or otherwise – is a powerful repository of social and erotic meaning. Even in the spaces of 'objective' representation, or the medicalization of andropause, its social effects are deeply imbricated in the information imparted. The achievement of a Davidian form through the use of testosterone that is implied by the speakers slide, points towards a subjective engagement that traverses the aesthetic, medical and phenomenological domains in one neat gesture. For the men requesting TRT the medicalization of the process allows them to become the object of desire, to become themselves, Davidian.

Theorists such as Turner (1984) have cautioned against biological reductionism, denouncing interpretations of the body that fail to recognize it as inherently social and cultural. Ultimately, Turner stresses the importance of appreciating bodies as sites of symbolic interpretation, where personal and social identities coalesce (Mangan 2000:32). Further to this, Haraway (1991) argues that personal and social bodies cannot be seen as natural but only as part of a self-creating process. In the context of testosterone, such interpretation may be called upon and extended to enquire as to how hormones may acquire their own agency, one that exists in conversation with the social, shifting and changing as it moves across a variety of domains (Mol 2002). Fundamentally, given the meanings that are often ascribed to an idealized body, we should recognize that the 'actions' of testosterone can very well be interpreted as imbued with sociocultural significance.

The use of an idealized male form by the speaker also exhibits (however unintentionally) the political, aesthetic and moral dimensions of the body as they exist within a specific gender regime. The achievement (or failure to achieve) a masculine ideal manifests in the accumulation of what Bridges refers to as 'gender capital' by groups such as male bodybuilders. That is, the cultivation, achievement and embodiment of specific gendered ideals – Davidian or otherwise – transforms the body into a bearer of gender capital. Physical improvement in particular implicates the body as a multidimensional project of the self and patriarchal systems of power – a space where power is both targeted and produced (Wagner 2015:235).

To communicate this bluntly, if you are a bearer of a 'buff bod' like Dave you are unlikely to be left wanting. The flipside of this is of course, is that the failure to possess such a body has connotations; where being physically strong is a marker of discipline and willpower, being overweight is readily interpreted as a marker of weakness or moral failure. Indeed, obesity is often narrativized as both an 'epidemic' and a moral crisis, with obese people themselves often being attributed with negative characteristic markers such as laziness and stupidity (e.g. Campos et al. 2006). Indeed, in the context of the presentation the use of the overweight David serves as comedic banter. The speaker chuckles at his own photoshop handy work and the rotund sculptural form becomes the target of derisive humour. He is positioned as 'less than' – his soft gentle edges the antithesis to desirable masculinity.

In the case of the David presentation the iteration of knowledge is clear. The speaker conveys a simple message: that testosterone will have the same observable effects in all men's bodies. The action of mapping testosterone in this way (with arrows moving in a linear trajectory all over an iconic statue/male body) fails not only to account for the complexity of the endocrine system, but also communicates a simple, linear causal pathway. We receive the message that specific hormones will deliver specific results. Categorical differences between hormones and bodies thus become crystallized, as existing gender models are firmed up. This firming up of gender roles reflects how hegemonic masculinity (Connell 1995) is able to capitalize on hypermasculine bodily performances and through the rhetoric of science 'fix' them as not only desirable, but 'natural' norms.

It is important to note, that desirability in relation to bodies however fluctuates, and that such fluctuation can often reflect material conditions as opposed to ardent scientific discovery. Industrialization, for example, transformed attitudes towards bodies due to the expanding access to food, transportation, and labour-saving technologies (Petrzela 2020). According to Alexander (2003:536) in their work on 'Branded Masculinities', social theorists (Baudrillard 1981; Derrida 1966; Lyotard 1984) have been able to demonstrate how shifts away from a modern industrial culture based on production to a postmodern culture informed by the consumption of products, ideas and knowledge have brought about changes in the ways in which bodies are both perceived and conceived.

While the positioning of testosterone as an attributable 'marker of masculinity' arguably began to take hold via the linguistic depictions of its synthesization in the early twentieth century (Hoberman 2005); it's more popularized conceptions well known to mainstream media came to the fore in the context of action stars such as Arnold Schwarzenegger and Sylvester Stallone (who were known to use androgenic steroids). As jaws clenched, muscles bulged and women were rescued, specific narratives about testosterone took seat.

Ideas that communicate a simple, linear model or pathway in which use of testosterone ensures the attainment of an embodied ideal masculinity, highlights how patriarchy is maintained and achieved in practise through the discourse of scientific rhetoric. Fundamentally, eroticism, virility and hierarchy are all tied to ideal bodies and it is promised that every man not only deserves but can possess such a desirable standard via the use of testosterone. In this sense, testosterone is made at once a figurative kingmaker and pardoner of the perceivedly inadequate man.

Science and culture

At the heart of the speakers presentation lies an important question. To what extent can science be seen as 'doing' cultural work? Though work within behavioural sciences frequently supports associations between testosterone and particular behaviours (e.g. an inability to cry or hold a baby) (Flemming 2018; Zilioli et al. 2015); more contemporary research challenges traditional stereotypes in which testosterone is linked to specific behaviours or attributes. Theorists increasingly highlight how responses from hormones may best be understood as existing in 'conversation' with each other (Fine 2017; Karkazis and Jordan-Young 2019) – a complex system of interrelated endocrine actors.

The linear, deterministic model in which specific hormones are thought to be tied to particular bodies, particular functions and particular genders is best problematized when considering research that examines relationships between hormones. For example, ties between testosterone and aggressive behaviour have been challenged by research which considers the role of cortisol (Popma et al. 2007). Widely accepted as having a modulating effect on testosterone, cortisol is believed to inhibit testosterone receptors through a binding process, impeding the relationship between testosterone and aggressive action. Through receptor reduction, cortisol is able to mobilize the body to escape impeding danger. The effect cortisol has on blocking testosterone receptors is, in this sense, akin to an instinctive threat management plan. We may like to consider the process to be like an automatic 'override' programme in the body: cortisol supersedes the effects of testosterone, encouraging the body to escape.

Processes such as aromatase further help to illustrate the manner by which relationships between hormones occur. Aromatase occurs naturally when hormone levels are out of balance in an attempt to maintain homeostasis in the body (Lakshman et al. 2010). For example, should large fluctuations of testosterone occur in the body (such as the injection of anabolic steroids) aromatization may occur in a bid to maintain and stabilize hormone levels.

The final slide in the presentation highlights how this concept of relational hormonal activity is ignored. It features a model of the endocrine system as a collection of linear arrows drawn upon the image of David like an electrical circuit. Such visual mapping misrepresents the dynamic character of the endocrine system; testosterone does not stand alone and its effects are as such, not accurately represented as complex – affected, superseded and impeded by other hormones in the body. The relationships *between* hormones are ignored and the message becomes absolute as opposed to relative. An image displayed in a subsequent presentation helps to articulate the difference. The arrows move in every direction, communicating a different story in which testosterone exists as part of a complex process and system, one that involves multiple hormonal 'actors' as opposed to a solitary isolated performer.

Appreciating the concept of 'conversations' or 'relationships' when considering the function of hormones within the body is, ultimately key. Much like contemporary understandings and imaginings of gender, it is important to remember that hormones are, by their very nature, fluid. They exist in a state of constant flux, unlikely to ever deliver the same specificity in their results day to day, or person to person. Just as we are individuals, so too are our bodies and our hormones. In the context of menopausal treatment for example, while one patient may only require one pump of transdermal oestrogen a day to alleviate their symptoms, another may well require four pumps of the same gel.

Structural instincts

Dualistic models in which testosterone belongs to men and oestrogen to women are inarguably seductive. Ordering offers a mechanism by which we may make sense of our surroundings (external and internal). We are able to box up otherwise confusing systems and complicated phenomena into neat categorical binaries, allowing us to apply order to an otherwise chaotic landscape. As hormones are neatly placed in pink and blue boxes, the highly complex nature of the endocrine system, formed of multiple collaborative relationships, lies forgotten in our consciousness. Hormones are taken in from the periphery and their fluid nature is made static. We sort according to inherited sociocultural structures. We manipulate and bend complexity, asking it to comply with structures that 'make sense': social structures that have existed and been passed down for millennia. Seeking out these correlations – and many others – is understandable. When we are able to observe and label natural phenomenon in a manner that supports deep-seated cultural assumptions, our understandings of the world are sured up. We are provided with an empirical touchstone – something that *feels* sound and real. But *is* it? In the case of testosterone, we may observe that men *do* produce more of the hormone naturally than women. How can it, therefore, be a manipulation to dub this hormone unequivocally male? The response to this is of course, as the saying goes, that size (or at least quantity) isn't everything.

The desire to apply order underscores much of our intellectual thinking around hormones. The question of whether this is a conscious process, however, is more complex. The allure of ordering the body is demonstrated by a dominant mid-twentieth-century theoretical model known as structuralism.[1] As opposed to thinking about the actions of individuals or groups, the structuralist perspective concerns itself with the underlying logic of social and symbolic systems. Claude Levi-Strauss (1963) argued that human culture is best understood as a manifestation of the human mind: a projection of its internal mechanisms and structures onto cultural phenomenon. Through the exploration of unifying systems such as kinship and the observation of similarities in the construction of myths and stories, Levi-Strauss considered how systems of belonging may be formed. Drawing upon the foundations of linguistics, wherein systems of relating are informed by the idea of opposition or binaries, culture becomes observable as a series of opposites. These dualities are found, Levi-Strauss argues in a wide variety of social-scientific thought; nature-culture,

---

[1]   As used by anthropologists; structuralism had wider meanings in other disciplines.

society-technology, rationality-emotion and so on; yet they also can be see to permeate conceptualizations of gender.

That which is masculine is that which is not feminine, just as that which belongs to 'technology' is not 'social'. The idea that the social world and its categories can be rendered intelligible, concrete and accurate through mediums such as 'science' is comforting. It represents natural, even cosmological axioms. Critical-theoretical currents have however come to query systems of opposites. 'Post-structural' analysis ultimately rejects the idea of categories such as masculine and feminine being fixed, instead preferring an understanding that positions them to be better understood as created through complex interactions and discourses. In the instance of gender, figures like Judith Butler for example turned their attention away from ideas of patriarchy as an immutable fact, towards how gender itself could be understood as produced (1993). Recent developments have moved towards a focus on dynamic, relational and shifting sets of relations between various actors (e.g. De Landa 2006; Latour 2005). Thus, while at times dualistic pairings may present overtly, and powerfully resonate with us as absolute, the deconstruction of oppositional thinking often reveals a more complex picture.

To move away from gender in the abstract, it is interesting to consider how biological sex may, upon reflection, be understood as less 'absolute' than perhaps first assumed. The biomedical processes involved in 'sexing' the body can arguably be seen to reveal insufficient objectivity and reflect deep-seated social norms, values and anxieties. Anne Fausto Sterling (2000) has explored the relative concerns with 'difference' through her work detailing the desire to biomedically categorize intersex individuals. In *Sexing the Body*, Sterling asserts that individuals should not be forced to compromise their individual differences to fit a flawed societal definition of 'normality'. In identifying variations in genitalia, Fausto Sterling hypothesizes that the need to categorize bodies into binary systems of male and female is more representative of a desire for social order than an actual biological need, thus demonstrating how inextricably linked concepts of body and biology are to social norms and the desire to categorize.

Though binary thinking continues to come under increasing scrutiny, the foundations of our biological teachings continue to rest upon deterministic models in which the identification of innate distinctions is commonplace. Moreover, while the conflation of sex and gender may be being addressed as problematic, in practice, the bleeding between these categories is not always easy to observe. As such, there are multiple instances in which the biological, or seemingly empirical, is in actuality heavily imbued with sociocultural context and gendered stereotypes that remain unchallenged in research.

Entering its thirtieth year, the relevance of Emily Martin's work (1991) is still profoundly relevant in the context of this conversation. Moving beyond the generalized representation of gender and the body, Martin's research looks at the domain of scientific and biological narratives themselves. Their work explores how the process of procreation relies upon gender normative narratives underscoring just how fluently biology becomes imbued with gendered meaning. Outlining the use of provocative gendered language, Martin explores how romance plots have been rehashed in the telling of conception. Though contemporary understandings of fertilization recognize the process as biologically collaborative (the egg drawing in the sperm as it makes contact), depictions in medical literature, teaching material and popular culture are outlined by Martin as chronicling conception differently (and more traditionally). Using extracts from educational textbooks, Martin highlights how both egg and sperm are anthropomorphized (the strong and courageous sperm greets the passive docile egg).

Ultimately, opening the door to begin thinking critically about the body and its processes as deeply intertwined with social narratives is challenging. It requires a curiosity of thought in which we must challenge ourselves to begin unpicking the stitches of the social fabric of our world. More than this, it asks us to commit the closest thing in our reach to secular blasphemy – it asks us to question the empirical. To return to the question raised from our David example: to what extent can science be seen as 'doing' cultural work'? We may respond that perhaps it is always doing cultural work. The inherently 'natural' is after all rarely born but rather made – sculpted from interpretation. This statement does not dismiss the existence of scientific rationale or 'fact'. Rather, it questions the objective, highlighting that it rarely remains value free.

Beyond a conference: Discussing hormones

The proliferation of testosterone in the UK is ultimately diversifying. As the parameters of hormonal care become increasingly blurred and testosterone is accessed across multiple platforms by both men and women, important questions are being raised regarding the relationship between this infamous hormone and our conceptualizations of it. Specifically, how conceptions of the hormone relate or are imbued with gendered discourse.

Testosterone is still presented in popular debate as exclusive to the male body (we need only think about the runner Caster Semenya and the accompanying discourse; as a woman, her levels of testosterone are often perceived as equivalent to those of a man – discussion has been had as to whether she should be barred from competing with other women).[2] This discursive action – in which testosterone is imbued with a unique masculine personality – ultimately serves a purpose. In retaining testosterone as 'the male hormone' and highlighting its impact only as it pertains to men's bodies, we maintain traditions in which medicine neatly aligns with existing gendered models important for sociocultural maintenance and personal comfort in a stable, knowable world. Aligning testosterone to gender also ensures we are able to draw upon sociocultural narratives for profiteering purposes. It is important to remind ourselves that hormones highly marketable. Firming up 'discernable' features, projecting expected impact, and marketing to a specific (gendered) target audience are all a part of this process. The crystallization of these factors ensures that a neat and straightforward causal pathway can be mapped out for the consumer. *Use X to achieve Y*. Or in the case of David *use testosterone and go from flab to fab*.

While andropause may only affect around 2–5 per cent of cis-men, we can see how the delivery of information by endocrine experts linking its effects to muscle mass and libido provides an easily manipulatable narrative for pharmaceutical companies to exploit. Whether intentional or not, it plants the seeds in which taking testosterone may grow to be viewed as the magic 'cure-all' for men who perceive themselves as insufficiently masculine. Offering a road to an attractive body, a great libido and an agile mind, testosterone becomes a highly sought-after form of gender capital facilitated by capitalism.

In drawing upon the concept of a 'natural' binary, unique and specific markers of masculinity are first distilled and then carved onto the body. The lack of such markers not only communicates a biological lack of testosterone – but also a cultural lack of masculinity. To the men diagnosed with testosterone deficiency, this positioning may complicate their diagnosis further by adding a negative psychological impact. It not only presents a particular version of masculinity that may feel unfamiliar and unattainable, but it also asserts a narrative of optimization – a suggestion that you can become better than you ever were before. This marketing of masculinity through the 'work' of testosterone reminds us of the familiar synthesis that exists between patriarchy and capitalism.

---

[2] For more information, see Brenner (2021).

The ramifications of these messages are significant and extend beyond TRT. In particular, how these messages are interpreted by communities where testosterone use has little or nothing to do with the concept of masculinity. As my research has shifted across spaces, places and networks, attention has been paid to the impact of what happens when conventional narratives about testosterone stop 'making sense'. Doing so has highlighted how, rather than being absent, gender issues continue to be embedded in the processes of pursuing treatment.

As outlined, testosterone serves an important function in all bodies – not just those assigned with the pronoun 'he/him' at birth. The depletion of hormones in peri-menopausal women, for example, can cause major and debilitating symptoms. The decline of hormones in perimenopause includes a reduction not only in oestrogen but also in testosterone, a hormone thought to contribute to the healthy functioning of mood, libido and cognitive performance in women as well as men. This being the case, when prescribing hormone replacement therapy (HRT), some professionals will opt to include testosterone in a patient's HRT treatment, should adequate improvements in symptoms not be observed after appropriately re-oestrogenizing the body. Despite this fact, there is currently no mainstream testosterone preparation designed for women widely available via the National Health Service (NHS) in the UK. Instead (if women are able to obtain testosterone at all via an NHS practitioner) they are likely to be prescribed preparations such as Tostran or Testogel which are designed to treat functional hypogonadism in older men. These preparations contain a higher dose of testosterone than is needed and consequently require patients to stagger applications, making the maintenance of a consistent testosterone level arguably more challenging.

Should women seek care through a private practice clinic (as observed in my own fieldwork) they may be prescribed AndroFeme – a preparation currently licenced in Western Australia for the treatment of peri-menopausal and menopausal symptoms. AndroFeme is designed with women's chemical makeup in mind, and therefore contains the more appropriate, targeted dose of testosterone required. As the product is not widely available in the UK however, the prescribing of the product is considerably more costly to patients, making it an inaccessible option for some. It is important to note, that during my observations, it became clear that women's decision to pay for private menopausal treatment was not something undertaken lightly. The long waiting list at the private clinic for an appointment with a consultant communicated a definite unmet need stemming from an overloaded state-funded system. Many spoke of the decision to 'go private' as a necessity, referencing the difficulties they had faced in gaining access to HRT from their GP regardless of how debilitating their symptoms were proving. Though HRT was outlined as difficult to access via the NHS, the prescribing of testosterone via publicly accessible healthcare was emphasized as near to impossible to obtain.

In multiple iterations of the same story, I observed women stressing to practitioners at the clinic the trouble they had experienced in obtaining HRT and testosterone from their GP. Women highlighted how, particularly in the case of testosterone, GP's had assumed they simply did not need it. At other times during my fieldwork, practitioners at the clinic took time to explore the assumption women did not need HRT with patients. As opposed to dismissing the advice of a fellow practitioner outright, they would explain the importance of particular hormones, stressing the processes by which adequate levels of these hormones serve to support our continued well-being (e.g. mood stability, cognitive function, libido etc.). They provided space for women to discuss their frustrations and validated their embodied experiences and ongoing discomfort. They explained how any assertion that a woman did not need HRT was ultimately, when considered in line with our knowledge of perimenopause/menopause and patients purported symptoms, ultimately problematic.

The measured response demonstrated in clinical consultations (in which hormones were positioned as part of a complex process that also interacted with lifestyle factors such as diet, exercise and alcohol consumption) is however, rarely communicated through popular discourse or the marketing material accompanying hormonal treatments. During this research, the iterations of gender as presented in the packaging of hormones were particularly thought provoking to observe. In the case of the presentation of testosterone preparations targeting women, traditional 'languages of gender' regularly recurred. We may observe how in the case of AndroFeme, great care has been taken to feminize the formula. The name weakens any association to testosterone by calling upon the term 'andro' as opposed to 'testo'. It also utilizes the suffix 'feme' to stress the targeted audience the product is designed for. The packaging enlists the assistance of a shocking pink colour scheme and graphically redesigns the chemical compound of testosterone to resemble prismatic honeycomb.

The information leaflet for the product continues and develops this theme. It employs the same colour scheme through a wide pink banner which introduces the formula as 'Testosterone for Women'. On the front of the leaflet a woman is pictured sitting on the lap of her supposed partner. She is laughing as he smiles, their faces pressed together. The image would suggest they are perhaps sharing a joke together. Their arms are wrapped tightly around one another and the man's hands are visibly pressed into the woman's waist, just below her breast. The angle of his face is positioned so his nose and mouth are pointed towards her ear and neck. It clearly suggests a sexual or intimate context.

Perhaps the most interesting thing to note about this image, however, is the suggestion that the impact of AndroFeme is not only for women, but for their partners too. In improving symptoms such as low libido, the benefits to heterosexual men are made apparent. These choices are important. Permission to use testosterone is arguably granted by patriarchy, and women are afforded use due to the potentially advantageous impact it could have on improving heterosexual men's sex lives. Moreover, while feminizing testosterone could be read as threatening to dilute masculine 'potency', in this instance we see a culturally protective mechanism at play. By rebranding the formula as 'testosterone for women' it is suggested that this hormone is not testosterone as traditionally understood. It is *different* to 'proper' testosterone. It is women's testosterone, something apart from 'regular' or 'men's' testosterone; its purpose is, for the reinforcement of a heterosexual patriarchal order.

Discussion of the marketing material was noted by practitioners, who highlighted the image on the information leaflet as 'a bit cheesey' before presenting patients with the material. AndroFeme as stated, however, remains the only testosterone preparation available on the market, designed with women's chemical makeup in mind, meaning there is no alternative for practitioners to prescribe. However, practitioners may not want another option. Though AndroFeme's marketing material may communicate gendered discourses, the product itself remains gender progressive by its very existence. In addition, the feminizing marketing discourse could be read differently, designed to comfort anxieties that testosterone remains fundamentally a 'male hormone'. In this sense, while AndroFeme may confirm certain patriarchal ideals and standards, it may also be seen as a progressive change maker, allowing women to access that which has been held close to the bosom of men for millennia.

This absence of options is interesting. In discussions with pharmaceutical representatives at the EMAS conference, the lack of interest in creating such a product for women was related to the assumption that it would not prove popular and, therefore, prove non-profitable. This rationale however is challenged when considering the increasing demand not only for menopausal care, but use of HRT that incorporates testosterone alongside oestrogen. Arguably, such an assumption communicates a discomfort beyond profiteering. It speaks to our blue and pink boxes in which testosterone, needs to remain the property of men.

In the case of the EMAS conference, multiple patriarchal practices can be observed. Not only are there the specific gendered messages in which hormones and the body are assigned pink and blue flags. There is also an uncomfortable intellectual encroachment of patriarchal power on feminine (and feminist) discourses. Andropause (though a term of disputed importance) is earmarked to close the conference and afforded half a day in lecture times and slots. The majority of speakers who are afforded larger spaces, longer speaking times, and bigger audiences over the preceding days at the conference are nearly all men, regardless of the fact that they are discussing an issue affecting women – menopause. The esteemed role of the discussion mediator was largely undertaken by men. Topical lectures taking place on Female Genital Cosmetic Surgery (FGCS) including discussions on labiaplasty, hymenoplasty, genital bleaching and whitening also occurred and were exclusively delivered by men. The technology on show at the conference including the use and 'display' of laser treatments promising to lighten tighten and brighten every inch of the ageing feminine form made a discernible project out of women's bodies.

Beyond this, there are also discernible implications for men. Within debates between conference attendees, andropause is consistently positioned as something that Frith describes as 'a joke subject' (2013). Yet despite this, lectures that deal with andropause foreground it as a state that needs to be corrected. In this sense, andropause becomes subject to the same patriarchal confines as experienced by women. It is illustrated as a threat, something that makes men less like men and more like women (just as testosterone makes women more like men and less like women). Consequently, andropause becomes a troubling category in need of correction.

Conclusion

Fundamentally, patriarchy rests upon clear categorical differences between men and women articulated in the (structuralist, dualist) gender binary. Testosterone, through its excess or deficiency in 'male' and 'female' bodies, is a disruptive substance that destabilizes these categories as it highlights its role in their construction. At a conference such as EMAS, even though professionals may readily accept bodily states as highly complex, they nonetheless reiterate distinctions that rest upon concepts of clear, natural and immutable categorical difference. However, what appears to unify gender within this patriarchal project is the ageing process. Patriarchy ultimately reveals itself to problematize ageing bodies, regardless of gender. Like more complex understandings of hormones and gender, this treatment may well be a consequence of the threat the ageing body poses in terms of eroding and blurring the boundaries of clear categorical difference. As women grow beards and men struggle to maintain erections, so the fabric of conceptual-categorical difference fades.

Following testosterone has led this research to uncover the depth and reach of patriarchal power, demonstrating its existence in medical discourse to extend further than we may first assume. Fundamentally, patriarchy is found to exist not only in obvious spaces but subtle ones too. The question is presented: were we not to follow patriarchy into obvious spaces, into talks on testosterone and sculptures of David, would we ever be able to observe it encroaching on the wider medical world around us? Yet the heresy of questioning the purportedly apolitical space of medical discourse is key to the task of anthropology. As this research has shifted across spaces, places and networks, paying attention to the impact of what happens when conventional narratives about testosterone stop 'making sense', many significant observations have been collected. These highlight how the issues embedded in the processes of pursuing treatment are not simply personal, but intensely political.

Observations from this research demonstrate empowering practice by committed clinicians. However, in the narratives of women discussing their struggles to attain HRT through an NHS pathway, it has also revealed the barriers facing innumerable women seeking essential menopausal care in the UK today. It has highlighted the manner in which links between patriarchal power and capitalism not only limit the access to available treatment options, but supress the development of options for women. Included within this is the reproduction of not only patriarchal power, but also wider systematic oppression in which women are unable to access treatment.

The intention of this research has been to explore the ways in which testosterone presents and is used in multiple spaces and places. In the case of the example this chapter began with, the categorization of a complex endocrine system highlights patriarchal power at play. Men's ownership of testosterone is outlined, and complexity is forgotten in the interest of a simplistic, knowable world. In cracking open the array of discourses and domains that testosterone 'moves through', bodies and selves can be repositioned away from a predisclosed fate of success or failure as it relates to a hormone's presence, lack or concomitant capacity to acquire it. Though the presentation of patriarchy in the instance of flab to fab David is perhaps overt, it does not imply that we should not deconstruct its messages. In doing so, we are better able to acknowledge the complexities involved in disentangling the actions of hormones such as testosterone from sociocultural constructs. Moreover, we may consider how these messages can present obstacles for professionals when explaining hormonal function and appreciate the difficulties involved in undertaking such a task without drawing upon shared metaphors or existing cultural scripts.

Exploring testosterone ethnographically exposes gendered imaginaries and market logics. It renders visible invisible patriarchal orders reified through scientific discourses and pierces the veil between the 'natural' and the 'social'. Deconstructing these messages encourages us to consider alternative ways to think about not only testosterone but the body and its processes in general. It tasks us to consider how we may better communicate messages about hormones and the body in a more gender-neutral and inclusive manner. In capturing multiple perspectives, my ongoing research hopes to continue to draw out the intersectional complexities associated with testosterone use. In pulling apart and documenting the experiences of those 'getting to know' testosterone intimately, we are challenged to think about alternative ways to engage with a hormone that can often feel so familiar to us.

Does testosterone belong to men? As this research demonstrates, though testosterone may be embroiled within a rich history of gender politics, it's function proves powerful in all bodies, rendering testosterone's 'identity' so much more than a mere masculinity maker.

Bibliography

Alexander, S. M. (2003) Stylish Hard Bodies: Branded Masculinity in Men's Health Magazine. *Sociological Perspectives*, 46(4), 535–54.

Baudrillard, Jean (1981) *Simulacra and Simulation*. Translated by Glaser, S. F. Ann Arbor: University of Michigan Press.

Brenner, S. (2021) Caster Semenya: 'They're Killing Sport. People Want Extraordinary Performances'. *The Guardian*. Available at: https://www.theguardian.com/sport/2021/apr/23/caster-semenya-theyre-killing-sport-people-want-extraordinary-performances

Campos, P. et al. (2006) The Epidemiology of Overweight and Obesity: Public Health Crisis or Moral Panic? *International Journal of Epidemiology*, 35, 55–60.

Connell, R.W. (1995) *Masculinities*. Berkeley: University of California Press.

De Landa, M. (2006) *A New Philosophy of Society: Assemblage Theory and Social Complexity*. London: Continuum.

Derrida, J. (1966) Structure, Sign and Play in the Discourse of the Human Sciences, in (trans.), Bass, A., *Writing and Difference*, 278–82. Chicago: University of Chicago Press.

Fausto Sterling, A. (2000) *Sexing the Body: Gender Politics and the Construction of Sexuality*. New York: Basic Books.

Fine, C. (2017) *Testosterone Rex: Myths of Science, Sex and Society*. New York: Norton & Company.

Frith, M. (2013) Is the Male Menopause Just a Convenient Myth?. *The Independent*, 21 October. Available at: https://www.independent.co.uk/news/science/is-the-male-menopause-just-a-convenient-myth-96478.html

Flemming, A. (2018) Does Testosterone Make You Mean?. *The Guardian*, available at: https://www.theguardian.com/science/2018/mar/20/testosterone-myth-male-hormone-behaviour-risk-taking

Haraway, D. (1991) *Simians, Cyborgs and Women: The Reinvention of Nature*. New York: Routledge.

Hoberman, J. (2005) *Testosterone Dreams: Rejuvenation, Aphrodisia, Doping*. London: University of California Press.

Jordan-Young, R., Karkazis, K. (2019) *Testosterone: An Unauthorised Biography*. London: Harvard University Press.

Lakshman, K. M., Kaplan, B., Travison, T. G., Basaria, S., Knapp, P. E., Singh, A. B., LaValley, M. P., Mazer, N. A. and Bhasin, S. (2010) The Effects of Injected Testosterone Dose and Age on the Conversion of Testosterone to Estradiol and Dihydrotestosterone in Young and Older Men. *The Journal of Clinical Endocrinology and Metabolism*, 95(8), 3955–64.

Latour, B. (2005) *Reassembling the Social: An Introduction to Actor Network Theory*. Oxford: Oxford University Press.

Lévi-Strauss, C. (1963) *Structural Anthropology*. New York: Basic Books.

Lyotard, J.F. (1984) *The Postmodern Condition: A Report on Knowledge*. Minneapolis: University of Minnesota Press.

Mangan, J. A. (2000) *Superman Supreme: Fascist Body as Political Icon – Global Fascism*. New York: Routledge.

Martin, E. (1991) The Egg and the Sperm: How Science Has Constructed a Romance Based on Stereotypical Male-Female Roles. *Signs*, 16(3), 485–501.

Mirzoeff, N. (1993) *Bodyscape: Art, Modernity and the Ideal Figure*. London: Routledge.

Mol, A. (2002) *The Body Multiple: Ontology in Medical Practice*. London: Duke University Press.

Petrzela, N.M. (2020) From Performance to Participation: The Origins of the Fit Nation. *Publisher Is the Transatlantica American Studies Journal*, 2: 2020.

PFLAG (2021) PFLAG National Glossary of Terms. *PFLAG*, 09 October. Available at: https://pflag.org/glossary

Popma, A., Vermeiren, R., Geluk, C., A.M.L, Rinne, T., van den Brink, W., Knol, D., Jansen, L.M.C., van Engeland, H. and Doreleijers, T, A.H. (2007) Cortisol Moderates the Relationship between Testosterone and Aggression in Delinquent Male Adolescents. *Biological Psychiatry*, 61(3), 405–11.

Sakran, J, V., Hilton, E, J., Sathya, C. (2020) Racism in Health Care Isn't Always Obvious. *Scientific American*, 9 July. Available at: https://www.scientificamerican.com/article/racism-in-health-care-isnt-always-obvious/

Singh, P. (2013) Andropause: Current Concepts. *Indian Journal of Endocrinology and Metabolism*, 17(3), 621–9.

Starn, R. (1986) Reinventing Heroes in Renaissance Italy. *Journal of Interdisciplinary History*, XVII, 2.

Turner, B.S. (1984) *The Body & Society: Explorations in Social Theory*. Oxford: Blackwell.

Wagner, P. (2015) Picture Perfect Bodies: Visualizing Hegemonic Masculinities Produced for/by Male Fitness Spaces. *International Journal of Men's Health*, 15(3), 235–58.

Zilioli, S., Ponzi, D., Henry, A. et al. (2015) Testosterone, Cortisol and Empathy: Evidence for the Dual-Hormone Hypothesis. *Adaptive Human Behavior and Physiology*, (1), 421–33.

Conclusion: Rupture and renewal, accountability and agency

Nikki van der Gaag, Amir Massoumian and Dan Artus

The contributions to this volume were gathered to ask a question: can masculinity be considered separable from patriarchy? We sought to find ways of answering this question through the examination of masculinity as patriarchy in practice, through presenting ethnographic studies, which we grouped in three sections. The first was dedicated to exploring contemporary crisis and change in masculinity. Many men proffer a sense of alienation and persecution, while in others it becomes easy to believe that some progress means enough progress. The risk of patriarchy consuming progressive discourses – of men uncritically participating in progressive work through symbolic gestures, dominating spaces and adopting leadership roles, without the necessary work on themselves. Yet equally, it is increasingly clear that inaction is not an option. The question of whether masculinity is separable from patriarchy was asked for the pragmatic reason of what it is that those who participate in, enact and embody masculinity can do, without harming or hindering. How can we balance critique with compassion, or accountability with agency? The juncture is precisely at the connective tissue between masculinity, patriarchy and those that enact both. Backlash becomes inevitable if one's sense of identity has masculinity tied to patriarchy or the exercise of hegemonic power.

Our remaining two sections looked to find spaces where masculinities were enacted outside of crisis, but in moments of contradiction and of re-shaping, by looking at different contexts where masculinity's relationship with patriarchy takes different forms through different actors. If we consider masculinities to be multiple rather than singular, enacted rather than essential, there is room to change. Only by paying close attention to what people 'actually do' can we start to unpick those relationships and explore the possibilities of dismantling patriarchy. We have aimed here to present open questions and provocations rather than proposing systematic solutions. The work of dismantling patriarchy, of men participating in the struggle for a better world, cannot happen with the assumption that they should lead from the front. It is not a call for men to heroically save the day, but to take a seat at the table, to listen to women. The consequences of nostalgia for a glorious past, for deeds of heroism and triumph, minimize the contributions of so many others, and women in particular. This makes the fabric of society, in the tacit and unspoken domains of the everyday, the thing that needs to be addressed through patient storytelling and the slow, painful work of healing.

This has been the role of our ethnographic material, yet it must be placed in large-scale events and wider contexts to mobilize mass action – at the grass-roots as well as in the corridors of power. As has been discussed in the first section in this book on contemporary politics, patriarchal narratives feature starkly and powerfully in the 'backlash' against perceived male disenfranchisement. Men attempt to maintain patriarchal order and their place in it through violence against women, railing at the incursion of a perceived 'matriarchy' that victimizes them. They believe that if women would just 'know their place', then everything would be as it was meant to be. Camaraderie forged in bitter loneliness and deteriorating mental health are the calling cards of the Involuntary Celibates or 'InCels' who congregate in the seedier parts of the internet. The anger spills out into real-world mass shootings that have taken the lives of dozens of young women whom they perceived as rejecting them. While power is not intrinsically masculine, patriarchy concentrates its power in a way that can make it appear as such. And yet the groups of men in this section rail at the *lack of power* they feel entitled to by birth. This sense of disillusionment cuts across economic and cultural spheres, channelled and manipulated by a cynical post-truth demagoguery.

While it was the events of 2016 that spurred us to organize the conference in 2019, recent events have shown in subtler, more insidious ways. As the COVID pandemic swept around the world, there were warning signs everywhere of the many threats to hard-won gender equality, the creeping reinforcement of patriarchal norms and accompanying social problems. In a particularly troubling example, extended lockdowns all over the world, with families confined to their homes, led to a huge rise in domestic violence, one which Phumzile Mlambo Ngcuka, then executive director of UN Women, called a 'shadow pandemic' (UN Women, 6 April 2020). Many countries around the world, from Lebanon to Zimbabwe, Malaysia to China, saw a doubling or tripling of calls to helplines from early on in the pandemic (UN 6 April 2020). A survey by the Australian Institute of Criminology (Boxall et al. 2020) found that of the nearly one in ten who experienced domestic abuse from a current or former partner since the start of the pandemic, two-thirds said their partner had been abusive for the first time, or that their violence had become more frequent and severe.

Other warning signs included the fact that women's paid jobs have been 1.8 times more vulnerable than men's during the crisis (McKinsey 2020). An analysis by UN Women (2020) found that in 2021, 435 million women and girls are likely be living on less than $1.90 a day, many because they lost their incomes because of the pandemic. The additional burden on the healthcare system has also had wide-ranging gendered effects. The United Nations Population Fund (UNFPA) warned in April 2020 that some 47 million women in 114 low- and middle-income countries were projected to be unable to use modern contraceptives, which could mean up to 15 million new unintended pregnancies (UNFPA 2020). Disruptions to healthcare are leading to an increase in maternal mortality and UNFPA also warned of increased in child marriages and female genital mutilation.

One of the other consequences was that women, who were already doing between three to ten times more unpaid care and domestic work than men, took on an ever-greater amount. Women of colour and those from more marginalized sections of society were particularly affected – research in the United States found that 57 per cent of White women said their daily domestic and care work had increased, but that this rose to 71 per cent of Black or African American women, 71 per cent of Latina women and 79 per cent of Asian women (Oxfam, Promundo-US and MenCare 2020). Yet men also increased their hours of care work at home in some places – in the UK, one study found that fathers had nearly doubled the time they spend on childcare – although mothers were still doing far more (Andrew et al. 2020). Equality here too is far from being reached (Barker et al. 2021). While gendered norms in the division of labour and patterns of abuse have in some cases been intensified from the pandemic, such things are not an inevitability. A close attention to the empirical conditions of resistance to those norms may provide insight into how to challenge them.

This was a theme we sought to address in the chapters on normativity and diversity, through examining spaces where masculinities disrupt and subvert patriarchy, or are even practiced in direct opposition to it. We saw that masculinity and sexuality easily become fluid when removed from visual hierarchies and cues by a simple flick of the light switch. Desire and personal proclivity are reconfigured as touch that does the talking – so patriarchies and masculinities are contextual, sensuous and embodied. Trans and queer identities highlight the porous borders between an entrenched gender binary; yet while fluidity is possible and liberating, the pressure to adopt the more problematic or 'toxic' parts of masculinity by trans people remains. Patriarchy may not vanish by wishing it was so, but the very existence of trans, non-binary and queer identities radically undermines fixed, biologically normative views of gender and questions the mandate for its border policing. These types of embodied subversions are also seen clearly in the rise of drag artists in popular culture. Through exploring the entanglements of capital, aesthetics, performance and stage identity other contours of masculinities can be seen. A tragic playfulness highlights the imbrication of stigma with glamour, of marginalization with assimilation and acceptance. Even when ground is won, capital and patriarchy remain resilient in their capacity to appropriate and mould the things that resist it. Across these and other chapters, the agency of different groups to disrupt patriarchal power structures – and open pathways to a different world – is seen.

Yet these possibilities should not lull us into a false sense of security. There is a real danger that the pandemic will have permanent and negative effects on gender and other equalities, reinforcing traditional gendered norms and giving increased power to authoritarian – masculinized – ways of governing, being and doing. An analysis of how power is mobilized in these scenarios is key to resisting it. As Arundhati Roy, Indian activist, noted, crises can also be opportunities for positive change: 'Historically, pandemics have forced humans to break with the past and imagine their world anew. This one is no different. It is a portal, a gateway between one world and the next' (*Financial Times*, April 2020). WHO Director-General Tedris Adhanom Ghebreyesus warned that the only way viruses have been vanquished is via 'permanent adjustments' to economics and societies, and added: 'We will not, we cannot go back to the way things were.'[1] 'Building back better' has become both a cliché and a rallying cry of the pandemic. But Theo Sowa, outgoing CEO of the African Women's Development Forum, had a note of caution: 'When people say "build back better" I hope we are going to say "Build better", because the "back" wasn't good for most of us.'[2] So what Sowa referring to? How close is the relationship between patriarchy, power and masculinities? And how have feminists articulated this over the years?

Systematic action and organized resistance are key, yet they must be rooted in an understanding of the lived experience and reflection on how we see masculinity

---

[1]   WHO warns a coronavirus vaccine alone will not end pandemic (cnbc.com).
[2]   https://www.youtube.com/watch?v=Xi6fFisz6Ew&t=20s

in both bodies, minds and a sense of self. Moving from a pronounced paradigm of neoliberal individualism and radical self-reliance, the pandemic has taught us lessons of profound vulnerability. It is quietly recognized that substance abuse, particularly alcohol, has been on the rise in the pandemic (e.g. Grossman et al. 2020). While self-control is something articulated as central to many models of masculinity, programmes like Alcoholics Anonymous offer challenges for men considering the values they attach to masculinity or what it means to be men. Through the work of service and 'sobriety', alternative subjectivities can be achieved that model a radical interdependence. An old trope is that 'no man (sic) is an island'; it is scarcely seen more starkly than in a world rocked by catastrophe. Likewise, physical disability highlights norms that attach to the body itself, presenting pressure to conform to impossible expectation. The 'double threat' of patriarchy for disabled men – the pressure to achieve patriarchal expectation and the experience of marginalization – should be cause to question our assumptions of how norms interact with somatic hierarchies that even extend within the body itself. Testosterone shows how the body – and its social possibilities – is plastic and malleable, whilst science itself can be shown to actively do social and cultural work. It is not that this work should not but done, but that can be redirected to serve us – and enable us to serve each other – better. Bodies and minds are less solid than we might think; acting as a nexus for a variety of complex interactions. If the pandemic has drawn out the worst in some cases, it has also materialized the best in community activism that prioritizes an ethic of local care for the most vulnerable.

In her short essay *Understanding Patriarchy*, bell hooks writes that 'to end male pain, to respond effectively to male crisis, we have to name the problem. We have to both acknowledge that the problem is patriarchy and work to end patriarchy' (2010:6). For hooks, there exists an 'essential goodness of male being' – a fundamentally *human* redeemability, a shared essence denied by narrow framings of masculinity. While we are opposed to the metaphysical bundling of human qualities into neatly gendered dualities; that any person can 'own' any virtue or vice is existential misappropriation. Those who are socialized as men are robbed of emotional expression and the authentic co-presence so fundamental to being human.

Yet for this optimism, we should be clear that the task that faces men who engage with feminism and the struggle for gender justice is very different from the emancipation of those directly oppressed by patriarchy and male violence. It requires a recognition of the present connection to forms of patriarchal power at different scales. Nyaradzayi Gumbonzanda, former General Secretary of the World YWCA, in a symposium run by the global pro-feminist network MenEngage, threw out a challenge to men:

> There are too many good men in the world who are doing nothing to dismantle patriarchy and yet who profess to be doing great stuff. There are too many in positions of responsibility who are irresponsible. They are the majority of leaders, parliamentarians, religious leaders, doctors … So when we ask where are the men, the men are there. But they are not making decisions that advance gender equality, human rights and dignity. It is not about involving or including men, it is about everybody in a position of responsibilities to use their power responsibly.
>
> (MenEngage Ubuntu Symposium 2021)

And Mbuyiselo Botha, former Commissioner for Gender Equality in South Africa, said in the same Symposium:

> There is nothing that inherently stops us[men] from caring. It is artificial, toxic, manmade, creations of what it means to be a real man that deny us the opportunity to be caring. And this is the sad part: that there is a system that really oppresses us as well. It divides us from our humanity. It denies us our own vulnerability.

This lies at the heart of the question of why men would and why they should challenge patriarchy, even though ostensibly they would seem to be its major beneficiaries.

Many scholars and activists of all genders have pondered this question; 'Not to buy into patriarchy means renouncing some historical privileges, but they are privileges which don't give you peace, don't give you happiness. What gives people happiness is being connected', said Oswaldo Montoya Telleria, Nicaragua, from MenEngage (quoted in van der Gaag 2014). Men's engagement with gender equality must involve engagement with the realities of their own experience of gender; its pains and its privileges. 'Building Back Better' at a systematic and policy level involves the slow, patient and existentially daunting work of men doing the same for themselves and each-other. Top-down policy shifts which re-engineer a world to be fairer for others and fairer for men; even if that fairness includes a diminution of socio-political privilege.
Srilatha Batliwala, longstanding Indian feminist activist, noted in 2014 at a MenEngage conference in Delhi, India that 'the root cause of injustice and our shared political agenda is the dismantling of patriarchy – not only because of

what it does to women and other subordinate genders and its dehumanizing effects on men, but also because it is the engine that fuels exploitative economic models and environmentally destructive development and all forms of war conflict and violence' (Batliwala 2014).

This is where ethnographic studies can be so useful, to examine the ways in which both power and patriarchy play out in daily life. They explore the richness and paradox of escaping from patriarchy; the profit and pain that comes from being entangled in it and the alienation and vertigo of trying to escape it. Making patriarchy visible to men, as well as their place in it, while providing room to explore alternatives. This plays out differently in different contexts and in different countries, as the chapters in this volume show clearly. The majority of authors in this volume are from the UK, but they also include critiques of the ever-evolving digital world, and insights from scholars in India, Indonesia and France. Together, we hope the chapters in this volume provide some insight into how masculinities relate to patriarchy – from anti-feminist digital spaces to the dark rooms of British sex clubs and pubs; from convicted male perpetrators in France, to the way in which trans masculinities play out in Indonesia; from Drag Queens to disability, politics and power.

Moments of rupture and crisis can shake up a recognition of a patriarchy that men are blind to, or forms of hegemonic masculinity that operate within it. Times are too dire for men to fruitlessly recriminate while others move to buttress unjust social orders. Action is needed, but it needs to be formulated with an unlimited cast of potential others – agency must be balanced with self-aware accountability. Put simply, men who need help only need ask in good faith. You need not be alone. You *are not* alone. There is joy, there is pain; yours and others, interconnected. We have both everything to gain *and* everything to lose. There is no discrete form of masculinity that will ever be more or less perfect; some failure is inevitable as a part of growth. We are all entangled in patriarchies and masculinities to varying degrees regardless of individual gender identity – which is why this volume contains a range of chapters that lays out how these play together to shape possibilities for future action. Our hope is that together they make a small contribution to an understanding of the ways in which patriarchy shapes us all, and therefore shapes our societies. While change must start with discussion, with ideas, it is not a substitute for action. For the slow work of healing and reconciliation, there also needs to be protest and activism, engagement with policymakers, and strategic action at the highest level. Ultimately, we hope that this kind of work on masculinities, grounded firmly in feminism, will make a small contribution to moving towards a world that is fairer, more equal and less violent – a truly post-patriarchal society.

Bibliography

Butler, J. (1990) *Gender Trouble*. London and New York: Routledge.

Crenshaw, K. (1991) Mapping the Margins: Intersectionality, Identity Politics, and Violence against Women of Color. *Stanford Law Review*, 43, 1241–99.

de Beauvoir, S. (1949) *The Second Sex*. London: Vintage Publishing.

hooks, b. (2010) *Understanding Patriarchy*. Louisville, USA: Louisville Anarchist Federation.

Lerner, G. (1986) *The Creation of Patriarchy*. New York: Oxford University Press.

Millett, K. (1970) *Sexual Politics*. New York: Doubleday and Co.

Van der Gaag, N. (2014) *Feminism and Men*. New York: Zed Books.

Blog articles

Andrew, A. et al. (May 2020) *How Are Mothers and Fathers Balancing Work and Family under Lockdown?*. London, UK: Institute for Fiscal Studies.

Batliwala, S. (2014) Carving a Space: reflections on the 2nd MenEngage Symposium. Available at: https://www.awid.org/news-and-analysis/carving-space-reflections-2nd-menengage-symposium

Boxall, H., Morgan, A. and Brown, R. (2020) *The Prevalence of Domestic Violence among Women during the COVID-19 Pandemic*. Statistical Bulletin no. 28. Canberra: Australian Institute of Criminology. Available at: https://doi.org/10.52922/sb04718.

Grossman, E. R., Benjamin-Neelon, S. E. and Sonnenschein, S. (2020) Alcohol Consumption during the COVID-19 Pandemic: A Cross-Sectional Survey of US Adults. *International Journal of Environmental Research and Public Health*, 17(24), 9189.

Oxfam, Promundo-US and MenCare (2020) *Caring under COVID-19: How the Pandemic Is – and Is Not – Changing Unpaid Care and Domestic Work Responsibilities in the United States*. Boston: Oxfam, & Washington, DC: Promundo-US.

McKinsey (2020) COVID-19 and Gender Equality: Countering the Regressive Effects. COVID-19 and Gender Equality: Countering the Regressive Effects (mckinsey.com).

MenEngage (2021) https://web.cvent.com/event/45bb0a94-a63b-4f48-a6fe-b1a97a9449dd/summary

UNFPA, with contributions from Avenir Health, Johns Hopkins University (USA) and Victoria University (Australia) (2020) *Impact of the COVID-19 Pandemic on Family Planning and Ending Gender-based Violence, Female Genital Mutilation and*

Child Marriage. https://www.unfpa.org/sites/default/files/resource-pdf/COVID-19_
    impact_brief_for_UNFPA_24_April_2020_1.pdf
UN news, April (2020) UN Chief Calls for Domestic Violence 'Ceasefire' amid
    'Horrifying Global Surge' | | UN News.
UN Women (April 2020) https://www.unwomen.org/en/news/stories/2020/4/
    statement-ed-phumzile-violence-against-women-during-pandemic.
UN Women (2020) *From Insights to Action: Gender Equality in the Wake of COVID-19.*

Index

Sadikin, A. 98
Sauvage, J. 44, 50–1
Schacht, S. 164
Schiappa, M. 45
   'Grenelle des violences conjugales' 46
School of African and Oriental Studies
   (SOAS) conference 1, 215
Schwarzenegger, A. 10, 236
Scoats, R. 116
secondary absence 74
Sedgwick, E. K. 155, 167
sex clubs (UK) 115, 118–20
   beyond masculinity and heterosexual
      performance 121–4
   cultures 127
   dark rooms 15–16, 116, 118, 120,
      122–8, 257
   desubjectification 125–6
   discharge of emotion 123
   eroticization 127
   ethos 119
   gay men's use 123
   gendered and sexual subjectivities 124–5
   heterosexual 116–17
   neo-liberal disposition 115
   playrooms 118, 121
   post-masculinity eroticism 124–7
   sexual appeals 115
   sexual consumption and
      commodification 115
   Swinger/Swap clubs 115
sexism 45, 53–4, 143–6
sexual and reproductive health and rights
   3, 98, 207–10
sexual freedom 45
Sexual Orientation, Gender Identity,
   Gender Expression, and Sexual
   Characteristics (SOGIESC) 100–1,
   110
Shuster, S. M. 108
Silverman, K. 127
Sivanandan, A. 62
Sleeping Giants 38
Slootmaeckers, K. 64
social identity categorizations 141
'Social Justice Warriors' 25 n.2, 134, 145
social micro-climate 68
social networking sites 55–6, 207
social personality 120
   gay bathhouse, anonymity 120, 123

social science and humanities approaches
   Essentialist 7
   Normative 8
   Positivist 7–8
   Semiotic 8
Sørensen, T. F., *An Anthropology of
   Absence* 62
Sowell, R. L. 123
Staiger, J. 164
Stallone, S. 236
Stevens, L. 139
Stick, M. 116
Stryker, S. 98
subordinate/marginalized masculinities 10
Swora, G. 185

Taylor, D. 125
tenuous masculinities 15, 96
   attaching value to masculinity 105–7
   evaluating masculine performances
      108–11
   Indonesia's transman identity 98–102
   inhabiting transman identity 102–5
testosterone 17, 229, 245–7, 255
   Andropause's big debut 230–2
   David case 233–5, 237, 240–1, 246
   ideal bodies 232–5
   as king maker 234–6
   science and culture 236–7
   structural instincts 238–40
   terminology 230
   'Testosterone for Women' 243–4
Testosterone Replacement Therapy (TRT)
   231–2, 234, 242
theatrical gender-bending 157
Thompson, S., *Hairspray* 165
Tilley, C. 68
Tinkcom, M. 158
tombois 99–100, 105–6
toxic masculinity 3, 13–14, 96, 104,
   108–10, 136, 227, 254
traditional masculinity 65, 73, 110, 183
Træen, B. 119
transgender 95–114, 119, 134, 165, 254
   transman (*see* transman/transmen
      (transpria))
   transition/transitioning 102–7, 109–10
transman/transmen (transpria) 15, 96, 96
   n.1, 100 n.3, 101, 111
   as cisgender man 107

www.ingramcontent.com/pod-product-compliance
Lightning Source LLC
Chambersburg PA
CBHW071353290326
41932CB00045B/1792